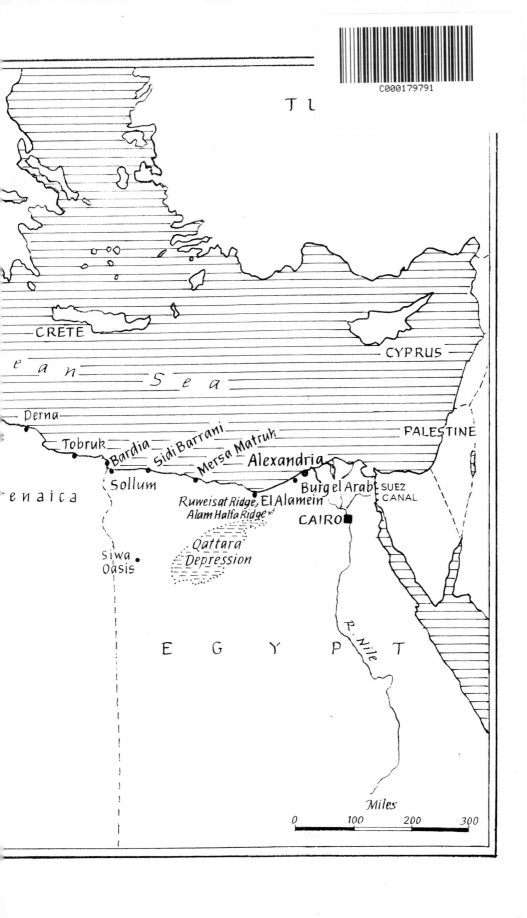

T L

CRETE

CYPRUS

e a n

S e a

Derna

Tobruk

Bardia

Sidi Barrani

Mersa Matruh

Alexandria

PALESTINE

e n a i c a

Sollum

Ruweisat Ridge, El Alamein
Alam Halfa Ridge

Burg el Arab

SUEZ
CANAL

CAIRO

Siwa
Oasis

Qattara
Depression

E   G   Y   P   T

R. Nile

Miles

0   100   200   300

WITH ALEX AT WAR

WITH ALEX AT WAR

From the Irrawaddy to the Po

1941 – 1945

by

RUPERT CLARKE

LEO COOPER

First published in Great Britain in 2000 by
Leo Cooper
an imprint of Pen & Sword Books
47 Church Street, Barnsley, S. Yorks, S70 2AS

ISBN 085052 717 1

A CIP catalogue record for this book
is available from the British Library

Dedication

To the Officers, Warrant Officers and Non-Commissioned Officers and Guardsmen of the Irish Guards. Also to those Irish regiments whose gallantry in the war in South Africa inspired Her Majesty Queen Victoria to establish the Regiment.

1900 – 2000
'Quis Separabit'

Army Order No 77 of April, 1900:
Her Majesty the Queen, having deemed it desirable to commemorate the bravery shown by the Irish regiments in the recent operations in South Africa, has been graciously pleased to command that an Irish regiment of Foot Guards be formed. This regiment will be designated "The Irish Guards".

CONTENTS

ACKNOWLEDGEMENTS

Service on the personal staff of a very senior Commander brings with it heavy responsibility, for one is working in an area and at a level at which mistakes cannot be tolerated, since the consequences of them may be extremely serious. Hence a new ADC or Personal Assistant (PA) will find himself quite suddenly working at a level which is completely foreign to him and not a little bewildering. In such a situation one's friends and colleagues who are working in similar circumstances and bearing similar responsibility become of immense importance.

What one might call the personal staff, or 'old boy network', has to provide much of the lubrication upon which the system of command must perforce rely. In making my acknowledgements to those who have been so helpful to me, I would now like to offer special thanks to those with whom I worked closely throughout the four years in which I served General Alex.

First and foremost must come Lieutenant Colonel W.M. (Bill) Cunningham MVO OBE MC and his wife Delia. Bill joined us from General Auchinleck's personal staff when we arrived in Cairo in 1942. His experience as a fighting soldier and as the former Commander-in-Chief's ADC was invaluable to the Chief. As his Military Assistant (MA), Bill ran the Chief's 'private office' whilst I went on tour with the General. As the head of our team he was a rock of calm and reliability and the stoutest of friends. I regard him as effectively the co-author of this book, for he has contributed so much and has generously allowed me to draw upon his personal diary for 1944, which is crammed with priceless material which I could not have got in any other way.

I wish to acknowledge the use of Sir David Hunt's papers, kindly loaned by Lady Hunt, covering the period that Colonel Hunt was GSO 1 during the North African and Italian Campaigns. At the conclusion of hostilities Colonel Hunt spent some time in Ottawa assisting the Field Marshal in writing his Despatches.

During the crucial period after General Sir Bernard Montgomery took over command of the Eighth Army and then fought his way forward until he finally linked up with the 1st Army in Tunisia, the link between him and General Alex was of special importance. In helping to maintain it, General Monty's two ADCs, the late Major John Poston MC and Major John Henderson MBE MC, became our fast friends and there was much for which we had to thank them as, indeed, there was later reason to thank another very good friend, Major Ion Calvocoressi MBE MC, senior ADC to General Sir Oliver Leese, who took over command of the Eighth Army from Monty in Italy. Oliver Leese's personal Auster pilot, Lieutenant Colonel Victor Cowley, has been immensely helpful during my researches, as indeed he was during the fighting – and I thank him too, most warmly. Victor had a very soft spot in his heart for Alex who, he said, was the only general ever to swing the propeller of his aircraft, with no self-starter, for him before take-off!

In addition I must thank Major Ralph Snagge MBE, MA to Alex's Chiefs of Staff in Italy, General John Harding, and later General (Monkey) Morgan, when General Harding became a Corps Commander in Northern Italy.

I also wish to thank Sir Stephen Hastings MC, Captain Ian Weston-Smith and Regimental Headquarters, Irish Guards, for their assistance.

I am most grateful to the Trustees of the Photographic Archive of the Imperial War Museum for permission to reproduce so many of their photographs and to John Delaney who devoted so much time to helping me make my selection.

My warmest thanks also go to Mrs Peggy MacDonald who typed so much of my manuscript and was so unfailingly helpful, and also to Mrs Harriet Friend. I must also thank Brigadier Henry Wilson (late Irish Guards) and the staff of Pen & Sword Books, my publishers, for their help, patience and advice.

Finally, I wish to record my thanks to Brigadier Bryan Watkins who has guided me and without whom I could not have completed this book.

The profits from this book will be divided between the Regimental Benevolent Fund of the Irish Guards and the Army Benevolent Fund.

Rupert Clarke

PREFACE

On 1 April 1998 I watched HRH The Duke of Gloucester unveil Martin Yeomans' portrait of his godfather, Field Marshal Earl Alexander of Tunis, in the villa at La Marsa, Tunis, by then the residence of the British Ambassador, but in 1943 the site of the Headquarters of the 18th Army Group, commanded by General The Hon Sir Harold Alexander, as he then was, whom it was my honour and privilege to serve as a member of his personal staff. As the curtain fell away from the picture, I at once felt those fifty-five years disappear. Once more I was standing in the Chief's Mess. Outside, the signals generators hummed in the garden and I could hear the tap, tap, tap of the radio antenna of our armoured car as it blew against the wall of the verandah in the evening breeze. All around me I could hear the multifarious sounds of a busy staff at work and the clatter of the defence platoon as they checked their wire and positions in the garden.

As I stood immersed in that happy dream, I resolved to write a personal memoir as a tribute to my Chief, covering the years that we were together, from the peaceful surroundings of Wilton House in 1941, through the nightmare of the First Burma Campaign of 1942, the days of his Command-in-Chief in Cairo and the Western Desert to Army Group Command in North Africa and Italy and, finally, Supreme Allied Command of the Mediterranean and the German surrender in 1945, after the crossing of the River Po.

* * *

'General Alex' or 'The Chief', as we all knew him, was a man in a million. Possessed of total physical and moral courage, a natural flair for command in battle and a priceless gift for getting the best out of all who served him, regardless of rank or race, he had a natural charm and arresting good looks, which radiated confidence and created a charisma which could not fail to captivate. That outward charm and easy-going manner, combined with a never-failing courtesy, concealed a very tough inner discipline. Field Marshal Montgomery, who, by his own confession, was as different from Alex as chalk from cheese, was

Caledon, Alex's boyhood home.

known to have said of Alex that he was 'The only man that any general would gladly serve in a subordinate position'.

The third son of the Earl of Caledon, Alexander was born in London in 1891. All his early years were spent in his beloved Ulster, which he regarded as his natural home. There he was free to develop his innate love of the countryside and his natural affinity with all the gamekeepers, foresters, farm labourers and staff who worked on the Caledon estate. A devoted family man, he was closest to his second brother, Herbrand, and the youngest, known always as 'Baby'. Both used to visit him during the Italian Campaign.

As he developed, Alex grew into an outstanding athlete and won the Irish Mile Championship. Had the 1916 Olympic Games not been cancelled, it was likely that he would have been selected to compete.

He had a lifelong ambition to become an accomplished landscape painter. Even when on campaign, he would paint whenever the opportunity occurred and, years later, when Governor General of Canada, he was still painting avidly.

Serious soldier though he was, he had a great sense of fun. Even as Commanding Officer, he would take part in regimental concerts and his act, which included tap dancing, was eagerly awaited by the guardsmen.

In the field Alex was always impeccably turned out, almost always wearing his Sam Browne belt and high, close-fitting boots, made for him by an old Turkish bootmaker in Cyprus. On his head he wore his Irish Guards cap, embellished with his red band and general's badge and often at a slightly rakish angle. In the years that I was with him, I never saw him wear a steel helmet, even under heavy shelling, bombing and machine-gun fire. His immaculate turn-out, combined with his dashing good looks and happy, relaxed expression, had a profound effect upon the confidence he inspired as he moved fearlessly around the battlefield, often at the wheel of his own jeep.

Commander The Baltic *Landeswehr*, 1919-20. Note that Alex is wearing the White Russian Order of St Anne.

After Harrow and Sandhurst, Alex was commissioned into the Irish Guards in 1911. His regimental record in the First World War was a source of great pride to him, for, as he would often tell me, he commanded at every level from platoon to brigade during those four years. Twice wounded, he was awarded the DSO and MC, and, as a subaltern, won the French Legion of Honour.

The war over, he volunteered to serve with the British Forces in the Baltic and was sent to join Stephen Tallents on the Armistice Commission. Tallents recommended Colonel Alexander for command of the Baltic *Landeswehr*, a force of almost divisional size, served by a German divisional headquarters. With this force he fought alongside the White Russians against the Bolshevik Red Army. He was wounded yet again, but served with conspicuous success, pushing the enemy back to their own borders and defeating a Russian army in so doing. This outstanding achievement brought about the independence of Latvia. It earned him the Baltic Cross of Honour and the White Russian Order of St Anne with Swords. Many years later, when he attended the Yalta Conference in February, 1945, as Supreme Allied Commander Mediterranean, Stalin would welcome him in Russian as the only general officer present who had defeated a Russian army, describing him as 'the best general on the Allied side' – a remark which, happily in the circumstances, was not fully translated to those present!

In the 1920s and '30s Alex lived a typical soldier's life: going to the Staff College and the Imperial Defence College, commanding his regiment and the Regimental District. In 1931 he married Lady Margaret Bingham, the younger daughter of the Earl of Lucan.

Unusually for an officer of the British Service, he was given command of a key formation in the Indian Army, the Nowshera Brigade, involved in operations on the North-West Frontier. This was yet another task that he carried out with distinction and for which he was long remembered by the Indian soldiers, not simply because he was a fine fighting soldier but because he took the trouble to master both Hindi and Urdu, the two lingua franca of

On 7 September 1939, just before Alex took his 1st Division to France, His Majesty King George VI visited Headquarters Aldershot Command. On the left of the front row is Brigadier Percival who, as GOC Malaya, would surrender Singapore to the Japanese in February 1942. Lieutenant General Sir John Dill (later CIGS) is on His Majesty's right. Alex is at the right-hand end of the front row.

the Indian Army, earning the unswerving respect and devotion of his Gurkha and Indian troops. The brigade covering the adjacent area to his was that of Brigadier Claude Auchinleck and based on Peshawar. He too was deeply loved by the Indian soldiers and stood head and shoulders above his contemporaries in the Indian Army. Little did either of them think that within a few short years Alex would relieve 'the Auk' as Commander-in-Chief Middle East. At the end of his tour of command Alex was appointed a Commander of the Star of India and, to him much more importantly, he was invited by the 3rd Battalion of the 2nd Punjab Regiment to become their Honorary Colonel.

In 1937 Alex was promoted to Major General, the youngest in the Army, and assumed command of the 1st Division in Aldershot, taking it to France on 19 September 1939 as part of the British Expeditionary Force (BEF). In May 1940, having fought a series of successful delaying actions as the Allies fell back before the German *Blitzkrieg*, the Division became part of the Dunkirk perimeter and General Alex was appointed Commander of the 1st British Corps, with responsibility for the whole of those elements of the BEF within the bridgehead. Lord Gort, the Commander-in-Chief, had been ordered home by Winston Churchill and handed over the bridgehead to Alex on 30 May.

It comes as no surprise that Alex should have been the last man to leave the beaches. He had patrolled up and down the embarkation areas in a motor boat, accompanied by his driver, Corporal Wells, shouting through a megaphone in both French and English 'Is anyone there?' Satisfied that the beaches were indeed clear, he returned to the harbour to embark on the last destroyer on 3 June. Well over 200,000 British and some 140,000 French troops had been evacuated. The gallant French rearguard surrendered to the Germans on the following day.

The story of General Alex's distinguished leadership at Dunkirk and his total disregard for his own safety made him one of the national heroes of the hour and, significantly, deeply impressed Winston Churchill, so that when, in 1942, the defence of Burma was in tatters and a firm hand at the helm was needed, there was only one name that came to the Prime Minister's mind, as Chapter 2 will reveal.

Chapter One

WILTON

April, 1941 – February, 1942

In April 1941, as my story opens, the state of the war gave few grounds for optimism. Britain and the Commonwealth still stood alone. London and many of our major cities were under nightly attack from the air. In the Mediterranean, Greece was about to fall to the Germans and the British and Anzac troops who had been sent there from the Middle East would very soon be fighting for dear life in Crete. In the Western Desert the fortress of Tobruk was under constant attack from Rommel's Afrika Korps and their Italian allies, and all attempts to relieve the garrison had failed. In the Atlantic the U-boats were taking a heavy toll of our merchant shipping. Yet, despite all this, there was still a quiet air of confidence that we would prevail. Hadn't we seen off the Luftwaffe only a few months ago in the Battle of Britain, and had that not put paid to Hitler's planned invasion of our islands?

Meanwhile, at home, the British Army was busily re-building, re-equipping and re-training to make good the damage of the disastrous defeat in France and the massive withdrawal from Dunkirk, in which my master to be had so distinguished himself.

In the Far East the Japanese, still fighting to gain control of more of mainland China, were beginning to play a double game. From their allies in the Pact of Steel, the Germans, they had acquired a Top Secret British document which not only revealed the parlous state of the defences of Hong Kong, Singapore and Burma, but also the sheer impossibility of providing them with any reinforcements or equipment. Thus armed, the Japanese military leaders had stepped up their preparations for what they saw as 'the move south', having already penetrated Indo-China with the connivance of the Vichy French, as directed by Berlin. As a safeguard, the Japanese had now signed a non-aggression pact with Russia, little knowing that within a matter of weeks their German allies would be launching over 180 divisions across the Russian western border in Hitler's Operation BARBAROSSA.

* * *

I came down from Magdalen College, Oxford, in November 1939 and was sent to the Royal Military College, Sandhurst, being

1

commissioned into the Irish Guards in May of the following year after a spell with the 5th (SR) Battalion, The Scots Guards, who were training at Chamonix with the French Chasseurs Alpins to go to support the Finns in their Winter War against the Russians. In the event we never went, for that war ended in March and the Battalion was broken up. Now, having served for the better part of a year as the senior platoon commander of No 1 Company, 1st Battalion Irish Guards, I was selected to become ADC to Lieutenant General Sir Harold Alexander, KCB, CSI, DSO, MC, General Officer Commanding-in-Chief, Southern Command, whose headquarters were at Wilton House, near Salisbury.

On 13 April 1941 I reported to Captain The Hon Hanning Phillips, Welsh Guards, the General's senior ADC. Hanning was some fifteen years older than me and at once became my mentor and friend.

As members of the Chief's personal staff, we lived in his private Mess in a small house a few minutes' walk from the office and looking out over the water meadows which were such a joy to General Alex. He loved to spend a few hours' relaxation out there on a Sunday, painting in company with our camouflage officer, the distinguished landscape painter, Edward Seago, with whom he had become fast friends. Those painting Sundays also gave Hanning and I a chance to have a break away from the office and get some exercise. We would walk about three miles along a hog's back of a ridge to a pub run by a retired Indian Army officer who produced the best curry you ever ate. After lunch, completely comatose, we would take a taxi back to Wilton and be back in post before Alex and Ted returned from the water meadows.

As is usual with the office arrangements for very senior officers, Hanning and I had our desks in an ante-room which gave access to the Chief. This enabled us to control the flow of visitors and ward off any who tried to gain admittance without an appointment. It also ensured that we knew where he was! On more than one occasion, when he felt, perhaps, like pulling our legs, we found him trying to escape through the window! Small wonder that we loved to work for him and would spare no effort to ensure that he got the service he had every right to expect.

Alex loved to be with the troops in the field and, almost daily, he would be out and about in the Command, watching training, assessing units and their commanders, listening to people's problems, which at once became his own. As the junior ADC, it was my responsibility to organize these tours, warn the formations and units and work out the itinerary and then to act as his map-reader and personal staff officer.

How well I remember those drives. The faithful Wells, long his driver and now a Sergeant, was at the wheel of the staff car. Getting the Chief to the right place at the right time was no easy matter, for all the signposts had been painted out as a counter to parachutist and invasion scares (of which we had two that year, each a red alert). So it was map-reading in earnest all the way!

While we were out, Hanning, acting more as Military Assistant than an ADC, kept the office and wrestled with the flood of paperwork – a division of labour which suited me to perfection and would be perpetuated later when Alex became Commander-in-Chief, Middle East, and Bill Cunningham, General Auchinleck's ADC, joined us as Military Assistant, with all his knowledge of the theatre and his experience of desert fighting.

Come on! Let's get warm! IWM H6286

After I had been in post for some months I was suddenly summoned to London by the Security Service (MI5) who had intercepted a letter to me from a German friend then serving in a Panzer division on the Eastern Front and complaining of the hardship and difficulties of the Russian winter. The writer was one of several German boys of my own age whom I had got to know well during the two summers I had spent in Bavaria before the war when perfecting my knowledge of German. Some of them were members of the *Hitler Jugend* and had even taken me to Munich to hear Hitler speak. Several such letters had arrived at my home in Ireland, but this one had clearly been redirected to me at Wilton by mistake. On the face of it, things did not look too good for me. However, I finally persuaded my interrogator that there was nothing sinister about all this, persuading him also to concede that there had been no way in which I could stop the letters coming without communicating with the enemy. Finally, with not very good grace, he let me go, saying that General Alexander would have to be informed.

As soon as I got back to Wilton I told the Chief the whole story, not without some trepidation. I should have known him better. Alex himself was a fluent German speaker, thanks to his time in command of the Baltic *Landeswehr*. Whilst holding that command he had had the staff support of a German divisional headquarters and had kept one eye on the progress of some of his better officers ever since; more than one had become a general by 1941. He listened to me with that charming smile of his and then burst out laughing, saying that my knowledge of German might prove useful. Indeed it did, for it gave us a private means of communication when he wanted to say something for my ears only! His response to my predicament had been entirely typical of him, for he had a great gift for putting junior officers at their ease.

The months flew by. We covered every corner of the Command as General Alex continued to instil confidence, keeping his experienced eye on progress and gently but firmly taking such action as might be required. Then, on 19 February 1942, at the beginning of what was to prove one of the most momentous years of his life, everything began to change. That was the moment when he received a summons from the War Office with orders to report at once to General Sir Alan Brooke, the CIGS. The relative calm of Wilton House had gone for ever.

Chapter Two

BURMA: A CHANGE OF COMMAND

March, 1942

In April 1941 Churchill determined that, in the light of the greatly increased German presence in the Middle East and Mediterranean, the main war effort in the immediate future must be concentrated there and, in his role as Minister of Defence as well as Prime Minister, issued a diktat to the Chiefs of Staff, whom he had not previously consulted, switching the national strategic priorities of the Middle East and Far East theatres. In that document he made it quite plain that no additional support, other than measures already in hand, could be sent to the Far East. He had completely failed to appreciate the true nature and scale of the Japanese threat and even suggested that, should America enter the war, the Japanese would stay out. Only the lone voice of Sir John Dill, then the CIGS, was raised in protest – and ignored.

From Singapore the Commander-in-Chief Far East had long been voicing his concern over the weakness of his defences throughout the Command and calling for reinforcements, particularly of modern aircraft. His pleas had fallen on stony ground. In the late summer of 1941, and again in September, General Wavell, the Commander-in-Chief, India, asked that Burma should be placed under his operational command as a matter of urgency. He knew that it had been regarded as a backwater by Singapore and that little or nothing had been done to put it on a war footing. Stressing how strategically important Burma was to the defence of north-east India, he reminded Whitehall that Rangoon was of equal importance to the Chinese in their fight against the Japanese, for it was the last port that they had through which they could pass warlike stores, ferrying material from there up the Burma Road from Lashio in central Burma to Chungking. He also expressed the view that to have Burma already under his logistic command but not for operations was thoroughly unsound. Not until 12 December 1941, four days after the Japanese had struck in Malaya, was that switch of command finally authorized – far, far, too late. Although Wavell at once sent a strong team of staff officers from Delhi to Rangoon to help with the urgent transfer to a war footing, and even sent his own Chief of Staff, Lieutenant General T.J. Hutton, a

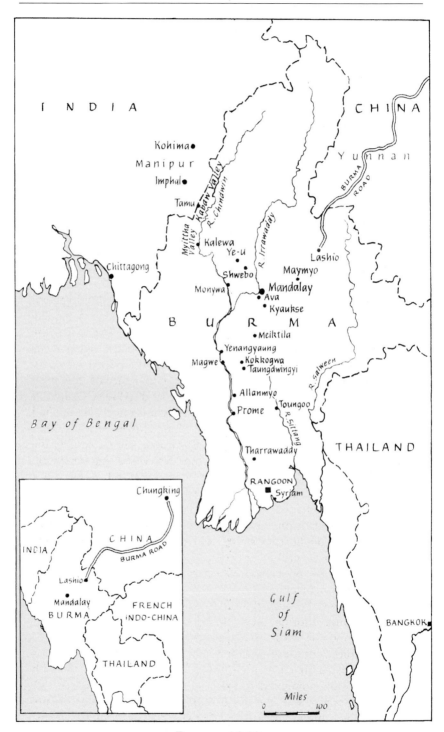

Burma 1942.

brilliant staff officer, to take command at the end of December, his excellent measures were frustrated by a piece of disastrous political folly.

On 7 December 1941 the Japanese attacked the American base of Pearl Harbor. On the 8th America entered the war and the Japanese invaded the north of Malaya. Two days later the Burma Independence Army (BIA), a clandestine force organized and trained by the Japanese, which had been lying in wait in Thailand, crossed the border into Burma with 2,300 men. The Japanese now had a built-in source of local knowledge of the country and a powerful and ruthless agency through which to exert control over the Burmese people. Meanwhile, General Iida's 15th Army, consisting of two infantry divisions, the battle-hardened 33rd and the well-trained but inexperienced 55th, and supported by the 5th Air Division, which had already alerted its formidable force of modern combat aircraft of all types in Bangkok, was beginning to move west to invade Burma.

Hutton teamed up with the Governor of Burma, Sir Reginald Dorman-Smith, as soon as he took over and things began to happen, but almost at once the disastrous plot hatched in Washington by Roosevelt and Churchill to establish a unified Allied Command for the Far East brought things in Burma to a halt. Burma was now switched once more and placed under command of this new American, British, Dutch, Australian Command (ABDACOM) with its headquarters in Java and negligible communications. Wavell had been appointed the Supreme Allied Commander, with General Chiang Kai-shek, the Chinese Nationalist leader, in command of the Chinese Theatre of Operations. Within five weeks this hopelessly unworkable, ineffective organization was dead and Burma once more reverted to Indian command. Wavell himself wrote later: 'It was during those five weeks that the fate of Burma was decided.'

The 5th Air Division began to bomb Rangoon almost as soon as Japan had begun hostilities. In early January General Iida's two divisions began the ground assault and, despite the gallant efforts of the RAF and the pilots of the American Volunteer Group, soon enjoyed air supremacy.

At that stage the Burma Army consisted of only the 1st Burma Division, a mixed formation of Burmese, Indian and Gurkha troops, with, initially, one British battalion. It was commanded by Major General Bruce Scott. It was neither trained nor equipped for war and quite unversed in jungle warfare. It was very soon joined by the 17th Indian Division, commanded by Major General 'Jackie' Smyth VC. This division, too, was untrained in jungle warfare and only lightly supported with mountain artillery. However, as it would soon show, whatever else it lacked, it did not lack courage or the will to fight.

The task of defending a vast country like Burma with two such divisions, which at first were without a coordinating Corps headquarters, was virtually impossible; the frontages were simply too great. With only the most limited and obsolete air support, the outlook was indeed grim. The Burma Army had perforce to keep giving ground whilst still desperately trying to cover the approaches to Rangoon, which by now was under almost constant air attack. Things were made no easier for Hutton by a large number of desertions from the Burma Rifles battalions which formed a substantial part of 1 Burma Division. The shock of encountering those tough, well-trained Japanese troops with their ample air support and the anxiety that many of the men were feeling for their families, who had been over-run by the enemy, proved too much for them.

In mid-February disaster struck once again. Through a misunderstanding, for which General Smyth later accepted full responsibility, the great Sittang River Bridge, which lay on one of the approach routes to Rangoon, was prematurely blown and a substantial part of 17 Indian Division was stranded on the wrong side of the river. Although some of those cut off got across on rafts or by swimming, they had lost their personal weapons and the overall strength of the Division was dramatically reduced. Smyth was relieved of his command and his Deputy Commander, Brigadier 'Punch' Cowan, who would prove to be one of the outstanding divisional commanders of the war, took over.

By the greatest good fortune, on the very day that the Sittang Bridge was blown the 7th Armoured Brigade, of two armoured regiments, the 7th Hussars and the 2nd Royal Tank Regiment, began unloading in Rangoon. Equipped with the American Stuart tank – the Honey – they had come from the battlefields of the Middle East and had seen a good bit of fighting. Here, at last, was manna from Heaven! Almost at once their presence began to be felt and from that time to the last days of the long, tortuous withdrawal to India, some 900 miles, they fought heroically to give the hard-pressed infantry the support they so desperately needed. Indeed, it has often been said by those who fought in that campaign that without those tanks the Burma Army might never have got away to fight another day.

By the beginning of March things were getting desperate. The threat to Rangoon and the consequent loss of his vital source of supply had driven Chiang Kai-shek to order General Joseph B. Stilwell, his American Deputy Commander, to send an officer to Rangoon to discuss Chinese support for the protection of the Burma Road. Earlier, at Wavell's request, he had released one of his two squadrons of the

American Volunteer Group (AVG) with its P40 fighters to assist in the air defence of Rangoon against the modern, high-performance aircraft of the Japanese, a task far beyond the capacity of the RAF's obsolete Brewster Buffaloes, of which they had a mere handful. Bravely as their pilots fought, they were simply shot out of the sky. It was not until January and February that reinforcements for the RAF arrived from Iraq. These included two squadrons of Hurricanes and a squadron of Blenheims. The aircraft were soon flying as much as three sorties a day and the lack of technical support available rapidly made itself felt.

By 5 March much of Rangoon was on fire and the city was in a state of chaos. The country simply had not been geared for war and the organization needed to keep such a situation under any sort of control did not exist.

* * *

The summons to the War Office had reached us on the Isle of Wight, where General Alex was inspecting some units. We at once returned to the mainland and Sergeant Wells and made for London at best speed.

When we reached the War Office that evening we were met at the door by Barney Charlesworth, General Brooke's ADC and a good friend, and taken up to the CIGS's office on the third floor. There Alex was ushered into 'the presence' and I sat in the outer office chatting to the staff and wondering what was afoot.

General Brooke lost no time in telling Alex that the Government was extremely concerned about the situation in Burma. ABDACOM had folded up a week earlier and Burma was now back under Delhi's command. The Viceroy had sent a signal to the Prime Minister suggesting that a firmer and more experienced hand than General Hutton's was needed if there was to be any hope of saving Rangoon. As things now stood, Rangoon was already being subjected to heavy air attack and should General Iida's two divisions be allowed to assault the city the chances of holding them off were pretty slim. The political importance of the port as Chiang Kai-shek's only source of supply from the West and the security of the Burma Road was worrying the Prime Minister considerably and he had issued instructions that Alex, whom he so admired for his performance at Dunkirk, should be sent out at once to assume command from Hutton. The CIGS explained that Hutton would remain in Burma as Alex's Chief of Staff. Alex would be promoted to the local rank of

General and was to take one ADC with him.

Looking as relaxed as ever, but with, I thought, just a shadow of unusual gravity on his cheerful face, Alex reappeared from this momentous interview and at once told me of his new mission, asking me if I would like to go with him as Hanning Phillips was unfit for overseas service. My immediate acceptance was one of the most important and certainly one of the happiest decisions of my life.

The Chief was then taken to Churchill's War Room. He later dined with him and Mrs Churchill in the Annexe. The next morning was taken up with a feverish round of briefings and talks before Alex lunched with Vice-Admiral Lord Louis Mountbatten, the newly-appointed Chief of Combined Operations. Mountbatten was pretty gloomy about Burma and voiced the view that the position there was hopeless, doubtless influenced by the naval appreciation issued soon after the Japanese had sunk the *Repulse* and the *Prince of Wales* off Malaya on 10 December. I was inclined to feel that his pessimism had little impact upon my Chief in whose book the word 'hopeless' did not exist and for whom the scent of battle was like champagne.

That afternoon, the 20th, we drove down to the Alexanders' house near Windsor for a farewell dinner with Lady Margaret. Their very understanding nanny gave me a splendid supper of bacon and eggs in the nursery. Then, later, we drove off to Hurn Airport outside Southampton to fly on the first leg of our long journey to Delhi, where Alex was to report to General Headquarters India Command.

Even for VIPs long-distance air travel in wartime was often a very uncomfortable and even hazardous business. We soon discovered that we were to go to Cairo in the bomb bay of a Liberator heavy bomber – unheated and unpressurized!

Despite the urgency of our journey, we were at the mercy of the weather which was still very wintery. After several abortive attempts to take off, we finally flew on 27 February, a precious week having been lost. Even General Alex's normal *sang froid* was affected, as he had no means of knowing what was happening in Burma while we endured that frustrating wait.

Because we were to be flying at between 19 and 20,000 feet we both had to undergo physical tests in the RAF's decompression chamber before we signed the 'Blood Chit' saying that we accepted that we flew at our own risk. To combat the cold we were then dressed in flying suits with padded bags of chemicals to keep the soles of our feet and our wrists warm. We had, of course, to wear flying helmets, as we would be on oxygen once we got to height, and heavy gloves. Even so, sitting in the bomb bay in my oxygen mask, with stalactites six inches long hanging from the mouth-piece, I had to keep stamping my feet to keep my circulation going until we got further south and into warmer conditions.

As we crossed Spain we were fired on, ineffectually, by the Spanish air defences, but it made quite a good fireworks display.

The Liberator had had to make a wide diversion over the Bay of Biscay to avoid a night fighter squadron of German JU-88s which patrolled off the French Atlantic coastline. After leaving Spain and Gibraltar behind us we came right down to a height of about 100 feet, wave-hopping over the

Alex, still GOC-in-C Southern Command, inspecting coastal defences on the Isle of Wight. IWM H6291

Mediterranean along the North African coast to Cairo. With our four tail guns and two more in the dorsal turret, we were pretty immune to fighters, who would not have room to dive on us and then pull out before hitting the waves. What a relief it was to us both to be able to discard our oxygen masks, helmets, gloves and flying suits and enjoy the sunshine, blue skies and warmth of the Mediterranean.

We landed at RAF Heliopolis on the outskirts of Cairo at about 8 am. General Alex spent the day at the British Embassy with Sir Miles Lampson. It was a stroke of luck for me to find that Graham Lampson, his son and one of my greatest friends, who had been up at Magdalen with me and with whom I had shared a house, was there. Although I had no inkling of it then, in less than six months we would be back in Cairo in earnest and my friendship with Graham was not only going to be invaluable but also provide me with a home from home when I was off duty.

On the following day, 1 March, we flew on to Delhi in a converted DC3, that great workhorse of the air, the Dakota. We had two RAF pilots and, mercifully as it turned out, a mechanic. The aircraft had been stripped down internally so that only two seats, near the door, remained. The rest of the fuselage was filled by an enormous extra fuel tank, leaving about 2 or 3 feet of headroom – enough to allow me to spread out my valise and enable me to get out of Alex's way, leaving him with the two seats so that he could spread his maps and reports of Burma on one as he worked. Nothing seemed to worry him. He was blithely indifferent to the fact that he was almost sitting on some hundreds of gallons of high octane aviation fuel. Climbing up onto my valise, I slept for an hour or two until we had to make a forced landing on a beach in the Persian Gulf at about midday. For some two hours that God-sent mechanic wrestled with our problem, which, with the aid of a few pieces of wire, he eventually defeated. Meanwhile, we took shelter in the shade of the wing; even there the temperature was over 100 degrees. On we flew to the nearest RAF base to refuel and check the aircraft and thence to India, landing at Delhi. There we were met by Wavell's ADC, Sandy Reid-Scott MC, who had lost an eye with the 11th Hussars in the Western Desert. At the Wavells' house we were warmly welcomed by Lady Wavell, who told Alex that, unfortunately, her husband, who was still commanding ABDACOM at that time, was visiting the war in Burma. Once more the Chief became involved in a series of talks and briefings for a couple of days and was given his mission in Burma by the Chief of Staff at General Headquarters, speaking on General Wavell's behalf. Quite simply it was to hold Rangoon if militarily possible, but if this could not be done he was to withdraw the Army to Upper Burma, keeping the Japanese out of India until the monsoon broke in May or June. At that time the Burma Army still consisted of two battered divisions with little or no air support and few heavy weapons. By the grace of God 7th Armoured Brigade had arrived a few days earlier and was already making its mark. Alex learned that General 'Bill' Slim was on his way back to India from his division in Iraq and, on arrival, would at once begin to form a Corps Headquarters (1st Burma Corps) to coordinate the operations of the divisions and 7th Armoured Brigade

GOC Burma. March, 1942. IWM IND 804

and to cooperate with the 5th and 6th Chinese Armies, who were arriving to protect the Burma Road under the command General Chiang Kai-shek's Deputy, the American Lieutenant General Joseph Stilwell (known to all as 'Vinegar Joe'). This Chinese Expeditionary Force would also come under General Alex's overall command. Joe was a noted Anglophobe and about as awkward a cuss as it was possible to find, but he was a magnificent soldier. As things turned out, he and Alex managed to hit it off through the mutual respect each had for the other as fighting men. Alex's natural gift for making things work and people to cooperate was going to be badly needed there!

While Alex was up at GHQ Sandy Reid-Scott very kindly took me in hand and helped with some very essential refurbishment of our kit, for we had been travelling with little more than we stood up in. I had some excellent Indian Army blue 'Masri' bush shirts made, such as General Alex had worn in India in the Thirties when commanding the Nowshera Brigade. They would be ideal for the hot, sticky climate of Burma and have the added advantage of making the Indian troops feel that they not only had a commander who could speak their language but identified himself with them by wearing the traditional dress of their own army. In that connection, it came as a very pleasant surprise to discover that we would now be on Indian Army rates of pay, which represented a most welcome increase to my small income.

On 4 March we flew on to Rangoon, stopping briefly in Calcutta, where Alex was able to have a short meeting with General Wavell on Dum Dum airport, surely one of the hottest places in the world; the heat hit us like a blast furnace as we climbed out of our Dakota. Wavell urged the Chief to hold Rangoon if humanly possible but not to get trapped there. On that not very happy note we flew on to a satellite airstrip outside

Maymyo, April, 1942. With the Governor, Sir Reginald Dorman-Smith. IWM IND 808

Rangoon, carved out of the jungle and rejoicing in the curious code name of Highland Queen. Although we did not realize it at the time, ours was to be the last aircraft to land at Rangoon. The RAF squadrons had already been withdrawn to Calcutta and the AVG squadron had returned to its base at Chungking. For a couple of days we would see a lonely photographic reconnaissance Hurricane around, making its routine sorties, and then even that disappeared, leaving the Burma Army bereft of all air support.

We were met at the airstrip by a staff officer and an armed escort and at once driven to Army headquarters in the University. The drive through the empty city was an eerie experience. Barely a soul was to be seen except furtive groups of looters doing their best to remain unobserved and a few lunatics from the asylum, who had been released in error by some civil servant. The looters doubtless included the prisoners from the jail, who had also been turned loose.

General Hutton and his staff had worked out a three-stage evacuation plan for the city, beginning on 20 February, and this was now well advanced, with the civil population, particularly the Indians, who formed so large a part of the working and clerical elements, now streaming north, some by train, some by car, but tens of thousands on foot. Under that plan the final evacuation should have begun that day, but one of General Alex's first decisions after we arrived at Army Headquarters was to delay that final move until he himself had had a chance to assess the chances of holding Rangoon.

On reaching the University we were greeted by General Hutton and later met the Governor, Sir Reginald Dorman-Smith, who was a an unimpressive character and was clearly very dependent upon Hutton. He seemed incapable of taking any decisions for himself. For the next hour Alex familiarized himself with the tactical situation and was brought up to date on the progress of the enemy. He at once decided that the gap which now existed between the two divisions of the Army must be closed and ordered two attacks to be launched by 1 Burma Division in the north and by 17 Indian Division, then sited about forty miles north up the Prome road. Having issued his orders, he drove up to 17 Division to take charge of the southern limb of the battle. Both attacks failed and, having issued further orders, Alex drove back to Rangoon to dine with the Governor and General Hutton. Hutton had protested over the use of 17 Division in an offensive operation as they were still suffering from the impact of the Sittang Bridge disaster, but Alex had been determined that no effort could be spared to stave off the seizure of Rangoon and had insisted that they should attack as ordered. Not surprisingly, dinner proved a pretty sombre affair. Hutton was, understandably, depressed at having been superseded and having to stay on as Chief of Staff and also by the disregard of his advice over the use of 17 Division. The Governor, who seemed to have been bowled over by the whole affair and to be conscious of his inability to shine in the present situation, was gloomy. The only light relief was the sudden appearance of dacoits in the garden, clearly waiting to loot the Residency when it was evacuated. I leaped through the French windows of the dining room and the would-be looters fled, leaving one of their number wounded.

The next morning Alex began his formal take-over from Hutton, which lasted until lunchtime. Meanwhile, while that was going on, I took myself down to the docks. There the scene was one of total chaos, a situation for which Alex had a splendid word, 'Bargo', a little code word which we would use all too frequently in the years ahead. Certainly Bargo was the only possible description of the sight that met my eyes. All the Indian and Burmese dock workers had long since fled and such unloading of ships as was possible was being done by troops, using the ships' own derricks. American kit was everywhere, the go-downs were packed with it and the docksides stacked with US $2\frac{1}{2}$ ton trucks and jeeps, which some American soldiers were beginning to destroy. British troops were moving from go-down to go-down scrounging whatever they could lay their hands on and might be useful in the fighting, a measure already tacitly agreed by Chiang Kai-shek, for whose armies the stores had been destined. As for me, I annexed a double-barrelled 12-bore shot gun and a bag of cartridges, which I felt would be better value in the jungle than a rifle. I also annexed a .45 Colt automatic pistol, which, together with a bandolier of thirty rounds of ammunition, I carried with me throughout the campaign.

On 6 March the Japanese cut the road between Pegu and Hlegu, cutting off 17 Division's 48 Brigade, and were beginning to move towards the vital Syriam oil refinery at the mouth of the

Rangoon river. This situation drove General Alex to decide that he could no longer hope to hold the city and wrote in his despatches:

> *In view of this situation, I considered that the retention of Rangoon was quite impossible with the comparatively small forces at my disposal, dispersed as they were and with parts of them already encircled.*

That evening, from Army Headquarters in the University, he ordered the final evacuation of Rangoon to begin at midnight. The programme of demolition to deny the enemy any facilities of use to them would begin in the afternoon of 7 March, with special emphasis upon the three oil refineries at Seikgyi, Thilawa and Syriam and all oil stocks in Rangoon itself. The demolition parties were under infantry escort as elements of the BIA had arrived in the area by sea. Meanwhile, Army headquarters moved up to the area of Taukkyan, a small town near what had been the RAF base at Mingaladon. Headquarters 17 Division and 7 Armoured Brigade were already there. It was then found that a Japanese battalion of 33 Division had established a very strong road block astride the Prome road just to the north of the town. An attempt by the 2nd King's Own Yorkshire Light Infantry, who had discovered the block, was thrown back. Two attacks by battalions of 17 Division with a detachment of the 7th Hussars also failed. That evening the situation was very serious, with the most important elements of the Army cut off. The dense pall of oily black smoke from the burning refineries did nothing to lighten the atmosphere and tension. As imperturbable and immaculate as ever, General Alex issued orders for a final all-out attack on the road block at dawn. When it went in, the leading elements found that the Japanese had gone. The battalion had received orders to screen the flanks of 33 Division when it crossed the Prome road before turning south and entering Rangoon from the west. Had that attack failed and the road block been reinforced, the consequences could only have been disastrous. Perhaps fortunately, I remember very little of that critical day as throughout most of it I was wrestling with an attack of dengue fever with a temperature of 102 degrees with alternating bouts of soaking sweat and cold.

Later, when I was capable of taking rather more interest in all that was happening around me, the Chief told me that he had been in tougher spots than the hairsbreadth escape they had just experienced. Certainly, as all around him during that day would swear, he had never once shown the slightest sign of doubt or apprehension.

During the night of 6–7 March continuous efforts had been made to get a message through to General Wavell to report the evacuation of the city, but all had failed. By a stroke of good fortune, however, a courier managed to get through before the Japanese blocked the roads and delivered a written message to the Governor in Maymyo (prounced *Mymew*) for onward transmission to Delhi. Maymyo, a pleasant hill station, was the new seat of government and within a matter of days we too would move Army Headquarters there.

Meanwhile, the Japanese entered Rangoon in triumph on 8 March 1942. Phase 1 of their invasion plan was completed.

Chapter Three

BURMA: THE LONG FIGHT BACK

March – May, 1942

Inevitably General Wavell now demanded reasons for the evacuation of Rangoon, upon the retention of which he had set such store. In his reply Alexander pointed out that his directive had been to hold Rangoon for as long as possible but not to allow his Army to be cut off or destroyed. 'This,' he said, 'has been accomplished, but only by a very small margin.'

The situation facing the Burma Army at this time was about as grim as anyone could imagine. General Bill Slim's 1st Burma Corps (Burcorps) Headquarters was still forming at the time of the fall of Rangoon and Slim himself would not be able to leave his division in Iraq until about 12 or 13 March, so that to have Burcorps deployed in Burma and functioning by the 16th was going to be a very tight squeeze. So the whole burden of tactical control of the Army would have to rest upon Alexander's own shoulders and those of his Army staff for the first eleven days of his tenure of command. It was indeed fortunate that his two divisional commanders, Scott and Cowan, were both Gurkhas and close friends of over twenty years' standing. Bill Slim, too, was a Gurkha and a friend of both. This was going to prove a most important factor over the months ahead, during which cooperation was going to be vital in the confused situation that was bound to persist – and did.

Overwhelmed as he was with work and problems, Alexander was first and foremost a high-class professional soldier and, as such, must have found the time to sit quietly and weigh up the pros and cons of his hazardous situation, for no one would know better than he that unless he got that appreciation right his chances of coming to the correct decisions which would enable him to extricate his Army and hold off the Japanese were non-existent.

We have no record of any such appreciation but it is not difficult to identify the principal realities of the situation on 8 March 1942.

His two divisions were in a parlous state, though for different reasons. Still suffering severely from the results of the Sittang Bridge disaster and a very severe 'friendly fire' incident, in which the RAF had hit some of its units hard as they were withdrawing to the Sittang River, the 17th was now being reorganized on a two-brigade basis, having recently been joined by a reinforcing brigade from India. In Punch Cowan it had a superb commander and the quality of leadership throughout the Division was high, as was the standard of discipline. Provided it could have even a short 'breather' while the reorganization was taking place, there were sound reasons for expecting that it would once more become a stout-hearted, effective formation. Although General Bruce Scott was an able commander, the very nature of 1 Burma Division (Burdiv) was a very different kettle of fish. The desertions already described were continuing and,

Discussing operations with the GOC 1st Burma Division, Major General Bruce Scott. April, 1942.

although many of the hillmen in the Division were made of sterner stuff than the men from lower Burma, they were much better suited to guerrilla-type operations than a fixed battle situation, as they would later show. So it was clear to General Alex that the lion's share of any rearguard work would have to be borne by 17 Division and the three regular British battalions who had recently arrived as reinforcements and were, as yet, unbrigaded. In that work, the newly joined 7th Armoured Brigade would have a major part to play.

A major concern was the absence of any air support and the lack of field artillery. There were two Indian Mounted Regiments, equipped with pack howitzers, both experienced in frontier operations and very efficient, but they lacked a serious punch. Burdiv had an Indian Field Regiment with 25 pdrs, like the Royal Horse Artillery battery with 7 Armoured Brigade. There were no medium guns.

A welcome asset was the existence of four Indian Sapper field companies and a field park company which had some heavy plant. In the light of the myriad Sapper tasks which would be an inevitable feature of the long fighting withdrawal about to begin – demolitions, route construction and repair, bridge-building and repair, the provision of fresh water in a country in which, despite its rivers, such water was hard to come by; the list was endless – those Sappers would be invaluable, as indeed they were to prove.

Transport was at a premium and the need to give such help as was possible to the tens of thousands of refugees streaming north was going to add seriously to an already difficult problem.

Finally came the $64,000 question, what about logistic support? Here there shone a bright ray of hope, for the Major General in charge of Administration, Major General E.N. Goddard, had already worked miracles, having foreseen that unless the ammunition, fuel and rations which the Army was going to need all the way back to India had been backloaded to safe dumps and unless new major dumps were created in northern Burma, stocked from India, the whole operation was a non-starter. A man of great ability, experience and ruthless drive, he had cut through every bureaucratic obstacle and ensured that the supplies would be there. In his book on the campaign *A Hell of a Licking* (Collins, 1986) Major General James Lunt, who fought through the campaign as a young officer with the Burma Rifles, wrote of Goddard, 'God knows where we would have been without him'.

Clearly the planning and handling of the tactical battle was going to spell success or failure. The Chief knew that until 16 March, when Burcorps would come into being under its dynamic Commander, General Bill Slim, the burden would continue to rest on his own very experienced shoulders. Not until Slim arrived would it be possible to establish a clear-cut chain of command and it was a mercy that in Cowan and Scott he had two stout-hearted dependable Commanders. The leadership given by all officers, from himself downwards, was going to be the critical factor in a successful withdrawal. Alex knew from his own experience of commanding Indian troops on operations that, given that leadership, they would respond magnificently. Without it, there could only be one outcome - to use his own word, 'Bargo'. That he had no less than six battalions of Gurkhas in the Army must have been a very welcome thought, for, fighting under their Gurkha Commanders, they would surely prove, as their forebears had so often in the past, that they ranked amongst the finest fighting soldiers in the world.

Meanwhile Chiang Kai-shek's 5th and 6th Armies were advancing down the Burma Road to come under Alexander's command. The 6th was heading for the Shan states and the 5th for Toungoo, where they would relieve 1 Burdiv, as agreed between General Wavell and Chiang Kai-shek. They would later be followed by the 66th Army. These armies were the equivalent of a British division. They were all under the command of 'Vinegar Joe' Stilwell,

With General Wavell (C-in-C India) and Generalissimo Chiang Kai-shek at Burma Army Headquarters, Maymyo. April, 1942. IWM IND859

although the chain of command was rather confusing. A real problem for the Burma Army was that the logistic responsibility for this Chinese Expeditionary Force would pass to them once the Chinese had deployed within Burma. They were only very lightly armed and without any artillery or armour, their heaviest weapons being a limited number of mortars. However, they were battle-hardened after years of fighting the Japanese and in the present circumstances any augmentation of fighting strength was welcome.

And what of the enemy? The Japanese plan for their invasion of Burma was in two phases, the first of which was the capture of

Rangoon with the two divisions we have already noted, the battle-hardened 33rd and the inexperienced but well-trained 55th. Despite endless references in existing accounts of this campaign to the jungle training these two divisions are alleged to have received, in fact they had had none, although a small pamphlet, designed to fit the soldier's pocket, which had been prepared and issued to all ranks and which was full of useful advice on how to fight in tropical conditions, provided very useful guidelines on the subject. Both divisions were well equipped and had ample artillery and air support. Their high standard of training and intense spirit of loyalty to their Emperor, often combined with suicidal bravery and an utter refusal to surrender, made them very dangerous and resolute opponents.

Fortunately they had an Achilles heel – a lack of motor transport. The transport regiments of the infantry divisions consisted of two horsed companies and one truck company only. This deficiency was bound to have a limiting effect upon their speed of advance and their ability to support the forward troops once their lines of communication began to stretch. Phase 2 of their invasion plan envisaged the occupation of the whole of Burma, the destruction of the Chinese forces and of the Burma Army on the plains south of Mandalay. The survivors were to be pushed back over the Indian frontier.

* * *

The 33rd Japanese Division had been charged with the restoration of law and order in Rangoon and not until 10 March did the 55th Division get its orders to begin advancing north towards Toungoo, some 85 miles away, to take on the Chinese 5th Army, who were relieving 1 Burdiv.

Also on 10 March General Alex moved Army Headquarters (AHQ) back to Maymyo, where the civil government had been established since it withdrew from Rangoon and so was the obvious location for AHQ. Maymyo was a pleasant little hill station standing at about 2,000 feet. Being the Governor's summer capital, it was well provided with good accommodation and, most importantly, good communications. All in all, it was a comfortable spot, set in well-laid-out gardens. As may be imagined, Alex had no intention of relaxing there away from the battle front for any longer than his business with the Governor or duties at AHQ required.

The Chief had a jeep, which he would either drive himself or leave the driving to me, as we traversed the extensive front. The never-ending columns of refugees, probably some 300,000 souls, mostly Indians, formed long black lines along the northbound routes. Sadly, it was all too common to see their dead and dying on the roadside or in the monsoon ditches. Women were having babies with no one to help them. Probably as many as 50,000 people died on that terrible trek.

The Chief was amazingly generous and I well remember how, when we had bully beef sandwiches for our picnic lunch, a rare delicacy at that time, he gave most of his sandwich to a young Indian woman who was carrying a child, and also half the contents of his water bottle. This impressed me deeply for it was extremely dry and dusty in the middle of the hot season and the heat was oppressive. We had only our army water-bottles to last us until nightfall, when a rather scratch meal would be produced. On another occasion I remember that we gave a lift to an elderly Indian who was struggling to rejoin his family. Very often, if we came across a marching column of Indian troops, Alex would get out of the jeep and march with them as they trudged wearily on, carrying their personal arms, Bren guns and ammunition and their big packs. As he loved to do, he would talk to them in Urdu and encourage them, with marked effect.

It was indeed lucky that the Japanese did not immediately follow up after the fall of Rangoon. This gave 17 Division, which had finally concentrated in the area of Tharrawaddy, the breather it so badly needed to complete its reorganization. It is a significant indication of what the Division had been through since the start of the campaign to find that of its sixteen British, Indian and Gurkha battalions, no less than eight Commanding Officers had been killed, five more wounded and one taken prisoner.

On 13 March General Alex had his first meeting with General Stilwell. At this first meeting Joe made no secret of the fact that he disliked Alexander. The quiet charm and impeccable turnout of this typical, aristocratic Briton were like a red rag to a bull to that dedicated anglophobe. Needless to say, Alex handled the situation with great diplomacy, for he knew, all too well, how vitally important it was that he should gain Stilwell's confidence. As a hard-bitten professional, Joe Stilwell knew that it was his duty to cooperate. In so doing he began to respect the Chief and realize that he was dealing with a very experienced and gallant soldier. So it was that after another two or three meetings relations became almost cordial and the mutual respect established was very evident, greatly improving the command situation. Nevertheless, Alex quickly came to see that Joe's own relationship with his Chinese masters was fraught with difficulty and that he would need all the help and support he could give him. This was going to be the first time that Chinese troops had ever served under foreign command and the situation was going to need very delicate handling, as would Joe himself, for, for all the mutual respect established between them, it was quite obvious that, as an American Lieutenant General, he would never feel very happy about getting his orders from a British officer.

Maurice Collis in his *First and Last in Burma* tells an amusing story about Joe Stilwell's relationship with the Chinese and the confusion which reigned over the question of command. On 12 March Joe had lunched with the Governor and Lady Dorman-Smith and had rather surprised His Excellency by telling him that he, Joe, commanded the 5th and 6th Chinese Armies in Burma. A little later the Governor met General Tu who said that he was commanding the Chinese forces, explaining, 'The American General only thinks he is commanding. To keep the Americans in this war, we give them a few commands on paper, as long as we do the work.'

This ambiguity was a major subject for discussion later when the Chief went to Chungking to see Chiang Kai-shek, but the incident on 12 March produced an amusing little piece of doggerel from the Governor's ADC, Eric Battersby:

> *Alexander, Stilwell and Tu*
> *Met at GH in Maymyo.*
> *They were somewhat perplexed*
> *And equally vexed,*
> *When trying to sort out who's who.*

That first meeting was the occasion of General Alex's Order Group at which he issued his directive to 1 Burma Corps to cover Prome. To my surprise, in addition to Generals Cowan and Scott, Slim was also present, his first appearance as Corps Commander. Like Alex, Bill Slim had his own charismatic aura. Just to see him was to feel the strong, quiet air of confidence which exuded from him and would inspire so many men of all ranks in the years ahead, not simply during the traumatic experience of this fighting withdrawal but throughout the Second Burma Campaign, from which he would emerge as a fighting general without peer. We had not expected him for at least another twenty-four hours. He had clearly come straight from his flight from Iraq without waiting for his headquarters. His most welcome presence lifted a huge burden from the Chief's overloaded shoulders.

After several more meetings with Stilwell, the Chief flew off to Chungking where Generalissimo and Madam Chiang Kai-shek had their headquarters. The Generalissimo, as he was known, was a small man with a narrow frame and long neck. We had christened him 'Pinhead'. Madam Chiang was a striking woman with a presence. She clearly wielded a good deal of power and was responsible for much of the decision-making. After three days of talks about the final arrangements for the Chinese Expeditionary Force coming under his command, General Alex flew back to Maymyo where he had a long talk with Joe Stilwell, who was still clearly unhappy about the thought of coming under command. The Chief subsequently ordered Slim to go on the offensive in order to support the Chinese armies. Three days later, on 1 April, Alex took the Commander-in-Chief, General Wavell, to Burcorps Headquarters at Allanmyo to see General Slim and give him orders to hold both banks of the Irrawaddy from his present location north to Taungdwingyi, to the north and east of which the Chinese were holding a line.

Whilst Alex had been in Chungking we had had our first experience of a formal Japanese attack – on Toungoo. Roughly speaking, their standard tactic was to fly a photographic reconnaissance over the objective some hours before launching a major high-level bombing attack by twenty-seven or more Mitsubishi twin-engined bombers, all of which bore such female names as 'Betty'. This would be followed by artillery concentrations upon our forward positions before the massed infantry came in. Some days later I went with the Chief to visit the headquarters of General Kan's 6th Army and had an opportunity to see these tactics in operation. Whilst Alex was talking to the Army Commander, I was idly watching a group of six Chinese soldiers playing cards. They were all tall, fair-haired, and often blue-eyed, young men, quite unlike the average small, dark-haired Chinese. Apparently it is believed that these fair-haired 'giants' are descended from the soldiers of Alexander the

Great, who had penetrated northern China some 2,000 years earlier in his great conquest of the then known world.

I had been told that a reconnaissance plane had flown over the headquarters on the previous afternoon, so a full-blown attack was expected at any time. To my surprise I also learned that the division's supporting elements, the mortars and transport, had been sent back to the next position, leaving the rifle companies to face the music. These fall-back positions could be anything from 20–50 miles in rear. Small parties of about three men each had also gone back to prepare the new company positions.

As I watched the game of cards I suddenly became aware of the sound of aircraft and then the explosion of the first bombs. One landed fairly close to where we were seated and one of the card players lost a leg. The raid over, the card game was resumed, the dying soldier's bets being divided among the other five.

Our liaison officer at the headquarters told me that this practice of making giant strides backwards when fighting a defensive battle was normal in the Chinese Army. One can only assume that it is a byproduct of the enormous size of their country, where ground will generally be of little importance, whereas the retention of trained soldiers is a matter of high priority. Whatever the reason may be, it was a disastrous policy for Burma and would later lead to the loss of the Burma Road, leaving the flank of 1 Burcorps exposed.

At about the time of the visit to 6th Army I took a young Shell engineer called Foster, who had supervised the destruction of the Rangoon refinery, to inspect the Yenangyaung oilfields, which were known to be a Japanse objective and which must, in any case, be denied to the enemy. We made our reconnaissance and reported back to the Chief Engineer at AHQ who was coordinating the extensive demolition programme. Before leaving, we dropped some spare parts and bits of piping down the wells. In the event the fields were demolished by Burcorps on 14 April, but I have since heard that it did not take the Japanese long to get them back into some sort of production.

April would prove an eventful month, with the Japanese pressing hard all along the line. Prome fell on the 2nd and 2,000 people were killed in Mandalay by Japanese bombing on the 3rd. Because there was no form of air defence, such raids could be carried out with impunity and the bombing could be pretty accurate, as could attacks upon troops in the field. Alex spent much of his time up with the rearguard or with Burcorps, now very firmly under Slim's inspired and experienced leadership. Earlier, soon after Slim arrived, the Headquarters had very nearly been overrun one night, an event which might have changed the whole course of the campaign.

On 8 April Slim had to evacuate Allanmyo and asked General Alex if the Chinese could take over the eastern end of the line. Although this was agreed with Stilwell, nothing, in fact, occurred.

Three days later Japanese attacks on Taungdwingyi and Kokkogwa were successfully repulsed. Slim had taken the Chief to visit both divisional headquarters at the start of the fighting and together they watched some of the battles. Slim later commented, 'Alexander, as usual, was quite unperturbed'.

The Corps was fighting bravely and well, but under the most appalling difficulties. The lack of air support not only exposed the troops to constant Japanese harassing attacks but denied Slim the means of acquiring tactical information about the enemy and of hitting at his units as they moved freely about the countryside undetected. Radio communications were almost non-existent below brigade level, except by making use of the tanks' sets, which were often also the best links between division and corps. At the lower levels much reliance had to be placed on telephones, runners and liaison officers.

Small wonder that vital messages and orders often failed to get through, the vulnerable telephone lines for ever getting cut or the bearers of written messages killed. By contrast, the Japanese were well provided with radios at all levels and handled their communications with expertise. The situation must often have looked dangerously near getting out of hand. Nevertheless, despite their many problems and their overpowering fatigue after so many days of fighting and marching in the heat and their lack of sleep – for the Japanese invariably operated round the clock and night was no time to 'switch off' – neither the troops of the Burma Army nor their fine commanders had any thoughts of doing other than to fight to the best of their ability in the light of their limited resources, making the Japanese pay as high a price as possible for every mile they advanced.

Late on 12 April General Slim withdrew Burcorps Headquarters to Yenangyaung and three days later destroyed the oilfields near Magwe as far as it proved possible to do so, Foster, the Shell man who had done the reconnaissance with me, being in charge of the demolitions.

Even as that important denial was being carried out, General Alex was in conference with Joe Stilwell, finding him in a state of profound gloom because of the increasing pressure on Mandalay. Realizing only too well how vital it was to bolster the Chinese in any way that he could, the Chief told Stilwell on the 17th that he had arranged for one of the two armoured regiments from 7 Armoured Brigade to go across to support 6th Army.

On the previous day the leading elements of the Japanese 18th Division, fresh from their victories in Malaya and Singapore, began to arrive in Toungoo with the 56th Division, which had been in reserve in Malaya, not far behind, thereby doubling the strength of the Japanese order of battle in Burma. The 18th Division had had three years' battle experience in China and the 56th, although a newish division, had a high proportion of battle-hardened reservists in its ranks, like the 55th. The scales were now beginning to tip against the Burma Army alarmingly.

Despite the arrival of the 2nd Royal Tank Regiment in their support, the Chinese 6th Army simply disintegrated on the night of 21 April, leaving the road to Lashio wide open to the enemy. As if he had not already got enough to worry about, Alex was dismayed to be informed by Sir Reginald Dorman-Smith on that same day that he was handing over all civilian affairs to him because he 'had shown himself quite excellent [in his] dealings with civilian officers and concerns'. Whilst it was true that Alex had a master's touch when it came to dealing with people under difficult circumstances, this was an added burden that he could well have done without.

For the next few days the Chief concerned himself mainly with the daunting problems of keeping the Chinese armies in being. He saw Stilwell on 22 April at Kyaukse and again on the 25th, this time accompanied by Slim and General Winterton, who had now taken over as Chief of Staff at AHQ from Hutton. It had become clear to General Alex that, with Meiktila exposed due to the 6th Army's collapse, all hope of holding Northern Burma had now gone. He therefore withdrew the 2nd Royal Tanks, who reverted to 7 Armoured Brigade, and ordered a general withdrawal to the north of Mandalay, so that he could at least carry out the second part of his directive – to hold the Japanese off from the North-East Frontier of India until the monsoon, which was due in mid-May.

* * *

With that decision of the Chief's the final stage of the defence of Burma had begun. As I look back to that unforgettable time, which would finally bring us to the safety of the Indian Frontier, soaked to the skin by the monsoon rain, dog-tired and very hungry, there are so many fleeting memories that keep flashing across my mind. Above all I recall the general feeling of pride amongst the fighting units that, weary and ragged though they might be, they still carried their personal arms and were still a disciplined fighting force which had given a much stronger and better-equipped enemy a hard fight for his gains. As for me, I was intensely proud to have served my Chief at that time. He had never wavered, never shown the least sign of despair, but was always his old cheerful, imperturbable self and a source of inspiration to us all. He had brought the Army out of Burma against seemingly overwhelming odds. To have been privileged to witness those two great fighting generals, Alex and Bill Slim, working together under such circumstances and to have seen the impact they made upon the British, Indian and Gurkha troops alike was an unforgettable experience. Who could forget their first sight of Mandalay? Pure Kipling, with those vast red walls surrounding the fort and the dominating outline of the Great Pagoda, which, sadly, there was no time to explore. A sad memory was my farewell to my faithful Kachin orderly who had been unfailingly loyal to both the Chief and me throughout all the ups and downs of the long withdrawal. The time had clearly come when it was right and proper for him to return to his hilltop village. It made no sense for him to cross into India and face an uncertain future. He had been ready for anything and always happy. The Chins and Kachins, from the hills, were so utterly different from the Burmese of the lowlands. Whilst the former were determined to fight, if necessary, for their right to remain a separate ethnic group in the mountain areas close to the Chinese border, too many of the lowlanders were either passive or actually assisted the enemy, especially the *Pongis*, or trainee monks, in their saffron robes. I sent my orderly on his way bearing my 12-bore shotgun and cartridges and with a pocketful of Indian silver rupees which I had kept by me in case of need. Off he went, the gun on his shoulder and thrilled beyond measure with what he told me was the finest present he had ever had. In complete contrast, how well I remember the unfortunate British liaison officers who had served with the Chinese armies. There were no faithful Kachin orderlies for them and all their personal belongings, including their watches, had been stolen by the Chinese soldiers! In Mogaung I had had a chance to acquire some Burma rubies but by then I was much more interested in laying my hands upon a couple of tins of bully beef to enjoy with General Alex as a change from the interminable rice. Who could forget our having to dump the contents of the paymaster's truck in the Chindwin at Kalewa, a load of silver rupees too heavy to be carried for the rest of the long trek? I have often wondered whether some enterprising Burman was able to recover them.

* * *

On 28 April General Alex ordered Slim to withdraw to India. Two brigades were to fall back astride the Chindwin with a detachment left in the Myittha Valley, 30 miles west of the Chindwin. The rest of Burcorps was to move to the crossing over the river at Kalewa via Ye-u, accompanied by General Sun's 38th Chinese Division, an American-equipped formation, still very much intact, which had been ordered to make for India.

Although the original divisions, the 33rd and 55th, who had taken Rangoon, were beginning to feel the strain of their long, fighting advance, they were still full of fight and hell-bent on destroying the Burma Army before it crossed the Chindwin. The two new arrivals, the 18th and 56th, were, of course, much fresher and the pressure on the eastern flank was growing by the hour.

On 29 April Lashio, which had been left wide-open when the Chinese 6th Army collapsed, was occupied by the Japanese. Realizing that the fall of Mandalay could only now be a matter of time, the Chief saw Stilwell on that same day and ordered the demolition of the Ava Bridge over the Irrawaddy, just south-west of Mandalay, at midnight. By this time AHQ had moved west of the great river to Shwebo and was preparing to move again, to Ye-u, en route for the Chindwin crossing at Kalewa.

After a brisk fight at Monywa the enemy occupied Mandalay on 1 May. AHQ and Stilwell's small headquarters were then at Ye-u and were joined there by Slim and Headquarters Burcorps. It was known that the Japanese were coming up the Chindwin, doubtless heading for Kalewa, so the race was on. If the Japanese won, the prospects of an opposed river crossing for the Army were depressing and would undoubtedly be very costly. The distance from Ye-u to Kalewa was just under 110 miles.

Fortunately it was possible to lift most of the marching units in trucks for part of the way to the river at least. Despite the weariness of the troops, somehow we got there in time. It was an extraordinary night. The river steamers upon which we had been relying to ferry the Army and its vehicles and equipment had almost all refused to run the risk; only one operated, and that briefly. So, as the units were transported in all sorts of makeshift ferries, rafts and boats, virtually all the Army's transport and heavy equipment had to be destroyed, even those stalwart tanks of 7 Armoured Brigade, to which the Army owed so much. Their rusting remains stand on the river bank to this day, with the grass and jungle growing through them. As the vehicles burned, the mountain gunners and the Bofors light anti-aircraft crews kept up a hail of fire on the surrounding hills, blazing off the ammunition which they could not take with them. The effect of this maelstrom seems to have stunned any Japanese who might have been up there, for the crossing was made without interference. There were some steamers about twelve miles up-stream and part of the force did get up there and a small number of trucks and jeeps were saved in that way.

For the bulk of the Army it was going to be a march of some 100 miles or more to Tamu on the Indian border. Our route passed through the infamous Kabaw Valley, which was ridden with disease, but there was no other way we could go. On Alex's orders, such trucks as were available were used to lift refugees – by now virtually all Indian women and children – an order that nobody questioned.

Even as the last of the Army left Kalewa on 12 May the monsoon broke. How well I remember that on the day we reached Tamu the rainfall was no less than twenty-four inches. Everything had become a quagmire and there could now no longer be any question of the Japanese being able to follow up to the border area and penetrate Indian territory. As we trudged on, soaked to the skin, we could not help envying the Nagas, the hillmen of the area, who went stark naked with just a blanket slung over one shoulder. The rain was nothing to them.

It would be nice to record that our weary, ragged, footsore

soldiers, who had fought so well, were given a hero's welcome, but so little did the military hierarchy understand what had been achieved that General Irwin was rude to Bill Slim about the withdrawal and little or nothing had been prepared to meet the obvious needs of the troops, not even the sorely needed medical support, for by this time almost half 17 Division was suffering from that march through the Kabaw Valley. It was a bitter experience. General Alex had already handed over command to Slim, as he had to report to the Commander-in-Chief, General Wavell, in Delhi. Having done so, he went to the Viceregal Summer Lodge, Naldera, at Simla to stay for a week's rest with Lord Linlithgow. On 23 May he flew back to Assam with General Wavell for a final meeting with General Stilwell and to enable the Commander-in-Chief to speak to the troops. He then returned to Simla to write his despatches, assisted by one of the Operations staff officers from AHQ. While all this was happening I too had fallen sick with a very nasty bout of dysentery. I went to the Lodge to recuperate. There I was very kindly looked after by Lord Linlithgow's daughter-in-law, who fed me vast quantities of Colossal Kaolin!

General Alex had fulfilled his mission. He had saved the Army and denied the Japanese any hope of penetrating Indian territory before the monsoon finally put paid to their ambitions. It is hard for anyone who was not at his side throughout those three months to appreciate the heavy burden of responsibility he bore or the complexity of the tactical situation he had to handle, particularly during those early days before 1st Burma Corps came into being and General Bill Slim took over command. The physical demands made upon him as he continuously crossed the face of the battle areas, maintaining touch with his subordinate commanders and doing all he could to sustain confidence throughout the Army, in what was, frankly, an impossible situation, were severe. Yet he was always his usual cheerful self and, as Slim put it, 'unperturbed'. Never did he give the slightest sign of the anxieties that must have lain upon him like a ton weight when the Chinese began to disintegrate or during that last desperate dash for Kalewa, and the threat of the enemy getting there ahead of us was so real.

Few British commanders in our history can have been pitchforked into a situation that matched that which greeted the

Chief in Rangoon at the beginning of March. Despite his orders to hold the city, if at all possible, there was never the slightest chance that he would be able to do so with the meagre resources at his disposal: two untrained divisions, one of which had just suffered a major disaster and the other utterly unsuited for full-scale warfare; no air support, enabling the Japanese to bomb and strafe at will; communications that were almost non-existent and the civil administration in tatters.

Burma's fate, as we have already seen, had been sealed in April 1941 when Churchill issued his diktat denying the Far East Command any further material support or reinforcement. In fairness to the Prime Minister, he would later accept full responsibility for the disasters which struck the Far East in 1942, but the blame cannot be his alone. Had Whitehall only been better aware of the total inadequacy of Burma's defences and of the great importance of Burma both to the defence of North-East India and to our Chinese allies, who relied so heavily upon Rangoon and the Burma Road as their lifeline in their fight against the Japanese, and had the Chiefs of Staff only listened to Wavell's pleas for Burma to be put under his command, it is possible that the story would have been different. However, in the light of the state of the war in the West in 1941, perhaps it was all too much to pray for.

* * *

So ended the First Burma Campaign of 1942 and General Alex, ordered to return to England in June, prepared to face the next demands made upon him.

Chapter Four

COMMANDER-IN-CHIEF MIDDLE EAST

August, 1942

As the Chief and I set off from Delhi for Cairo, whence, by stages, we would be making our way to Lisbon, where we would catch a civil flying boat to take us home to England, more than ready for a rest and a spell of leave, Alex must have been wondering just what this summons to London held in store for him. Clearly a further command was in the offing.

The first six months of 1942 had been one long tale of disaster and nobody, at that stage of the war, could have been blamed for wondering just how it would all end. However, one man, Winston Churchill, invigorated by his recent contacts with President Roosevelt and the agreement that had been reached over a common Allied strategy for the conduct of the war, had already declared his absolute confidence in the outcome. On 23 March, the day before Alex had flown to Chungking for his talks with Chiang Kai-shek, Churchill stated:

> It now seems likely that we and our Allies cannot lose this war – except through our own fault.

That he should have been able to say that less than a month after the fall of Singapore and Rangoon and the surrender of the Americans' last toehold in the Philippines, Bataan, reflects an astonishing pre-science, but one of which Alex himself would have instantly approved, for thoughts of defeat simply never entered his mind. There were very few indications at that time that the war was about to make an unexpected turn, so that by the end of 1942 the whole scene would be changed and the prospects of victory would have become very much easier to identify. Ready for whatever duty fell to him, and to shoulder whatever burden was put upon him, I have often wondered whether, at that stage, the Chief had any idea of the importance of the task he was about to be allotted or where it was going to lead him.

Just as we, while in Burma, had felt that Whitehall and even Delhi had little knowledge of the immense problems we faced in trying to maintain a coherent front against the swarming Japanese or of the grave lack of support, especially from the air, from which we suffered so severely, so had we had little time, as we battled on, to give much thought to what was happening elsewhere. Not until the fighting was over and we were in the calm of Simla and once more in contact with people who did have access to that sort of news had we been able to bring ourselves up to date.

The most important event which heralded the 'turn of the tide', as Sir Arthur Bryant has put it, had occurred well before we had left England for Rangoon – the entry of the United States into the war. Unprepared, as we had been, for the Japanese onslaught, they had paid heavily for that unreadiness. Nevertheless, by the middle of April, despite the loss of the Philippines, they had made their first air attack on the Japanese mainland and on 4–6 June had won the decisive Battle of Midway which marked the beginning of the end for the Imperial Japanese Navy and so of the Japanese dominance of the Pacific basin. At home the Germans had launched their series of heavy air attacks on our cathedral cities, known as the 'Baedeker' raids, on 23 April, although, a fortnight earlier, the RAF had given them something to think about when they dropped the first 8,000lb bomb on Essen and on the night of 30–31 May had replied to Baedeker with the first 1,000-bomber raid on Cologne, with devastating results. In the Atlantic the U-boat war was at its height and by the time we were back in England nearly 1,000 ships would have been lost since January, of which almost 600 would have been sunk by U-boats. However, despite a severe hold-up in the use of Ultra to keep track of the wolf-packs, when the German Navy introduced a fourth encoding 'wheel' into the naval version of their Enigma encryption machine, by the end of the year the tally of U-boats sunk would have begun to rise quite sharply and the grave anxiety caused by those shipping losses would have abated.

Perhaps the greatest change was about to occur in the Middle East, where things had been going very much awry. So much so that General Auchinleck, the C-in-C Middle East, had felt driven to write on 23 June to General Sir Alan Brooke, the CIGS, offering his resignation in these terms:

> *Fresh blood and new ideas at the top may make all the difference between success and stalemate. For this theatre originality is essential and a change* [is] *quite probably desirable on this account alone... It occurred to me that you might want to use Alexander, who is due here in a day or two. Personally, I do not think Wilson could do it now.*

Auchinleck had felt impelled to write as he did because of the disaster at Gazala, which had been abandoned on 15 June, sending the Eighth Army headlong back to the Alamein line, only 40 miles from Alexandria, and the fall of Tobruk on the 21st, from which only some elements of 201 Guards Brigade had broken out. On the 25th the Auk (as he was known to all) assumed personal command of the Army and sacked General Ritchie, the Army Commander. He at once set about reinvigorating the Army and pulling it together once more, fighting a series of sharp actions with Rommel with some success, a series that later became known as 'First Alamein'.

The rot had been stopped, temporarily at least. However, it was clear to all that a complete change of commanders at the higher levels was urgently needed.

* * *

Alex and I spent three days at the Embassy in Cairo before flying on to Gibraltar. As birds of passage we had to lie low, for it was abundantly clear that all was far from well in the Western Desert, but that was none of our business. I was not privy to any private talks Alex had with the Ambassador, but when we left Cairo it was plain that he was very preoccupied with what he had seen and heard.

At Gibraltar, then a very dull but necessary transport hub for the Middle East, we had another two days' enforced wait during which Alex received orders to return to the United Kingdom to take command of what was then called Force 141, which was being assembled for the Anglo-American landings in North Africa which had been agreed at the Washington Conference in December, 1941.

In order to reach Lisbon we had to cross Spain and Portugal by car in plain clothes. Alex was given a passport as a mining engineer from Burma, while I travelled on my own civilian passport as a law student from Oxford. I shall never forget the sight of the Chief in his ill-fitting blue and white striped jacket, such a contrast to his smart Indian blue Masri bush jacket or khaki service dress.

In Lisbon we had to spend two days in the best hotel before catching the weekly civil flying boat service to Shannon in Ireland. It was bizarre to find ourselves sitting at a table for two in the dining room with a table of Japanese beside us and a number of Germans at other tables. It was, of course, important for us to maintain our incognito, so I was a bit worried when a man with a camera suddenly took a photograph of us as we came out of the hotel in the street and immediately disappeared. Fortunately that was the last we saw of him and there were no undesirable consequences.

We duly caught our flying boat early one morning and made a

safe passage to Shannon. In that we seem to have been lucky. In 1943 a similar aircraft was intercepted over the Atlantic by JU88s from France and shot down. The well-known actor Leslie Howard was on board, but not Winston Churchill, as the Germans had been led to believe.

On arrival at Shannon, much to General Alex's displeasure, a young Irish Army officer boarded the aircraft to check the passengers. That this young man was wearing light brown rubber boots with a Sam Browne belt did nothing to improve matters!

From Foynes we flew to London and went to the War Office where the Chief reported to General Brooke and I spent some time with Barney Charlesworth, his ADC, who had been so friendly last time we had come, before going to Rangoon. He very kindly fixed me up with a War Office pass which showed me to be attached to the CIGS's staff and would prove invaluable.

The headquarters of Force 141 was in London. I spent some time at Leconfield House and Alex himself managed to fit in a few days' leave, as indeed did I a bit later.

Deeply concerned about the general state of affairs in the Western Desert, Churchill and the CIGS left London on 1 August. Clearly there had to be some firm action taken to sort out the very unsatisfactory command situation. Auchinleck, as he himself had suggested, would have to be replaced and a new Army Commander found for the Eighth. Meanwhile Alex began to work on the planning for TORCH, as the projected landings in North Africa were called. On 3 August he called upon General Kennedy, the Deputy CIGS, who took him, as Commander Designate of the Mediterranean Sector Ground Force for Operation TORCH, to meet Lieutenant General Dwight D. Eisenhower, who had been appointed Supreme Allied Commander for the operation, which included General George S. Patton's landings on the Atlantic coast of Morocco. In his book *The Business of War* (Hutchinson, 1957), Kennedy records:

> Eisenhower talked a great deal in his forthright way. Alexander, on the other hand, was very silent and listened to all we said imperturbably, without comment. I felt that there was little doubt that he and Eisenhower would get on well together.

Eisenhower's Aide, Captain Harry C. Butcher USNR, in his *Three Years With Eisenhower* (Heinemann, 1946), commenting upon the luncheon that followed this meeting, relates:

This was an important luncheon, for with Ike junior to General Alexander in rank, with no actual battle experience, with his appointment as Commander-in-Chief not yet confirmed by the President, with Alexander having commanded at Dunkirk during the evacuation and more recently in Burma, there was the touchy question of how acceptable Ike might be to Alexander...I was in Ike's office, visiting with Colonel William Stirling of the Secretariat, British Chiefs of Staff, when Ike returned from luncheon. His first comment was, 'That guy's good. He ought to be Commander-in-Chief instead of me.' That evening I asked how he felt they would click. 'Fine,' he said. 'The last thing Alexander said as we were going out of the door after lunch was, "You're off to a good start".'

Little did we realize how important that successful first meeting would prove in the months to come.

Meanwhile, Churchill and Brooke were deeply immersed in Cairo in the thorny problem of appointing a new Commander-in-Chief and Army Commander. Much has been written about the various combinations of names considered, not least that of Brooke himself and his refusal of the top job, though it nearly broke his heart to do so, for he knew that only he could control Winston in his wilder moments and so his duty had to lie in Whitehall. Finally, as proposed by Brooke, a message was sent to the War Cabinet informing them that Alex had been selected. He should fly out at once so that Churchill and Brooke could see him before they left for their meetings in Teheran and Moscow.

On 7 August, after a frantic scramble to sort out our kit and make final arrangements at home, Alex and I flew off to Cairo where we were met early next morning at Heliopolis by the Prime Minister's PA, Commander Tommy Thompson.

While they waited for Alex to arrive, Churchill and Brooke had been up in the Desert and had had meetings with the Australian and South African commanders and had visited Headquarters Eighth Army.

We were driven to the Embassy where Brooke at once dashed into the Prime Minister's room to tell him that Alex had arrived. He then grabbed Alex himself and had a talk with him before they both went in to see Churchill and have a long discussion.

Alex learned that the Auk was to return to India and resume his old appointment as C-in-C India, Wavell having been appointed Viceroy. No man was better equipped to care for the Indian

Army than Auchinleck. It was his life and the soldiers venerated him. Fine fighting soldier though he was, he was not equipped to cope with the demands of mobile warfare. The sad story of the Eighth Army since he had replaced Wavell in 1941 had been greatly influenced by his inability to apply the principle of Concentration. All too often his scattered brigade 'boxes' or mobile columns* had been defeated in detail, not because of any failure of courage in the troops but because his tactical concept was wrong. That his senior commanders were often inadequate simply added to the problem. Nothing could have been clearer to Alex as he listened to Brooke than that his whole command, and the Eighth Army in particular, was in urgent need of drastic change and firm hands to apply it. He had no doubt whatever that Montgomery, who had been ordered out on his recommendation to take command of the Army, was the ideal man for the job. Not only was there no better trainer of troops in the British Army but he had the flair and charisma to win the soldiers' confidence, a commodity in very short supply at that time. The quality of the troops was good, but they had lost all faith in their senior commanders and in General Headquarters. Between them, he and Montgomery had to restore the situation without delay. Small wonder that Alex's first words to me as he emerged from his talk with Winston and Brooke were, 'Bargo again, Rupert!'

The whole attitude in Cairo at that time was unreal. It was almost like arriving in Rangoon all over again. Officials and staff officers were burning their records and looking over their shoulders beyond the Suez Canal to Palestine and Syria. Small wonder that they were often described scornfully by the desert soldiers as the 'Gaberdine Swine'! Of course the situation was quickly recognized by the Egyptians and the civil population as a whole, who were already showing their lack of confidence in the British Army. They made no bones about their readiness to welcome the new wave of conquerors and to salvage their own futures thereby.

A subtle aura of defeat and retreat hung over the whole city. Alex's first instruction to all was that there was to be no more talk of withdrawal or retreat, the Army would stand and fight, and if need be die, at El Alamein. Like Alex, Monty, when he arrived on 13 August, saw at once that there was no time to be lost in restoring the morale and sense of purpose of the Army.

*Known as 'Jock columns' after their originator, the late Brigadier Jock Campbell VC.

Before he left for Teheran on 10 August the Prime Minister handed Alex a single sheet of Embassy notepaper on which he had written that memorable Directive:

Your prime and main duty will be to take or destroy at the earliest opportunity the German-Italian Army commanded by Field Marshal Rommel.

What was needed was a quick and punishing victory. By God's grace, one was waiting just round the corner.

Our first few days in our new surroundings were very much taken up with the Cairo Conference. While Alex was closeted with the Great it was possible to begin to get ourselves sorted out, draw up such desert kit as we would need and organize the Chief's office arrangements.

A most welcome addition to the Chief's personal staff was Captain W. M. Cunningham MC of the 11th Hussars, the Auk's former ADC and now to be senior ADC to Alex. At last we had someone with an intimate knowledge of GHQ and who was well acquainted with all the senior personalities. Bill Cunningham was six years older than me and was an original 'Desert Rat'. He had been wounded in Wavell's legendary 'push' at the end of 1940, had taken over 1,000 prisoners and had been awarded the Military Cross. He and I would share a twelve-foot tent for some three years and I cannot recall a single serious disagreement between us in all that time. Because of his wide GHQ experience, it was agreed that Bill would 'run the office' and that, as heretofore, I would be the Chief's map-reader, personal staff officer and companion when he went into the field.

The ADCs had a small room in the Semiramis Hotel, the home of GHQ, which gave access to the C-in-C. As it had been in the old days with Hanning at Wilton, the Chief could not escape without us knowing and, this time, being up on the third or fourth floor, had no window through which he could climb when he wanted to play 'hooky'.

Another very welcome addition to the personal staff was Guardsman Williamson, Scots Guards, who arrived to be Alex's soldier servant, and would, quietly and efficiently, keep the Chief's uniforms and boots spick and span, something of great importance to Alex, who, whatever the circumstances, liked to look immaculate.

Although Alex had necessarily to have an office in GHQ, as a fighting soldier he could not stand the cloying atmosphere of Cairo and liked to live as much as possible in what was known as 'The Commander-in-Chief's Camp'. This spartan set-up consisted of the C-in-C's caravan, a map lorry and a Mess 3-ton truck which served a large Mess tent. In addition, we had an armoured car and a signals tentacle under an officer who was a specialist in handling the top-secret traffic from the Prime Minister and the War Office known as Ultra and containing material based on Bletchley Park's extracts from the Germans' Enigma transmissions. The secrecy of that traffic had to be absolute. Only the most senior commanders were allowed access to it and anyone handling the messages had to go through a rigorous vetting process. When such a signal arrived, the Signals Officer would bring it by hand to Bill who passed it on to Alex. In Bill's absence, that task fell to me.

There were tents for the personal staff and a couple for visitors. In addition, there was accommodation for the Chief's two principal staff officers, General Dick McCreery, the Chief of General Staff, and, later, General Brian Robertson, the MGA, who, like Eric Goddard in Burma, would perform logistic miracles in the years ahead.

The Camp was run by Captain Cedric Yates, whose parents ran a small hotel in London, near the Cavendish. He was assisted by a Mess Sergeant and had about a dozen soldiers as Camp staff. Later, when we got to North Africa, we would also have a defence platoon.

At first the Camp was set up under the lee of the Great Pyramid of Cheops, near the Mena House Hotel, and I could contemplate the massive pile from my tent. Once the fighting began again and Alex wanted to be forward, we would always set up within a short distance of Monty's Tactical Headquarters so that the two Chiefs could be in immediate touch and we, the 'Indians', could be in equally close touch with Monty's Aides and Liaison Officers, which would prove of inestimable value. It was a very happy set-up and we were all absolutely devoted to Alex, by whom those feelings were reciprocated. He was the most perfect leader that any soldier could wish to serve under.

During the handover period between the Auk and Alex, which also involved them both in Churchill's Cairo Conference, we lived at the Embassy. This was, of course, particularly enjoyable for me, as my good friend Graham was there and we were able to make the most of our time together. However, there was one little problem for me and one that was not going to go away if I was to continue to enjoy the warm and generous hospitality of the Embassy. Sir Miles Lampson had a second wife who was only a very few years older than her stepson. She loved the bright lights and to go out to the nightclubs. When Graham went out with his girlfriend, Lady Lampson, known to all as 'Jackie', would often go too, escorted by her husband's RAF ADC. When he was not available, Sir Miles would ask me to do the escorting. Jackie was a fun-loving and most attractive girl, but it was clearly important not to have any problems with one's hostess, so, unlike Graham, I had to watch my step. As I was always made welcome when I came into Cairo or had forty-eight hours' local leave, I can only assume that I got it about right!

On 12 August Monty arrived from England to assume command of the Eighth Army. He was accompanied by his ADC, Captain Spooner, both looking very 'un-desertworthy'. Because I had met Monty when he had South-Eastern Command, I was sent to meet him. After breakfast he went to meet General Auchinleck and I took Spooner to Kasr-el-Nil Barracks to get his General kitted out for the desert. Now a sort of multiple Supply Depot, the barracks had been the home of the 1st Battalion Irish Guards in the mid-thirties, so I had a sneaking regard for the place. There we laid hands on two essential items, an Australian Digger's hat and an excellent New Zealand sweater. It was that hat which Monty used to pin on the cap badges of all the units he saw on his way up to Eighth Army Headquarters. The result was a hat so heavy that he could not hold his head up in it. Some

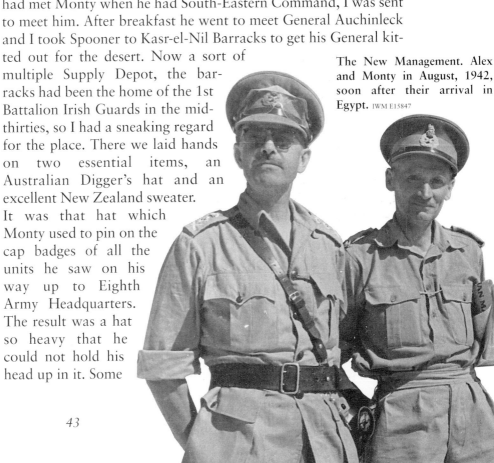

The New Management. Alex and Monty in August, 1942, soon after their arrival in Egypt. IWM E15847

time later, as all the world knows, he was offered a black beret by the commander of his command tank, and this he adopted, wearing only the badge of the Royal Tank Regiment as well as his General's badge, a much more workable and comfortable solution.

During his meeting with the Auk Monty was disturbed to hear that Auchinleck was intending to retain command until 15 August and that, if Rommel attacked before then, he would resume command of the Army. It was indeed unfortunate that the Auk and Monty had long been in conflict and the fault most certainly did not lie with the Auk. As would often be the case in the years ahead, Monty had been grossly insubordinate when the Auk had Southern Command soon after Dunkirk and Monty was one of his Corps Commanders. That long-standing enmity lay behind the bitter and unjust attacks that Monty would make about the Auk's plans for the defence of Egypt.

From the Auk's office Monty came to see Alex. They sent for Brigadier John Harding, already one of the brightest stars in the Middle East firmament and now Deputy CGS to General Corbett. He was asked to produce a *Corps de Chasse*, an armoured corps, and went off to do that. Harding was a brilliant staff officer and more than made up for all Corbett's shortcomings. He had already deeply impressed Alex and from that day on his star was in the ascendant. He would very soon be selected to command the 7th Armoured Division, which he was to do with great élan and distinction until severely wounded. While Harding was assembling his plan, Alex and Monty went to see Sir Miles Lampson, returning to the Semiramis at 6 pm to find Harding ready for them. While he was in our office, Monty asked Bill Cunningham if he could recommend an ADC who could navigate in the desert and use a sun compass. Bill at once suggested John Poston MC, another 11th Hussar, who had just returned to Cairo with General 'Strafer' Gott's car and kit. The General had been a strong contender for command of the Army until he was tragically killed while trying to save fellow passengers from an aircraft in which they had been shot down. John was given the job and was Monty's favourite Aide until the end of the war in North-West Europe, when he was killed during the last week of the fighting. John was a very good friend to Bill and me and until he went back to England with Monty in 1943 worked very closely with us, serving the needs of our respective masters, as did Johnny

Henderson, Monty's other Aide.

On the following morning, full of determination to execute Alex's firm directive that the Army should stand and fight or die at El Alamein, Monty drove off to visit his new Army. On his way he picked up an old protégé of his, Brigadier de Guingand, then the Brigadier General Staff at GHQ. As they drove, Monty invited Freddy to become his Chief of Staff, which was unquestionably the best decision he made in the whole of his military career, for Freddy would prove not only a tower of strength but a supreme diplomat who would save Monty's bacon on many occasions after he had been guilty of some unpardonable indiscretion.

Appalled by the lack of morale and the air of indecisiveness he found at Army Headquarters, Monty at once assumed command, despite what he knew about the Auk's planned date of handover. He immediately issued orders to the effect that the Army would stand fast and cancelled all the Auk's existing plans. He then made his historic speech to the staff announcing his intentions and policies. The effect was electric. The morale of the Headquarters rocketed. Here, at last, was the firm and determined leadership they had longed for. That speech would be repeated several times throughout the Army, with similar results.

The Alamein line, upon which the Eighth Army was now based, was some forty miles long, with the sea on the north and the impenetrable sand sea of the Qattara depression forming a secure left flank. The Intelligence staffs had already appreciated that Rommel would renew his attacks in about a month and would attempt to outflank the Army from the south. Montgomery at once realized the importance of the Alam Halfa feature, a dominating height some 15 miles north of the Qattara Depression. Knowing full well the problems of Eighth Army at that time, he determined to fight a resolute defensive battle based upon Alam Halfa.

This was to be very much a 'last man/last round' affair and Monty at once began to request the additional troops that he needed and, above all, to concentrate all the artillery he could lay his hands on to forge a massive hammer with which to strike the German attack. Gone were the days of 'penny packets'; the golden rule of concentration and centralized control of artillery would be applied. Furthermore, he asked the RAF to make available all the striking power it could muster. He knew that a convincing victory against Rommel was the one tonic that would really put the Army back on its feet and begin the process of preparation for a return to the offensive.

Meanwhile, back in Cairo, Alex too had been making changes, the first of which was to replace the present Chief of General Staff, General Corbett, with the forceful and capable Dick McCreery, who had in fact been sent out in 1941 by Brooke to be CGS to the Auk. The two men had fallen out and Corbett had come in from India to replace McCreery, who was relegated to the role of armoured adviser. Now Alex had restored him to his original position from which he would never look back, finally commanding the Eighth Army in the last stages of the war in Italy. Like Monty, Alex had already made a deep impression upon his staff, whose eyes were once more firmly traversed to the front.

On his very first evening in command Monty told Freddy de Guingand to have the 10th Armoured Division, newly formed, and the 44th Infantry Division, which had just arrived from England and had yet to complete its desert training, sent up to the Desert. When McCreery was given the message requesting 44th Div he refused, on the grounds that it was not yet completely concentrated with all its units. However, de Guingand saw Alex at the Embassy, where he was talking to the Ambassador, and Alex at once sent a message to John Harding, the DCGS, telling him to issue the instructions for the move. Monty had also decided, having met his new staff and Corps Commanders, that he needed some new blood for his team and had already asked that Major General Horrocks and Brigadiers Kirkman and Simpson should be sent out from England at once.

There is a serious misconception that Alex was like clay in Monty's hand and that the latter only had to ask and it was given. I have often been asked about this.

The two men were professionals to their fingertips, but very different characters, although they had one thing in common: both were absolutely without physical fear and the presence of either on the battlefield had a dramatic effect upon all around them. Although four or five years Alex's senior, Monty, who had been badly wounded in France in the First World War, had never commanded a unit larger than a company in battle until he took the 3rd Division to France in 1940. A brilliant trainer of soldiers and a master tactician, he was, sadly, a natural egotist with a profound belief in his own infallibility, rarely willing to give credit to anyone else, which makes his utterance about Alex quoted on page xi all the more remarkable. In stark contrast, Alex had effectively commanded a division in Latvia with outstanding success, defeating a Bolshevik army as long ago as 1919–20, and a brigade on the North-West Frontier of India in mountain operations, with distinction, in the Thirties. When Alex went to the Staff College, he was already a Colonel and voluntarily accepted reduction in rank to Major so that he would not outrank all the instructors, of whom Montgomery was one! Monty had never regarded Alex as one of his star students. Nevertheless, it was Monty who persuaded Lord Gort, on 30 May, 1940, to replace General Barker, who had collapsed, by Alex as GOC 1 Corps, thereby giving Alex responsibility for the defence and evacuation of the Dunkirk bridgehead. Alex was promoted Lieutenant General in the field and so was always one step ahead of Monty in rank thereafter. Alex knew exactly how to get the best out of Monty, as he would later with difficult Allied generals. He was never a man to seek kudos for himself or even acknowledgements, but always ready to allow his subordinates the principal credit for any victory. I well remember him saying to General Lemnitzer, his American Deputy Chief of Staff in 15th Army Group, that 'Army Groups exist to support and make possible the successful operations of their Armies'.

When it came to operations, Alex would always discuss Monty's plans and requirements with him before any major battle to ensure that he had the commanders, formations and logistic support he needed to secure 'his victory'. He saw it as his job to formulate the strategy, to move heaven and earth to get his Army Commanders the resources they needed and to keep the politicians off their backs. If Churchill was demanding action, it was his, Alex's, job to handle him.

Monty's famous Tactical Headquarters (Tac HQ) was as frugal as our Commander-in-Chief's Camp: the Army Commander's caravan and map lorry, a large camouflaged Mess tent and several small tents for his team of young Aides and Liaison Officers. Monty refused to have anyone other than junior officers to stay the night: all Colonels and Generals were sent packing after they had said their piece. This inflexible rule was to bear bitter fruit when I brought the US Generals Patton and Bradley to visit Monty in Tunisia.

Because our Camp and Tac 8th Army were always so close to one another in the field, Alex had many unrecorded meetings with his dynamic subordinate. The strength of that relationship is reflected in the fact that when Alex wanted to get from Monty the details of the formations and commanders he wanted for Operation HUSKY (the invasion of Sicily), at a time when the First and Eighth Armies had yet to link up in Tunisia, he sent me flying over the German lines to get this information from Monty himself. Monty's private hand-written letters to Alex and the latter's replies demonstrated very clearly how high was the regard in which they held one another and the strength of their professionalism. When we come to consider the events of the Battle of El Alamein we shall see there proof of Alex's genius for handling Monty at a time when he was probably least ready to accept any interference with what he saw as 'his' battle. It was an occasion upon which Alex showed not only his sure touch as a fighting soldier but the depth of his understanding of how best to influence a situation at a delicate moment.

Both Bill and I were always made very welcome at Tac Eighth Army by the ADCs and Monty's young Liaison Officers, who did such a remarkable job for him. Smoking was absolutely taboo, but, while Monty was a strict teetotaller himself, whenever I came over to see him with a message from the Chief he would always send me across to the Mess for a gin and tonic.

* * *

It has to be said that the new management in the Middle East had arrived at a propitious moment, when new formations and new equipment were beginning to arrive from England or America. With great generosity, the Americans had allotted Britain no less than 300 new Sherman tanks, withdrawn from their own 1st Armoured Division. At a time when they themselves were trying to raise new armies at top speed, it was a noble gesture. For the first time the British would have a tank with a 75mm gun, matching anything other than the long-barrelled gun of the Germans' Mark IV 'Special', of which a few had appeared in the Desert just before Montgomery's first battle at Alam Halfa. The American Grant, which had first appeared at Gazala, had indeed had a 75mm gun, but it was mounted in a sponson low on the hull, making it impossible to achieve a hull-down position, and this, together with its high profile, had made it very vulnerable to German anti-tank guns, particularly the 88mm. Now the Sherman, with its turret-mounted 75mm, would give them the vital hull-down capability and the range at which to engage anti-tank guns with a good high explosive (HE) round. It is not generally realized that it was the Germans' anti-tank guns and their skilled use of them, rather than any great superiority in tanks, that had played havoc with British armour. The new British 6pdr anti-tank gun had recently arrived in good numbers and to this would soon be added the superb 17pdr. Handled correctly, as they would now be, these new weapons would make an immense difference to the armoured battle. Rommel of course knew about these new reinforcements and equipments and had realized that he must strike hard in September before they arrived in the forward area.

* * *

On 17 August Churchill and Brooke returned from their meetings in Teheran and Moscow and held a conference to discuss the future of the Persia and Iraq Command (known to all as Pai-Force), since it had been decided at Moscow that a main supply route for Russia would be established through Iraq and Persia, with Basra (popularly known as 'the arsehole of the world') becoming a port of major importance. A strong rail link from

The Prime Minister visits Egypt. August, 1942. IWM E15905

The PM is briefed on future plans. *(L to R)* Alex, General Sir Alan Brooke (CIGS), Lieutenant General Sir Brian Horrocks (13 Corps), Winston Churchill. IWM E15913

there across Persia to the Russian border would be built by the Americans. This was a development of considerable strategic importance to Alex as C-in-C Middle East, as it had been decided that a new command would be set up there under General 'Jumbo' Wilson. Churchill had earlier tried to persuade Auchinleck to accept this appointment but, very naturally, the Auk had declined and asked to go back to his old command in India, which, as we already know, had now been agreed.

The conference was attended by Sir Miles Lampson, the Iraqi Ambassador, Alex, Air Marshal Tedder (the AOC-in-C Middle

East), Admiral Cunningham (C-in-C Mediterranean), General Lindsell (representing the Quartermaster General) and Colonel Ian Jacob (a senior member of Churchill's personal staff). The meetings in Moscow had been pretty gruelling for both the Prime Minister and Brooke and it was plain that Winston was now burning to get up into the Desert to see Montgomery and the troops for himself. This he did on the following day, accompanied by Alex.

They drove from Cairo up past the Pyramids and on about 130 miles to the sea at Aboukir. From there they went to Monty's headquarters, arriving at 7.30 in the evening for dinner, where they were also joined by Brooke, who had been lent Alex's caravan for his stay. Over dinner, Monty accurately predicted the timing and nature of Rommel's next attack and described his plans to meet it. He then went on to detail his plans for a resumption of the offensive, stipulating an absolute requirement for six weeks' delay in order to get the Eighth Army in proper shape for the battle, the Sherman tanks modified for the desert and all the new divisions which were now arriving trained for desert warfare and deployed for battle. On the following day Churchill and Brooke were taken to see the Ruweisat Ridge, a key feature of the Alamein position, and to meet Churchill's old friend General Bernard Freyberg VC, commanding the 2nd New Zealand Division. Freyberg was an outstanding leader and a brilliant divisional commander, but time would show that his desire to be in the middle of the action and to exercise his personal leadership would not fit in with the requirements for command of a Corps.

On the last day of his stay in Cairo the Prime Minister visited the Tura caves and then inspected the newly arrived 51st Highland Division before having a final discussion with Brooke and Alex about the Middle East situation, at which they were joined by Lampson. Brooke later had a talk with Jumbo Wilson about the forthcoming partition of the Command and his part in it. On 23 August, the following day, Churchill and Brooke left for home, both well satisfied with the local changes they had brought about since they had first come out and delighted with the very obvious impact which both Alex and Monty had clearly had upon both the Army and the General Headquarters – not least the replacement of Corbett, whom Churchill described as 'a very small, agreeable man, of no personality and little experience'.

That the Auk should have chosen him as CGS was a very clear indication of a major weakness of his, the inability to pick horses for courses, as he had also shown when appointing Ritchie to Eighth Army and the eccentric, self-opinionated and tiresome Brigadier 'Chink' Dorman-Smith (brother of the Governor of Burma, who had been such a broken reed during Alex's time there) as Corbett's deputy.

Describing the events of August, 1942, Churchill would later write of Alex:

> He was the Supreme Authority with whom I now dealt in the Middle East. General Montgomery and the Eighth Army were under him. Alex, as I had long called him, had already moved himself and his personal HQ into the desert by the Pyramids; cool, gay, comprehending all, he inspired quiet, deep confidence in every quarter.

On 28 August Churchill signalled Alex about the probability of the Axis attack, codenamed ZIP. Alex replied, 'ZIP now equal money every day from now onwards.'

Chapter Five

FROM EL ALAMEIN TO TRIPOLI

August, 1942 – January, 1943

On 19 August the Chief set the seal upon his 'Stand Fast' policy by issuing this directive to Montgomery:

1. Your prime and immediate task is to prepare for offensive operations against the German-Italian forces with a view to destroying them at the earliest possible moment.

2. Whilst preparing this attack you must hold your present positions and on no account allow the enemy to penetrate east of them.

He instructed that the contents of that directive should be made known to all troops.

On 15 August, the day on which Alex had assumed command, General Brian Horrocks, for whom Monty had asked, arrived in Cairo and was at once ordered to assume command of 13 Corps, filling the gap left by the death of General 'Strafer' Gott. Horrocks had originally been intended for the new *Corps de Chasse*, 10 Corps, but he very wisely protested that he was by training and experience an infantryman and that General Herbert Lumsden, an armoured officer who had made his name in command of the 12th Lancers in France in 1940, was much better equipped than he for that task.

The next two weeks were a period of frenetic activity as the 44th Division and 10th Armoured Division were moved up to take up positions on the Alamein Line and the Alam Halfa Ridge in particular. At the same time nearly 260 guns and 200 anti-tank guns were also mustered there and the machinery of artillery control, designed to maintain command at the highest level, was established. Meanwhile the minefields covering the position were widened and strengthened.

Deeply conscious of Rommel's Achilles heel, the supply of fuel for his armour and transport, Alex arranged with Air Marshal Tedder for maximum air effort to be concentrated against Axis shipping in the Mediterranean and tankers in particular, whilst sweeps across the desert, aimed at his supply convoys, were maintained. At the same time the Desert Air Force was made ready to lend all its weight to the defence of the Alam Halfa position, a role in which it would play a significant part. To assist the RAF three squadrons of the 9th United States Air Force had been made available to fight as a part of Air Marshal 'Maori' Coningham's command. A major success was achieved by the Royal Navy when one of their submarines sank a large tanker carrying fuel outside Tobruk harbour.

Meanwhile the pattern of events world-wide was beginning to reflect a change for the better. In the Pacific the United States Marines had begun their historic defence of Guadalcanal and had already inflicted very heavy casualties on the Japanese who, nevertheless, were still extending their operations throughout the Far East. As the Battle of Midway had shown, the tide was just beginning to turn.

In England, Alex's former Force 141, now designated the British First Army and commanded by General Anderson, was putting the final touches to its preparations for TORCH and General Eisenhower had been confirmed as the Supreme Allied Commander for the operation.

On 19 August the Canadians had suffered a severe defeat in their raid on Dieppe, with something like fifty per cent casualties, although it was claimed that valuable lessons had been learned for future operations against a defended coastline. That operation did mark the first appearance in combat of the superb new American long-range fighter, the P51 Mustang, which would from then on prove such an asset wherever the Allies would be fighting.

In India, just as General Wavell was about to assume the position of Viceroy and the Auk would reassume his old post as Commander-in-Chief, serious civil unrest and violence had broken out in support of the Independence movement. There was a strong anti-British movement afoot and this was causing real problems over recruiting and the return to battle with the Japanese.

In Russia, General Paulus's 6th Panzer Army, with more than a million men under command, was taking heavy casualties as he drove them to capture the key city of Stalingrad. Little did he realize at that stage that this was the start of the greatest disaster suffered by the German Army in the Second World War and, unquestionably, the turning point of Hitler's fatal campaign in Russia.

In contrast, who in the Eighth Army at that juncture would have foreseen that the battle they were about to fight would mark the first step on a long, rocky road to victory that would end on the banks of the River Po?

* * *

On the night of 30–31 August Rommel struck, opening his offensive with three feints on the 30 Corps front. Then, at 0100 on the

31st, the Afrika Korps, spearheaded by 15 and 21 Panzer Divisions and by 90 Light Division, began to breach the minefields in the south, opposite General Horrocks's 13 Corps. As Monty had already appreciated, it was now clear that Rommel's intention was to hook behind the Alam Halfa Ridge and cut through the rear areas of 30 Corps to reach the sea.

Montgomery's carefully controlled but devastating response was immediate. While elements of 7th Armoured Division harassed the breaching operation, the gunners of the New Zealand Division engaged them in enfilade, the whole of the massed field artillery on the Alam Halfa position joining in and blasting the assembled armour behind the breaching operation. Later the Desert Air Force played havoc not only with the armour but also with the transport further to the rear.

The Germans responded with vigour and for two days the battle raged without ceasing. By the evening of the second day Alex, who had been watching the battle intently, judged that, as the enemy had achieved no significant success, the turning point had been reached.

Up in the north, on 1 September, General Leslie Morshead's 9th Australian Division attacked Tell el Eisa and forced a gap through which a raiding force was to be passed, but the enemy counterattacked and the gap was closed.

Montgomery, who was controlling every movement of his troops, now estimated that by the night of the fourth day Rommel would begin to withdraw. Both sides had suffered heavy casualties, but Rommel's supply echelons had taken a beating and there was no doubt that he would soon be faced with a fuel crisis, made all the more certain by the damage being inflicted upon the Axis shipping bringing in new supplies.

Throughout days 4 and 5 the Eighth Army harassed the enemy with short, sharp counter-attacks, chiefly by the armoured brigades. Although the German withdrawal had taken them back to the line of the minefields by the end of the fifth day, Monty would allow no pursuit. He knew how vital it was that his Army should emerge from this battle not only victorious but intact. On day 6 Rommel went firm along the line Deir el Munassib to the high ground round Himeimat, from where he had excellent observation of our positions up as far as the Ruweisat Ridge. At great cost he had secured one small advantage. On day 7 the battle was called off. Later, writing in his Despatches, Alex observed:

> *This meagre gain of some four or five miles of desert could in no way be set off against the material losses. Forty-two German tanks and eleven Italian and nearly seven hundred motor vehicles were abandoned on the field, together with thirty field and forty anti-tank guns. Casualties were more difficult to assess but we estimated that the enemy had lost two thousand Italians and two thousand five hundred Germans killed and wounded; three hundred were taken prisoner. Our own losses were sixty-eight tanks, one anti-aircraft and eighteen anti-tank guns; killed, wounded and missing numbered sixteen hundred and forty. But the battle of Alam Halfa was far more important than would appear from any statistics of gains and losses or the numbers involved. It was the last throw of the German forces in Africa, their last chance of a victory before, as they calculated, our increasing strength would make victory for them impossible. It was hard to realize it at the time, but the moment when the Africa Corps began to retreat...marked the first westward ebb of the tide which had carried the Axis arms so far to the east, an ebb which was about to begin to the north as well...To me at the time the great features of the battle were the immediate improvement in the morale of our own troops and the confidence I felt in General Montgomery, who had handled his first battle in the desert with great ability. The valuable part played by the RAF during the battle was a good omen for future air support. I now felt sure that we should be able to defeat the enemy when we were ready to take the offensive.*

Alex was, of course, far too imperturbable to have shown the least sign of anxiety during the battle, but I have often wondered how many people have ever given a thought to the consequences had the enemy achieved his aim. Whilst all thought of further retreat had been discarded on Alex's orders, as Commander-in-Chief, bearing the full responsibility for the conduct of military operations within his Command, it was not a subject that he could possibly have dismissed entirely from his mind, no matter how great his confidence in Monty might have been. Between them they had done much to raise morale during the brief period between taking command and the start of the battle, a period of only a fortnight, during which considerable movement of troops had had to take place as reinforcements were brought forward and the whole line was strengthened and reorganized, vast quantities of ammunition, mines and engineer stores had had to be dumped and the minefields extended. Despite the improvement of morale over that all too short period, the troops were yet to be convinced by the performance of their new commanders. Brian Horrocks had only had 13 Corps for about four days before Rommel attacked and it was his Corps that had had to bear the brunt. In the eyes of the world the credit for Alam Halfa has always gone completely to Montgomery and certainly he gave the performance of his life in that battle, but much credit must also go to Alex himself, the firm, patient overall commander whose support of Montgomery must have done much to boost the latter's own confidence. One might be forgiven for thinking that self-confidence was one commodity which Monty never lacked, but he was far too able and shrewd a soldier not to have been acutely aware of the issues at stake. Whilst the plaudits rained down upon Monty, we, the personal staff in the Commander-in-Chief's Camp, had been very conscious of the supreme importance of that battle for the Chief, the first blow struck by his troops in the fulfilment of the formidable mission given to him by the Prime Minister. That he was to record in his despatches that the battle confirmed his confidence in Montgomery's ability is proof enough that he, at least, had not dismissed the possibility of a less successful outcome, for, in the final analysis, it is the individual soldier and his officers who win the victory. That Alex put the improvement of the troops' morale as the first satisfaction he derived from the outcome shows very clearly what a born field commander he himself was.

* * *

There were a number of senior Americans visiting Cairo at about the time of Alam Halfa, one of whom was a presidential aspirant named Wendell Willkie, a man whose political self-confidence and ambition matched the military equivalents in Monty, so it was, perhaps, not altogether surprising that he should have appeared at Monty's Tac HQ for dinner on 4 September. The Personal Staff found him rather fat, sweaty and unimpressive. In contrast, Alex had discovered that General Brereton, the Commanding General 9th US Air Force and of all American ground forces in the Middle East, had received no such bidding and, indeed, had been ignored by Monty at a time when three American squadrons of fighters had been playing a valiant part in the air operations supporting Monty's own battle. With his usual charm, Alex invited the General to dine with us in the Camp. This small incident was a perfect example of Alex's constant awareness of the need to show courtesy and, where appropriate, appreciation to Allied colleagues, which would prove a source of his popularity with them over the months and years ahead, during which his involvement with them, some of whom were notoriously 'difficult', would increase considerably. By contrast, there were few senior Allies who had much regard for Monty, though they usually respected his unquestionable military skills.

The reader cannot fail to have wondered why it was that the British lost nearly half as many tanks again as the Germans at Alam Halfa, considering that the Germans had been taking such a hammering from the air and from the Eighth Army's massed artillery, in addition to large numbers of tank and anti-tank guns. The answer lies largely in the design fault of the Grant tank, described on page 48. When the armoured brigades were launched from their dug-in positions to make their short, sharp counter-attacks, these massive vehicles, with their main armament sited so low in the hull, had perforce to expose themselves on forward slopes and were easy meat for the German 88mm and long 50mm anti-tank guns, not to mention the long 75mms of the six Mark IV 'Specials' that were making their debut in that battle.

* * *

After the battle the Chief and Monty attended a Service of Thanksgiving in the desert and signals of congratulation began to pour in. This had been Monty's first opportunity to see his senior commanders in action and, as a result of his assessment of their performances, a number of changes were now made, the most important being the removal of General Ramsden from 30 Corps and his replacement by General Sir Oliver Leese, one of Monty's protégés from England who had been commanding the Guards Armoured Division and would later succeed Monty to the command of the Army in Italy. General Renton of 7th Armoured Division was replaced by Brigadier John Harding, a significant step on the latter's path to his Field Marshal's baton in the years ahead. The 51st Highland Division, now reconstituted after the disaster of St Valery in 1940 and lusting to strike a blow at the Germans, was brought up into the line. The *Corps de Chasse*, 10 Corps, was given to General Herbert Lumsden, as Brian Horrocks had suggested. Finally, Monty issued his training directive for preparation for the renewal of the offensive, an outstanding document which left no man in any doubt of what was expected of him.

Alex was delighted with the way things were now shaping and when Churchill, true to form, demanded an advance in September, he had no hesitation in fighting Monty's case for a D-Day of 23 October, when a nearly full moon would be so important a factor in the execution of the extensive minefield clearance that was an inescapable part of the initial advance, which Monty had already determined must be a night attack.

We had already moved the Chief's Camp to Burg el Arab before Alam Halfa and it remained there throughout the coming battle, now known as LIGHTFOOT. Not only did this enable Alex to keep in close personal touch with Monty but also to get to know as many formation and unit commanders as possible.

On 16 September Montgomery presented his plan for LIGHT-FOOT to his Corps and Divisional Commanders, explaining his concept of the penetration and ultimate breakthrough of the enemy's defences – the clearance of the routes through the minefields, the subsequent 'dog fight' as he called it and the 'crumbling operations', which he described as a 'real roughhouse' and which, he warned them, could last seven days, followed by the breakthrough and the pursuit of the broken enemy by the *Corps de Chasse* (10 Corps). The intensity of the prospect was lost on no one who heard him, but his determination and confidence were infectious.

As I sat at the back of the audience with Monty's personal staff, the sheer ferocity of the task facing the Eighth Army became clearer and clearer. No wonder that his training directive had placed so much emphasis upon the need for the soldiers to be not only extremely fit but also very hard. Six weeks was going to be little enough to get that toughening process completed on top of the mass of weapon and tactical training that had to be done. Such was the magnetism of Monty's own personality when delivering such a challenge to his audience that there can be no doubt that all who heard him on that September afternoon were fired with his enthusiasm. I have often wondered how those commanders felt later as they sat in their own headquarters preparing their orders and made ready to speak to their subordinate commanders, for the prospect could not be other than a sobering one and some thousands of their soldiers would unquestionably become casualties.

The prod from Winston came on the following day when he

signalled Alex: 'Anxiously awaiting some account of your intentions'. The Chief went across to speak to Monty who answered that he could not possibly be ready in September for he needed a superiority, which he had not yet got, of three to one in guns and armour. A reply was drafted mentioning the October date and signed by the Chief. The Prime Minister was furious, for TORCH (the North African Anglo-American landings under Eisenhower) was due to begin on 4 November. Finally, with ill grace and reluctance, a signal was sent back to Alex on 23 September, just one month before D-Day, agreeing to the postponement of Monty's offensive but reminding him that the delay was enabling Rommel to strengthen his defences and minefields.

We actually received that signal in Jerusalem where we had gone to stay with the Governor of Palestine, Sir Harold MacMichael, because, of course, Alex's 'empire' was very widespread and his responsibility for the territories beyond the Egyptian borders inevitably made demands not only on his time but also upon his presence. Because of the immense importance of the events in the Western Desert and the measure of public interest which they created, it was all too easy for people to forget the full scope of the C-in-C Middle East's commitments. This was the first time that Alex and I encountered that remarkable woman Hermione Ranfurly (wife of the Earl of Ranfurly, who was at that

On 10 October 1942 Alex visited the Fighting French at Bir Hacheim and presented gallantry awards for their historic defence of the fort. Seen here inspecting Foreign Legion infantry, he is accompanied by General Pierre Koenig, their heroic commander. Bill Cunningham is behind the Chief. IWM E17846

time a prisoner of war in Italy, together with General O'Connor, whose Aide he was). Hermione was the Governor's personal secretary. She was a most efficient woman and a very good-looking one too. She would soon be carrying out the same duties for General Jumbo Wilson and would wield considerable influence as his Personal Assistant in Persia-Iraq, Cairo and at Allied Force Headquarters at Caserta. Hermione was undoubtedly a person to have on your side if you worked in that tangled 'old boy net' of the personal staff world.

Alex had a mischievously boyish sense of humour, which he was quite liable to exercise on those of us who worked closest to him. On that evening in Jerusalem I took the Governor's daughter Priscilla to the King David Hotel after dinner, as it had a night club. After bringing her safely back to Government House I walked into an open door in the blacked-out corridor leading to my room and sported an enormous black eye at breakfast in consequence. The Chief immediately enquired whether I had collected this from Priscilla after taking her out to the night club!

A visit I well remember was to the newly completed railway line through Syria to the Turkish frontier, where, to Alex's delight, he drove in 'the last spike' and had a chance to drive an engine, something he had not done since the General Strike in 1926. That

The act of completion. Alex drives in a silver spike. IWM E20478

Dog River, Palestine, December, 1942. Inspecting the Guard of Honour mounted by the Royal Australian Engineers at the ceremony to mark the completion of the Beirut-Tripoli Railway. IWM E20478

line was an important link and supply route for the Turks, who we hoped would remain neutral and resist the blandishments of the Germans, as, indeed, they had resisted all Churchill's efforts to persuade them to join the Allies. In addition to those trips to Palestine and Syria, we also went to Khartoum and visited Abyssinia, all part of 'the empire', with various units dotted about or in training.

The build-up period before El Alamein gave the Chief a chance to visit Trans-Jordan. On landing, our C47 blew a tyre and we had to stay a little longer than planned while a spare was flown out from Egypt.

After he had inspected the Trans-Jordan Frontier Force, commanded by the legendary British general, Glubb Pasha, Alex dined with the ruler, the Emir Abdullah. The Emir, who had all the charm and manners of a true Bedouin, loved to talk about the war and explained to Alex how to drive the Germans out of Africa and land in Europe. The Chief listened and agreed politely with the Emir's ideas. Later, when Abdullah produced the Visitor's Book, Alex signed his name in well-written Arabic script, to the delight of all present. *Iskander* had been the most famous of soldier's names in the Middle East since Alexander the Great had successfully invaded Egypt. The excited Emir put his arms round Alex's neck and kissed him, saying, '*Mahaba*,' meaning 'I love you', a sincere expression between Arab men.

While Alex was with the Emir, I gave some training in pistol shooting to the Ruler's sons and nephews. They thoroughly enjoyed themselves and I got some practice with my American 9mm Colt automatic pistol. I allowed them to use my British .38 revolver, to their great delight, so we were soon the best of friends, for, like all Arabs, they had a great love of shooting, which was their main pastime.

Nearer home, in Cairo, a quite different matter began to raise its head. Before the victories of Alam Halfa and El Alamein King Farouk had begun to show strong sympathy with the Italian Government. Perhaps this was not so surprising for the King was a pleasure-loving young man and, unlike the British, who had given him a Rolls Royce for his last birthday, the Italians had sent some very attractive dancers, who were much more to his liking. His restlessness with the British was probably also fuelled by the instruction that he had been receiving from the Ambassador – perhaps guidance was the word – on the government of the Anglo-Egyptian Sudan and Egypt's foreign policy with regard to the Axis powers. All this came to a head in February of 1943. Farouk had been growing increasingly uncooperative and something had to be done to bring him to his senses. It was clear that he must now be shown the iron hand in the diplomatic glove. The method employed was certainly effective. A tank was used to smash the locked gates of the Abdin Palace and the Ambassador marched through to present His Majesty with an ultimatum. Either he cooperated fully with the British Armed Forces or he would be flown immediately into internment. The thought of being separated from his favourite belly-dancer at the night club of the Mena House Hotel, where he would frequently take a table and entertain the girls, proved too much for him to contemplate with equanimity. He quickly made up his mind to accept Sir Miles's ultimatum and guidance. However, he never forgave or forgot that he had been driven to accept British instructions under duress.

∗ ∗ ∗

Time flies so fast that it is hard for those of us who were there to realize that nearly sixty years have gone by since 23 October 1942, when almost 1,000 guns opened the barrage which marked the start of LIGHTFOOT, now known to all the world as the Battle of El Alamein. With the passage of time and the greatly reduced scale of warfare since the end of the Second World War, it is all too easy grossly to underestimate the scale of the achievement of Alex's Command over a period of little over two months in which the Eighth Army was not only reinvigorated and mustered to fight a brilliant defensive victory at Alam Halfa but then reconstituted, retrained and redeployed to fight a massive offensive action against a very determined and well-protected enemy.

It was indeed fortunate that, despite the disasters of the recent desert battles and the loss of Tobruk immediately before Alex and Monty arrived in the Middle East, a highly organized and most efficient Middle East Base had been established and stocked in the Delta, now under the brilliant direction of General Wilfrid Lindsell, one of the Army's leading logisticians. It was equally fortunate that at Eighth Army Headquarters the responsibility for logistic planning and execution was in the hands of Brigadier Sir Brian Robertson, whose administrative genius outshone even that of Lindsell, as we shall see in later chapters.

It was the existence of the Middle East Base that made possible the massive reinforcement and re-equipment programmes upon which LIGHTFOOT was contingent. One writes casually today of the arrival of 300 Sherman tanks from America in early September and their involvement in the great battle, but between their arrival and their issue to three armoured brigades of the Army each had had to be rigorously checked and then made fit for desert fighting in sufficient time for their new owners to become familiarized with them and trained in their use – the Army's first tanks with a turret-mounted, long-range gun with a good HE performance in addition to an anti-tank capability with solid shot. The base workshops had not only to cope with re-equipment tasks like that but with a massive repair programme, making good past battle damage and preparing a huge fleet of transport so that the Army could be supported in mobile operations over hundreds of very tough miles of desert going. Two fresh infantry divisions had had to be kitted out and hundreds of thousands of tons of stores of all types – rations, ammunition, engineer stores, mines and so on – had to be brought forward by road and rail to stock the forward dumps in great secrecy. Six major new tracks had to be built and massive deception operations, involving the creation of a dummy logistic organization and the hiding of hundreds of tanks disguised as lorries, not to mention a dummy pipeline, had to be executed in order to deceive the enemy over Montgomery's planned deployment.

On top of all this the troops had to carry out their very intensive hardening and tactical training. As I well remember, there was precious little sleep for many people during those six weeks following Alam Halfa. Alex took the most intense interest in every facet of this great build-up and especially in the deception plan and operational security, for, experienced soldier that he was, he knew only too well that an intelligence failure could spell disaster. Despite the massive burden of work he had to tackle, he spent every hour he could visiting the troops and, as he did so, his confidence in the outcome of the battle and his delight in their greatly increased confidence in the new leadership, and hence their morale, grew and grew.

✳ ✳ ✳

The Battle of El Alamein has been described many times and there is no room in a short memoir to go into its progress in any detail. It was, however, a major milestone in Alex's fulfilment of his mission, given to him only two months earlier by the Prime Minister.

Alex with Brian Robertson, who is wearing his 'goonskin' coat, and General Sidney Kirkman.

After twelve days' intense and bitter fighting a magnificent victory was won and Rommel's fate was sealed. It was now only a matter of time. As Field Marshal Lord Wavell would always teach as a brigade commander, no battle ever goes to plan and once the fighting starts chaos will reign. Monty always claimed that Alamein went to plan, but, although that was very broadly true, he had his fair share of setbacks, and muddle and chaos frequently reigned as the Eighth Army struggled to penetrate the German minefields and their deep defensive positions. So it was that after two days' intense fighting, with casualties mounting alarmingly, and little progress made, he withdrew much of his armour into reserve and made a new plan designed to penetrate the northern corridor of the enemy's defences. Alex, who had been watching the progress of the battle minutely but never interfering, now decided that the time had come for him to influence events, for he knew that a second attempt in the north would prove unacceptably costly and had little real chance of success. Accompanied by Dick Casey, the Australian British High

Alex and the Right Hon Richard Casey, the Minister of State in the Middle East, watch an aerial dogfight over the El Alamein battlefield. 30 October 1942. Note the desert-type domestic arrangements and the washing hung out to dry! IWM E18786

Commissioner, and General Dick McCreery, the Chief of Staff at GHQ, Alex went across to have a talk with Montgomery. It was at once apparent that any suggestion of a new direction of attack would be adamantly rejected. Knowing Monty as he did, and very conscious of his subordinate's extreme sensitivity to what he would see as interference in *his* battle, Alex withdrew, telling McCreery to get together with Freddy de Guingand, Monty's Chief of Staff, and to seek to persuade Monty to listen to reason and shift his point of attack further south, west of the Kidney Ridge feature. De Guingand begged McCreery to keep out of this discussion and to leave it to him to put the idea into Monty's mind in such a way that he believed that he had thought of it himself. It worked like a charm and on 2 November SUPER-CHARGE, as the new attack was called, was duly launched, spearheaded by the New Zealand Division and the 51st (Highland). The breach in the enemy's line was achieved and 10 Corps was passed through to break out and cut off the whole of the surviving elements of the Axis armies. Sadly, the *Corps de Chasse* was not driven hard enough and a golden opportunity to end the war in Africa was lost. To crown it all, a violent rainstorm then turned the desert into a quagmire and all hope of a rapid pursuit was also irretrievably gone.

Monty never acknowledged Alex's part in the re-direction of SUPERCHARGE, but it was, in fact, a striking example of his skill at dealing with a difficult commander at a critical moment.

* * *

The hold-up in the process of the battle had infuriated Churchill, who had drafted a strong signal to Alex demanding more action. Mercifully, for all his faults in dealing with commanders in the field, the Prime Minister almost invariably sought the approval of the Chiefs of Staff for any action he was proposing, normally by addressing General Brooke as their Chairman. This draft, when shown to the CIGS, provoked a blazing row between the two men, with Brooke vigorously defending both Alex and Montgomery, so it was never sent. The incident was just one of many examples of Brooke's supreme importance in the conduct of the war and proof positive that his unselfish rejection of the Command-in-Chief and his nomination of Alex for the post that he would so dearly have loved to accept was completely right.

The lion's share of the blame for the lack of progress in LIGHT-FOOT has traditionally been awarded to the armour and the lack of thrust on the part of its senior commanders. Certainly there was the feeling among some of the infantry divisions that they had been let down, but, as General Sir David Fraser says in his superb *And We Shall Shock Them* (Hodder & Stoughton, 1983), when Montgomery blamed the armoured commanders for their lack of drive at Alamein, part at least of the blame should have been directed inwards at his own failure to comprehend what tanks can and cannot reasonably be made to do. Field Marshal Lord Carver has explained with great clarity how great were the difficulties within

January, 1943. Australian troops, paying a last visit to the scene of their heroic success at El Alamein, examine a burned out Sherman tank. Author's collection

the breaching lanes in the minefields and how easily tanks could get lost in the chaos that persisted in the clouds of dust that hung over the battlefield, drifting off the marked lanes, only to become casualties and thereby adding to the confusion. However, as one who was present in the battle, as GSO I of 7th Armoured Division, he is certainly critical of some commanders and their formations.

The battle as a whole was a great demonstration of courage and determination in the face of very tough opposition. The 'men of the match' have to be the 'Diggers' of Lieutenant General Leslie Morshead's 9th Australian Division. Of them Montgomery later wrote:

> *We could not have won the battle in twelve days without the magnificent 9th Australian Division.*

Churchill too wrote:

> *The 9th Australian Division had* [struck] *what history may well proclaim as the decisive blow in the Battle of Alamein.*

There was a price to be paid for victory and some 13,500 men fell in the battle. Since July 1942 General Bernard Freyberg's New Zealand Division had suffered 6,000 casualties and the 9th

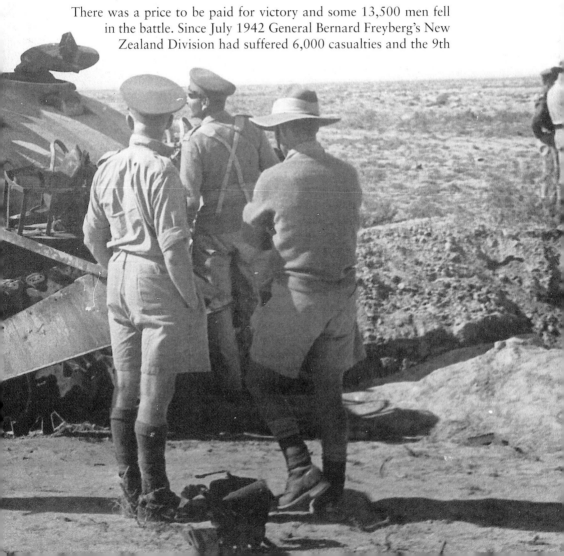

Gaza, December, 1942. The Chief is accompanied from his aircraft by Lieutenant General Sir Leslie Morshead on his arrival in Gaza for the Farewell Parade of the 9th Australian Division. IWM E20441

Australian Division 5,800. The percentage of casualties for the Eighth Army in the battle was 8 per cent, a remarkably small figure in the circumstances, but in line with Monty's forecast. Hence the losses of the two 'Anzac' divisions were disproportionately very high.

* * *

On 4 November, the Chief sent this signal to the Prime Minister:

> *After twelve days of heavy and violent fighting, the 8th Army has inflicted a severe defeat on the German and Italian forces.*

Then, two days later:

> *Ring out the Bells. Prisoners estimated now 20,000, tanks 350, guns 400, MT [Mechanized Transport] several thousand – 8th*

Army is advancing – heavy rains slow down pursuit of Rommel.

* * *

Two days after that signal was sent the Army crossed the Egyptian frontier in pursuit of Rommel. On the same day, 8 November, Operation TORCH was launched in North Africa, with British and American armies making three simultaneous landings, the 1st British Army being commanded by Lieutenant General Sir Kenneth Anderson. At Alamein Churchill had been given the victory he sought to boost the morale of the British people and give them confidence in this new venture, the first Anglo-American operation of the war.

On 13 December the Eighth Army, having recovered control of the whole of Cyrenaica, attacked the remnants of Rommel's forces at El Agheila, the start point of his own dramatic advance in April 1941. Three days later the Germans withdrew, Rommel having decided that until he could rebuild his armies he would avoid any further major clashes with Montgomery and would gradually with-draw from Tripolitania altogether. He first stopped briefly at Buerat on the Gulf of Sirte and by 18 January had gone back to points just east of Tripoli itself, ordering the destruction and evacuation of the port on the 19th. At 0500 hrs on 23 January the 11th Hussars entered Tripoli together with the 1st Gordons. The Army had come 1,400 miles from Alamein and it was time for a pause, although Montgomery would not allow the troops to move into the town. Meanwhile, as the Army had moved on Rommel's heels, great efforts had been made by the logisticians to get the ports of Tobruk and Benghazi in working order and to begin to build up stocks so that the long lines of communication, which were stretching daily, could be served effectively.

* * *

A major conference had been called by Churchill and Roosevelt to begin at Casablanca on 13 January to which Alex had been summoned. A major review of Allied strategy was to be made, addressing not only the Allies' future plans for the Mediterranean Theatre but also the preparation for Operation OVERLORD, the invasion of Europe, planned for spring or early summer of 1944. Although Alex was not very heavily involved in many of the meet-ings, Casablanca was to prove another milestone in his career, for reasons explained in the next chapter. The conference over, Churchill decided to pay a visit to the Eighth Army in Tripoli. There, on 3 February, he addressed the troops in the great

After the Conference, the Allied Commanders-in-Chief met to discuss future operations in the Mediterranean. (Front row, L to R) General Eisenhower (Supreme Allied Commander), Air Chief Marshal Sir Arthur Tedder, Alex, Admiral Sir Andrew Cunningham. Harold Macmillan and Major General Bedell Smith are standing on the left of the second row. IWM NY8657

amphitheatre. He ended with these famous words:

> *In days to come, when people ask you what you did in the Second World War, it will be enough to say: I marched with the Eighth Army.*

On the following day he took the salute at a Victory Parade led by the massed pipes of the 51st Highland Division. In company with some armour, the marching troops came principally from the 51st (Highland) and New Zealand Divisions. It was an unforgettable occasion.

Flanked by Alex and Monty, Winston stood there on the saluting base with the tears pouring down his face. Brooke, who was also present, noted those tears with some relief, for he was deeply conscious that he had a lump in his throat that would have made speech impossible and that his own cheeks were wet. And who could blame them? As the then Colonel Ian Jacob wrote in his diary: 'It was an occasion that made all the disappointments and setbacks of the Middle East campaign seem to be robbed of their sting'. I, for one, will never forget the impact of those massed pipes and the marching of rank upon rank of bronzed, battle-hardened soldiers – 'Every man an emperor,' as Winston later put it. That the Eighth Army could put on a show like that after slogging some 1,400 miles from Alamein speaks volumes for the calibre of its soldiers. For both Alex and Monty it was, of course, a morning of high personal achievement.

Churchill returned to Algiers after this momentous visit. There

4 February 1943. After the luncheon given for Winston Churchill by Lieutenant General Oliver Leese (30 Corps) to celebrate the Tripoli Victory Parade. (L to R) Oliver Leese, Alex, Winston, Brookie and Monty. IWM E222/1

he received this signal from the Chief on 8 February:

> *Sir, the orders you gave me on the 10th of August, 1942, have been fulfilled. His Majesty's enemies, together with their impedimenta, have been completely eliminated from Egypt, Cyrenaica, Libya and Tripolitania. I now await your further instructions.*

Churchill read that signal to the assembled Members of the House of Commons on 11 February to the acknowledgement of wild cheers.

Chapter Six

18TH ARMY GROUP: 'WE ARE MASTERS OF THE NORTH AFRICAN SHORES'

February – May, 1943

When Winston Churchill had read out Alex's famous signal to the Commons on 11 February 1943 he added these words:

It is not the end. It is not the beginning of the end, but it is, perhaps, the end of the beginning.

They were singularly appropriate, for events of equal or even greater magnitude had been occurring across the whole span of the war. Nine days before Winston spoke, all German resistance in Stalingrad had ceased. Over 147,000 men had been killed and 91,000 surrendered. It was certainly the turning point in Hitler's mad adventure in Russia. On the same day, 2 February, the Japanese had begun to evacuate Guadalcanal and the United States Marines had secured their greatest victory after months of extremely bloody fighting. That triumph had followed hard on the heels of the first Allied success on land against the Japanese in Papua New Guinea, which had fallen to the Americans and the Australians on 22 January, the 'Diggers' once again on the crest of the wave, but, on this occasion, much nearer home.

But it was not all plain sailing and Winston's caution was perhaps justified, for the Germans had now occupied all Vichy France. In Burma the campaign in the Arakan was not going well and, as we shall see in this chapter, there were serious problems to be tackled in North Africa which had led to a decision at the Allied conference at Casablanca in the middle of January to appoint my Chief as Deputy to General Eisenhower and commander of all Allied ground operations in the drive for Tunis. In the Atlantic the submarine war still raged and massive orders for new anti-submarine shipping and maritime patrol aircraft had had to be placed in the United States, whose factories and shipyards were already producing truly astonishing results.

* * *

We must now turn back to those developments in Operation

TORCH which were causing the Combined Chiefs of Staff and their political masters such concern.

For all his sterling qualities General Eisenhower lacked any previous experience of command in battle, let alone of the duties of a Theatre Commander, and Lieutenant General Anderson, the GOC-in-C of the British First Army, who was charged with the coordination of the land operations designed to secure both Tunis and Bizerta and so to check any further German reinforcement of North Africa, though a good soldier, was not cut out for that role. An initial dash for Bizerta had been made by the British 78th Division with elements of the Second US Corps under command. A combination of logistic confusion and a lack of drive in the forward area enabled the enemy to react with considerable vigour and as many as 1,000 reinforcements a day were being poured into Tunisia. To make matters worse, the weather was appalling and the whole operation came to a grinding halt some 25 miles short of Tunis in a sea of mud.

It must be remembered that all this was happening only about one year after Pearl Harbor and America's entry into the war, a war for which the US Army had been totally unprepared. That TORCH had been mounted at all in so short a space of time was a pretty remarkable achievement, but, inevitably, lack of training and battle experience put the Americans at a very serious disadvantage against the tough, well-led, battle-hardened Germans of von Arnim's 5th Army. It had soon become apparent that General Fredendall, the commander of the Second US Corps, was enjoying the confidence of neither his superiors nor his own troops. Meanwhile, a very confusing political tangle had landed on General Eisenhower's plate as the question of the command and role of the French troops in Algeria had to be sorted out.

Finally, it was now only a matter of time before the Eighth Army would be seeking to link up with the Allies in Tunisia and joint operations would become the pattern of the campaign. A man of stature and tact, with experience of command at the highest levels and a proven leader who could handle not only a mixed Allied force but also the cocksure Montgomery, had to be found and found quickly. There was only one answer to that requirement: the Land Force Commander and Deputy to Eisenhower had to be Alex. Fortunately no one was more keenly aware of this than Eisenhower himself, whose admiration of Alex's qualities was made so clear after their first meeting.

* * *

On 2 January 1943 a most important personality was added to the Algiers scene, Harold Macmillan, who had arrived as British

Alex chats with his close friend and colleague Harold Macmillan, the Resident Minister, with whom he would work so successfully and in such complete harmony. IWM NA3524

Resident Minister, accompanied by his charming and most able Secretary, the Hon John Wyndham who, incredibly, served him in an honorary capacity. In the months to come Macmillan would quickly become as staunch a friend and supporter of Alex as General Ike himself. We dubbed him 'our Commissar'! Like Alex, he had a wonderful gift for handling difficult personalities, even General de Gaulle, who was just about as hard to handle as it is possible to be. His quiet but highly reassuring presence made an invaluable contribution to the business of untangling the political web that so enmeshed the general situation. A former officer in the Grenadier Guards in the First World War, during which he had been wounded, he felt an instinctive affinity with Alex. There was nothing he enjoyed more than his honorary membership of the Chief's Mess where Alex's quiet cultured charm was a most welcome tonic, in sharp contrast with some of the more tiresome characters who daily crossed his path, which had quickly become something of a minefield.

* * *

The Mediterranean Commanders-in-Chief, Alex, Admiral Sir Andrew Cunningham and Air Marshal Sir Arthur Tedder, together with Harold Macmillan, had all been summoned to attend the Casablanca Conference. This seemed to the Chief to be a good chance to give Bill Cunningham a trip away from the drudgery of his desk and I was left to 'mind the office' in Cairo.

Bill's diary records the lighter side of that visit, which must have given Alex a very welcome break:

We flew with Tedder in his Liberator in modest comfort, high enough above Rommel's panzers to need oxygen masks, and eventually landed in Casablanca and drove to the Hotel Anfa and its surrounding villas. The Heads of State dined in their own quarters while the Combined Chiefs [of Staff] and the rest of the assorted generals, admirals and air marshals and their hangers-on fed in the hotel restaurant. Alex and I had a table on our own and were joined by a former destroyer Captain just promoted to Rear Admiral, who was rather surprised to find that the senior full Admirals at the top table thought him too junior to be admitted to their company. His Flag Lieutenant came too – a nice boy but one who copied his master's rather blasé attitude a bit too closely.

Alex's [presence] at the meetings was not too much in demand, though Winston seemed to like his company. One morning my master said, 'Can you fix up a jeep, Bill? I hear the Americans bombed the French battleship Jean Bart *during the landings. She is said to be in the harbour with a damned great hole in her foredeck and I wouldn't mind having a look.'*

I called upon the American transport officer and begged a brand new jeep, granted with great courtesy and generosity, together with a box of so many razor blades (at that time like gold dust in Cairo) that I used them for years after the war. We drove down to the harbour and pulled up alongside the Jean Bart; *rather a domestic scene, the crew's washing hanging on the rail, sailors lying around on deck playing cards to accordion music. Alex's red hat brought the officer of the watch down the gangplank and we were invited on board for a glass of red wine before being taken to inspect the damage done by the American dive bombers, which had indeed made 'a damned great hole in the foredeck' and a tangle of twisted deck plates and pipework had resulted. We left this very cordial reception and returned to the hotel for lunch.*

Lord Louis (for our newly promoted Rear Admiral was none other than Mountbatten) was already at the table. 'Oh Alex,' he whispered, 'I have a treat for you this afternoon.' 'What is it?' asked my master. 'Quietly, very secret,' said Lord Louis. Considering where and in what secure company we were lunching, it was not easy to imagine the need for the hushed tones. 'Got the car fixed, Flags? Then off we go,' said Lord Louis.

We finished our lunch and went outside where Flags whistled up a staff car which pulled up beside us, its windows obscured by oil and dust, except for a small patch. 'Isn't this fun?' said Dickie Mountbatten as we drove down the other side of the harbour from the Jean Bart, *perhaps a mile away. There Flags produced field-glasses, through which we examined the ship, not very effectively. 'Why all the mystery, Dickie?' asked Alex. 'Any closer and they see who I am; it would be most embarrassing,' was the reply. I could see Alex suppressing a smile with difficulty. 'What a treat, Dickie; thank you so much.' And we drove back to the Anfa Hotel in silence.*

Alex was required to address the Conference and described the plan for the seizure of Tripoli, which he forecast would fall in the near future. Churchill wrote, 'Alexander made a most favourable impression on the President who was greatly attracted to him, and also by his news [about the forthcoming fall of Tripoli].' The Conference then endorsed the proposal that Alex should at once become Eisenhower's Deputy, with responsibility for all Allied ground operations in North Africa and command of a new Army Group, the 18th, composed of the First and Eighth British Armies. Air Marshal Tedder was to assume overall command of the Allied air forces. The decision to invade Sicily in July 1943 had also been taken by the Conference and the responsibility for planning was also given to Alex. As always, he took on his new responsibilities with smiling equanimity. Being at heart a dedicated battlefield soldier, the prospect of some 'hands on' command and of driving the Germans out of North Africa delighted him. However, he had no illusions about the problems which now strewed his path. Meanwhile, he had still got the battle for Tripolitania on his plate and the need to sort out a small battlefield headquarters, drawn from his existing staff in Cairo. 'Jumbo' Wilson was to take over the Middle East Command.

It was patently obvious that the sooner he could get to know Ike really well the better, for so much was going to hang on their close cooperation and mutual confidence. He therefore decided to spend two days with Eisenhower after the Conference for this purpose and to get the feel of the overall situation in Tunisia. Bill Cunningham went with him and has this nice little touch of light relief in his diary:

> On the way back to Egypt from the Casablanca Conference Alex and I spent a couple of days in Algiers with Eisenhower; it seemed to be tactful and useful for the future to establish some personal contact and liaison with Eisenhower's personal staff [so] I duly appeared at Allied Force Headquarters for that purpose.
>
> I was met and entertained by a Lieutenant Colonel whose name I had forgotten until the other night, when I watched the film Patton on TV. There he was, listed as the co-producer of the film. Tall and handsome in beautifully tailored battledress of smooth serge, he at once offered me the conventional 'cuppa cawfee' whilst we sat down to 'get acquainted'. His left breast was ablaze with two rows of decorations and, out of politeness, I asked him what they were. 'Purple Heart comes first,' he said. 'I got that for being wounded in London; a big piece of shrapnel from one of your Ack Ack guns fell on me and ruined my best uniform, so I reckon I earned that. Next comes the Order of the Lion of Morocco, then the Star of Tunis. Next the campaign medal for serving in Europe, then ditto for Africa and the something French – I can't remember what.' He eyed my chest, bare but for the unspectacular purple and white of the Military Cross; our own Africa Star came out many months later and I must say I felt rather naked. 'How did you acquire your spectacular medals?' I asked. They were indeed quite dazzling, particularly the Star of Tunis, which was almost fluorescent orange. 'I'm the guy who distributes them,' was the answer. 'Who else would have first choice?' He glanced again at my left breast. 'Did you say you had been a General's aide for a year?' he queried. 'Only one medal? Jee-zus, you must be slow,' was the comment. However, he apparently condoned my lack of opportunism and afterwards became a helpful and friendly wangler of air priorities and provider of PX (Post Exchange) goodies and beds in his boss's villa.

On 16 January, during the Conference, the CIGS had attended a discussion with Eisenhower and Alex to consider the coordination of attacks on Tunisia. He later wrote:

> Eisenhower's original plan (a wild dash across Southern Tunisia to Sfax, leaving his flanks exposed) was a real bad one... a better plan was drawn up.

Ten days later Brooke and the Prime Minister met the Chief in

Cairo to discuss the clearing of Tunisia and the subsequent Sicilian operation (known as HUSKY).

On the following morning 'Brookie' (as he was known to all) attended the Chief's staff conference at which all intelligence matters were reviewed. He then went to say goodbye to General Morshead before he left with the 9th Australian Division for Australia. They were leaving with heads held high, having distinguished themselves in the Eighth Army as a fighting formation without peer. Now their great fighting qualities were needed closer to home. By good fortune, not only was General Morshead married to my future wife's cousin but his ADC, Tim Collins, was a cousin of mine. Tim kindly offered to take any letters for my family back to Australia for me. General Jumbo Wilson also arrived on that day to discuss the arrangements for his takeover from the Chief. The operational scene had so changed that the principal task for Headquarters Middle East would now be the logistic support for Alex's armies in North Africa and Sicily.

Before Brookie and Winston left for Turkey Alex gave the CIGS a memorable day off by flying him with his ADC to the legendary Siwa Oasis, a veritable Garden of Eden in the middle of the desert. Its Beau Geste fort had for some time been the forward operating base of the Long Range Desert Group. From there its patrols would set out for their daring cross-desert drives to their hides, from which they would produce a vast quantity of invaluable intelligence about the movement of the enemy, or to transport raiding groups of the Special Air Service on their harassing tasks against the German and Italian airfields.

There was a great deal to be done before we could establish 18th Army Group. Thanks to the change in the operational scene, it was possible for the Chief to take General Dick McCreery and other senior members of his present headquarters to man the new set-up. Alex visited Monty in Tripoli to discuss the forthcoming operations which would finally enable the First and Eighth Armies to meld into the new Army Group. Monty assured him that once his Army had broken through the Gabes Gap 'we will roll the whole show up from the south'. In the event, it was not to prove quite as simple as that!

On 17 February Ike sent his personal Flying Fortress to collect the Chief and his personal staff, General Dick McCreery and the team of experienced staff officers from Middle East Command who were to form the nucleus of 18th Army Group. First and foremost the new headquarters would command the two British Armies, but the 2nd United States Corps would also come under command. Essentially, it was organized on British staff lines which were much more economical in manpower than their US counterparts and since the intention was for it to be fairly mobile, 'small was beautiful'.

Once more Alex was faced with 'Bargo'! On 14 February 1943 Rommel had won his last great victory. The Germans had broken through the front of the 2nd US Corps at the Kasserine Pass, inflicting 6,000 casualties and destroying eighty tanks and hundreds of wheeled vehicles. On the day that we flew in, Kasserine, Fériana and Sbeitla were all occupied by Rommel's troops. Having spent the 18th talking to General Eisenhower, Alex assumed command of the Army Group two days ahead of schedule and at once began to get a grip on a very untidy situation.

While Alex was in discussion with Ike I took the opportunity to get to know some of Ike's personal staff, notably General Bedell Smith (known to all as 'Beetle'), his Chief of Staff, and his PA, Commander Harry Butcher, who was very helpful. I also met Ike's attractive British driver, Kay Summersby. They all lived in a nice villa overlooking Algiers where we had lunch and dinner and spent the night. As in Cairo, Alex decided to get away from the fleshpots and settle his Camp some ten miles west of Algiers at Bouzarea, using the buildings of the *École Normale* and pitching our tents among the pine trees. Hardly had we got settled there than we moved camp to Constantine, much nearer the front.

Alex was convinced that the Germans were heading for Tebessa and that the Americans had been defeated in detail because they were too widely dispersed. He was determined to get forward and see things for himself. As I shall show, he found things worse than he had feared.

In pouring rain we headed out from Algiers for a five-hour easterly drive over bad roads to Constantine, which stood 1,000 feet above sea level. Conditions there were pretty miserable, but we were near First Army Headquarters and the forward troops and we set up our first North African Tac HQ there, originally in buildings, but General Dick wisely moved the headquarters into tents, though the bitterly cold weather made this a rather unpopular decision.

Alex wasted no time in getting around the front. In his Despatch he describes what he found on the 2nd Corps front and this quotation gives a very fair picture of the problems he now faced as he sought to get the battlefield under proper control:

> *I then went on to the II Corps sector...I found the position even more critical than I had expected and a visit to the Kasserine area showed that, in the inevitable confusion of the retreat, American, French and British troops had been inextricably mingled, there was no coordinated plan of defence and definite uncertainty as to command.*

One of Alex's first steps was to signal Monty, asking for assistance in easing the pressure on the northern and central sectors of the Tunisian front where things were pretty desperate. He explained:

> *The battle area is all mixed up with British, French and American units, with no policy and no plan. I have issued the necessary directives but need time to make them effective. The present battle*

A typical picture of the Chief at the wheel of his jeep – a very familiar sight in the forward areas during fighting. IWM1526

situation extremely critical.

Although he was not yet ready to launch his new offensive, as his logistic position was still building up, Montgomery at once despatched the leading elements of the Eighth Army to Medenine, a road junction south of his next major objective, the Mareth Line, which patrols had occupied on the 18th. There, with a strong infantry presence of the New Zealand Division and 201 Guards Brigade supported by some 400 tanks, no less than 500 anti-tank guns had been dug in. The Germans were about to be hoist with their own petard, as indeed they were, losing fifty-two tanks in four attacks, the greatest single day's loss of the whole African campaign and something like fifty per cent of all the tanks involved. Medenine, which must rate as a classic, was Rommel's last battle in Africa. On 9 March he left Africa for ever, von Arnim assuming command of all the Axis forces in Tunisia.

The mauling given to the Germans at Medenine produced an immediate alleviation of the worst of Alex's problems in the 2 Corps area and he sent Monty a signal: 'Well done! I am greatly relieved'.

* * *

We left Alex still making his personal assessment of the battle situation as we drove from formation to formation, the Chief making a personal intervention on occasions in order to restore some sort of order out of chaos. Though never by the flicker of an eyelid did he reveal it, even to us, his personal staff, he must at times have felt very like despair. Not long after we left Algiers he wrote bluntly to Brookie:

> They [the Americans] *simply do not know their job as soldiers and this is the case from the highest to the lowest, from the General to the private soldier. Perhaps the weakest link of all is the junior leader, who just does not lead, with the result that their men do not really fight.*

Later he would be the first to acknowledge that, with great determination and the inspiration stemming from a dynamic and outstanding new commander, they soon began to fight bravely and well.

As far as the British 1st Army was concerned, Alex at once realized that he was going to have to hold General Kenneth Anderson firmly by the hand. Described by Monty, in a typically unkind way, as 'a good plain cook', Anderson simply did not have the flair for Army command and needed all the help and encouragement that Alex could give him. The final battles and the breakthrough to Tunis would all be fought under Alex's personal control.

It was an education for me, as a very young officer, to accompany Alex to and fro across the front, exerting his almost magical influence upon the formations as they struggled to pull themselves together and get the situation stabilized so that the advance towards Tunis could be resumed. I remember so well that there was very little friction but rather a sense of relief, as the fighting troops had received little or no information or direction from Allied Force Headquarters. Now, at last, they had an experienced commander and staff right up forward and a new grip had been taken which did much for their confidence and morale.

Once his main headquarters had been established at Constantine, Alex took his small mobile Tac HQ forward to get closer to the fighting. We were first at Ainbeida, then at Le Kef, which was still on high ground, some 3,000 feet up, but an attractive mountain town covering the entrance to the plains and

March, 1943. Arriving at Allied Force Headquarters where he gave a Press Conference to a gathering of American and British Press Correspondents, his first after assuming his appointment as Deputy to Ike and Commander 18th Army Group. IWM NA1035

the approach to Tunis and sited more or less centrally between the First Army and 2nd US Corps, once Alex had sorted out the muddle and had regrouped after Kasserine, with the British, French and Americans each in their own areas. In fact we were sitting on the traditional approach route of all who had conquered Tunis throughout history, leading on to the Medjez Valley.

We had arrived in North Africa with only our normal desert uniform, unlike the First Army whose soldiers wore battledress and were glad of it in the biting cold. Luckily, we had brought from the desert what were known as our 'goonskin' coats which we could wear in the Chief's open car or jeep. These rather unusual garments were made of khaki-coloured material with a sheep- (or goat-) skin lining, with the inside lining continuing round the collar. Where they originated I know not, but they were real life-savers in the winter weather. The Chief, who wore his with a belt round his waist, his peaked Irish Guards cap and plastic eyeshields, looked rather like a German officer. Those eyeshields, so valuable in the desert to keep the sand out of our eyes, now gave us protection from the wind and driving rain, for the windscreens of our vehicles had to be kept flat on the bonnet to avoid sun flashes. To reduce damage from road mines, I put sandbags on the floor of the car, but I doubt if they would have given us much protection, judging by the wrecks of countless carriers we saw on the verges of roads and tracks, having run over anti-tank mines, usually with fatal results.

General George Patton, who had commanded the Western Task Force in the TORCH landings with commendable skill and determination, arrived in Algiers on 5 March and was told by Ike to relieve General Lloyd Fredendall in command of 2 Corps. He then flew to Constantine to meet Alex who told him that he had asked for the best Corps Commander he could get and that he had been assured that he, Patton, was that man, as indeed he was, for Patton was without doubt the best fighting general in the US Army at that level. Colourful figure though he was and often foul-mouthed, the troops loved his salty harangues and would follow him to the death. On 6 March he assumed command and on the 9th we visited him, General Dick McCreery coming with us. Alex was impressed by the degree of immediate improvement which had appeared in only three short days but he was still concerned about the greenness of the US troops in general. But Georgie Patton was not only an inspired leader, he was a consummate trainer of men and had a wealth of experience. We came away from that visit feeling a great deal happier about 2 Corps.

A soldier cannot become a battle-hardened veteran overnight and the average American soldier had not got the faintest idea of how to live on the face of the battlefield. I well remember Patrick Stewart MC, one of our liaison officers sent over to help 2 Corps, telling me how the soldiers gathered around him when he brewed up, using a little petrol in a tin of sand to heat up some bully beef stew and a mug of tea. As the stew cooked the GIs began to sniff the air appreciatively, saying, 'Gee, we haven't had a hot meal for a week'. This failure to recognize the importance of feeding the troops seems to be a characteristic of new-born American armies in the field, for they had had just the same problem in the Argonne in 1918, when some soldiers literally starved in the forward trenches. I hardly need to add that the lesson was soon learned this time. Poor Patrick was very badly wounded after Kasserine, guiding American tanks in his open jeep. Although confined to a wheelchair, he later became Second-in-Command of the Security Service in London.

* * *

17 March, St Patrick's Day, is, of course, our regimental day in the Irish Guards. So 17 March 1943 is one St Patrick's Day that I will never forget. On that day the 24th Guards Brigade, which included the 1st Battalion Irish Guards, landed in Bône. Alex sent me down to the docks to meet them and to take the Shamrock, with the message, 'Welcome to the Micks. Now we'll get cracking!' After the traditional Battalion parade and church service, conducted by the Regimental Chaplain, Father 'Dolly' Brooks MC (who had fought with the Battalion as a Platoon Commander in the First World War and was then a master at Downside), the officers saw the men sat down to a gargantuan meal, washed down with quantities of rough red wine which was quite foreign to the Micks and, I suspect, must have produced a number of sore heads. Then the officers, about thirty of us in all, tucked into a very ample and convivial lunch. Sadly, that was the last St Patrick's Day for many. From the set-piece company attack launched on Recce Ridge at midnight on 26 March, just nine days later, only five men out of 103 officers and men of 2 Company survived to get back to the Battalion. There was only one officer

survivor, Lieutenant Lesslie, who was wounded and taken prisoner. He later escaped from his Italian prison camp and was taken into the Vatican City by an Irish priest, Monsignor O'Flaherty, described by Father Dolly Brooks as 'The Vatican Pimpernel'. At immense personal risk, he smuggled Allied prisoners of war out of Rome into such Vatican enclaves as the Abbey of St Paul's-without-the Walls. Lesslie was liberated when we captured Rome on 4 June 1944.

Father Dolly was a legendary figure himself and on 4 January 1945 Alex had him posted to his own Supreme Allied Commander's Headquarters in the Palace of Caserta, the royal palace of the former Kings of Sicily.

After the Recce Ridge attack the Irish Guards went on to take and hold Djebel Bou Aoukaz (hereafter 'the Bou'). This was the key to Medjez el Bab. Corporal Kenneally was awarded the Victoria Cross for his part in that battle and Captain Colin Kennard an immediate DSO. The Scots Guards captured the other side of the Bou, Captain Lord Lyell being awarded a posthumous VC.

* * *

Meanwhile Monty was not letting the grass grow under his feet and attacked the Mareth Line on 18 March. After two days' bitter fighting, during which the 50th (Northumbrian) Division took very heavy casualties but were unable to break through, he sent Bernard Freyberg's New Zealand Corps, together with the 8th Armoured Brigade and General Leclerc's Free French, in an outflanking 'left hook' to the west. They crossed a piece of desert considered impassable by the French when they built the line, following a passable track reconnoitred by the Long Range Desert Group. The Corps went on to take Matmata and to threaten El Hamma, forcing von Arnim to evacuate the Mareth Line on 27 March and withdraw to the Wadi Akarit, a formidable position north of Mareth. A very tough, bloody battle ensued, described by Monty as 'the heaviest and most savage fighting we have had since I have commanded the Eighth Army'. The debouchment by the 10th Corps was a disappointment and the defenders got clean away to fight another day. However, on 7 April an armoured car patrol of the 12th Lancers made the first link-up between the Eighth Army and the US 2nd Corps. Two days later the Army took Sfax, enabling Monty to make a triumphal entry (of which more anon!). On the 12th Sousse also fell and the 12th Lancers made contact with units of the First Army. 18th Army group was coming together and the noose around von Arnim's neck was beginning to tighten.

* * *

While Monty and the Eighth Army were making these advances Harold Macmillan arrived at our Tac HQ for a visit, the first of many. We left camp on 21 March in the open car with the Chief and Macmillan sitting in the back, which was slightly raised and so a pretty cold spot whilst we were up in the mountains. The faithful Sergeant Wells and I sat at a lower level in the front. Unlike those behind us, we had no sandbags, but, being a bit more sheltered, were warmer, for which we were duly grateful! We made a tour of a series of formation headquarters, from Corps downwards, coming down from the mountains and into the great plains. Macmillan loved those visits. He was deeply impressed by our Chief's simple Camp and Alex's ability to receive signals and issue orders without interrupting his guests as the battle rumbled on, in this case ending when the New Zealanders entered Gabes on 29 March.

As if he had not already got enough on his plate, Alex was wrestling with the thorny problems of the planning for HUSKY, with which he had also been charged. It will be recalled that when we came back from Burma he had become the Commander designate for TORCH and involved in the planning that was going on in London. HUSKY too had begun to be planned in London and this process had been continued in Algiers. Alex knew that Monty had not thought much of such plans as he had already seen and would probably be wanting to have all his most experienced Corps and Divisional Commanders, complete with their battle-hardened divisions, nominated for the operation. However, there was a view being taken that some of those divisions, who had been fighting for two or three years, needed a bit of a rest and an opportunity and time to absorb and train their reinforcements. Alex decided to send me to see Monty for him and get his views. He would often send Bill Cunningham or me on such trips as we were both privy to all the planning already in hand and the current operational situation. On this occasion I was sent in a Beaufighter, flown by a young and very inexperienced pilot who could only fly in daylight. As the armies had yet to link up, this meant flying across the German lines, but we did so without interference from the Luftwaffe. I flew along the coastal road linking Mareth and Medenine, assuming that I would find Monty's Tac HQ somewhere there. We landed at a desert strip beside the road from where I managed to get a lift in a passing armoured car to Monty's headquarters. After my discussion with him and memorizing the details of his requirements, I realized that time was pressing and that I must get back to my Beaufighter if we were to make the trip back in daylight. Monty very kindly told me to take his staff car, which was a great help, as the only road was clogged with transport and guns moving up and the Army Commander's car gave me a sort of right of way. The car began to boil and the driver wanted to stop. However, I had to tell him to press on as the Chief needed Monty's views urgently. Just short of the airstrip the car seized up and I had to cadge a lift in another armoured car to get me to the plane. We took off just before dark and I got back safely. Not surprisingly there was an aftermath. Monty had been planning a triumphal entry into Sfax in his open car and was forced to use his jeep instead. I received a signal from John Poston saying, 'Don't come back again'!

By 19 April, fighting hard much of the way, the Eighth Army reached Enfidaville. By then it had shot its bolt and Alex had decided that the final assault on Tunis would be carried out by the First Army and the 2nd US Corps. Two divisions, 4th Indian and 7th Armoured, together with 201 Guards Brigade, were switched to command of First Army and Horrocks was moved to command First Army's 9 Corps, as General Crocker had been injured.

VULCAN, as Alex had christened his final breakthrough, which was to be followed by STRIKE, the capture of Tunis itself, was to be under his personal control, its main thrust being up the Medjez Valley.

The 9 Corps operation began on 22 April and from then on it was bitter, hard fighting all the way. On 25 April Alex signalled Winston:

The enemy continues to resist desperately, but this evening there are definite signs that he is weakening.

Meanwhile 5 Corps was advancing down the Tunis-Medjez road. The intensity of the fighting may be judged from the fact that three VCs were awarded. The Irish Guards had all this time been fiercely defending their position on 'the Bou', the lynch-pin to the valley. When some eighty survivors of the Battalion finally left that feature, no less than 700 German bodies were counted on its slopes. So relentlessly had the Germans attacked that, when their casualties began to mount, fresh troops were bussed straight into the battle from Enfidaville.

After the battle the Battalion went into rest at Hammamet. There they received a message from Alex which was read out to all ranks on Sunday 9 May by Lieutenant Colonel Andrew Scott:

> *Heartiest congratulations to you and all ranks of the Battalion for your magnificent fight, which has not only added fresh laurels to the illustrious name of the Regiment, but has been of the utmost importance to our whole battle. I am very sorry about your losses. H.R.G.A.* *

On 6 May the final attack went in on either side of the Medjez-Tunis road, with both Bizerta and Tunis being entered on the 7th. Eisenhower had given Alex a directive to the effect that the 2nd Corps was to be given a major objective and Patton's men

* From *The History of the Irish Guards in the Second World War* by Major D.J.L. Fitzgerald MC (Gale & Polden)

With his jeep well laden, the Chief drives up to a forward brigade during Operation VULCAN. RC sits behind him as map reader. IWM FLM1528. A British Newsreels Picture

Special Order of the Day

HEADQUARTERS
18th ARMY GROUP
21st April, 1943

SOLDIERS OF THE ALLIES

1. Two months ago, when the Germans and Italians were attacking us, I told you that if you held firm, final victory was assured.

2. You did your duty and now you are about to reap its full reward.

3. We have reached the last phase of this campaign. We have grouped our victorious Armies and are going to drive the enemy into the sea.

   We have got them just where we want them—with their backs to the wall.

4. This final battle will be fierce, bitter and long, and will demand all the skill, strength and endurance of each one of us.

   But you have proved yourselves the masters of the battle-field, and therefore you will win this last great battle which will give us the whole of North Africa.

5. The eyes of the world are on you—and the hopes of all at home.

FORWARD THEN, TO VICTORY

H. R. Alexander

General,

Commander, 18th Army Group

triumphantly captured Bizerta, a very important victory for them in the light of all that had happened during the Kasserine battle and the determination they had shown ever since under their inspiring commander.

On the 8th Alex signalled Churchill, who was on the *Queen Mary* en route for Washington:

The Axis front has completely collapsed and disintegrated.

Only 633 Germans escaped from Tunisia and by 25 May the number of prisoners taken totalled 238,243.

On 12 May Colonel General von Arnim, the Commander of Army Group Afrika, surrendered. A typical member of the landed aristocracy, he had come to Africa from the Soviet Union, where he had commanded a Corps and assumed command of the German 5th Army. Always at loggerheads with Rommel, he was also disinclined to cooperate with his Italian allies. Alex declined to invite him to his mess but told me to look after him and see that he was treated correctly. After an interview with Colonel David Hunt, our GSO I, I got von Arnim a tent in our Tac HQ and arranged for the mess to give him dinner. I told him that I had spent several years at Murnau-am-Staffelsee in Bavaria, staying in the Schloss Rieden, which stood at the other end of the lake to his family home. Before he left for Algiers the General said, 'I probably will not need these,' and gave me his Zeiss binoculars and Leica camera. He was flown to Maison Blanche, near Ike's headquarters. Like Alex, Eisenhower decided not to see him. However, while he was waiting at the airport to be flown to the Senior Officers' Cage at Latimer (in England), he was interviewed by General Strong, Ike's Director of Military Intelligence, a British officer. At Latimer Intelligence Officers listened intently to the chat between the various German generals housed there, the flow always increasing with each new arrival.

On the day after von Arnim's surrender Alex sent Churchill another of his historic messages:

Colonel General von Arnim, Commander Army Group Afrika, at Le Kef after surrendering on 12 May 1943. Bill Cunningham

Sir, it is my duty to report that the Tunisian Campaign is over. All enemy resistance has ceased. We are masters of the North African shores.

On 20 May the Victory Parade was held in Tunis. Eisenhower and the French Commander-in-Chief, General Giraud, stood side by side on the saluting base. Behind them were the three fighting Commanders, Admiral Sir Andrew Cunningham, Alex and Air Marshal Sir Arthur Tedder. With all names changed since independence from Vichy France, the main Avenue, flanked by tall, graceful palms throughout its length, made a perfect and most impressive setting for this truly historic occasion. First came the colourful Zouaves and Goumiers of the French Forces, followed by the quietly marching serried ranks of the Americans and then, an unforgettable sound and sight, the massed pipers of the Scots and Irish Guards and of all the Highland regiments of the 51st (Highland) Division, leading rank upon rank of the infantry of the First and Eighth British Armies. They were followed by the guns, armoured cars and tanks and, finally, General Leclerc's magnificent Free French Forces, who had marched all the way from Lake Chad to join the Eighth Army, with whom they now insisted upon marching rather than their

The Supreme Allied Commander and his Deputy at the Tunis Victory Parade, May, 1943. IWM CNA1074

With General de Gaulle at the Parade. IWM NA3816

former Vichy French brethren, with whom they had no wish to associate.

* * *

As in Tripoli, this was a very moving occasion and one that inspired many memories, not least of good friends lost in that wonderful stand on the Bou by the Irish Guards, mingled for me with a certain regret that I had not been there to fight with them. Above all, I was thinking of Alex, as he stood there so smartly turned out with that air of quiet charm and modesty, combined with an aura of authority which bred unquestioning but willing obedience. What a long way we had come from those quiet days at Wilton in 1941! Yet, unbelievably, only fourteen months had passed since we landed in Rangoon and Alex had found himself landed with the first of the three 'Bargos' which those who ran the war had seen fit to drop on to his plate – three drastic situations, each formidable enough to have lasted one man for his lifetime as a soldier, and all three sorted out and crowned with success, though the success in Burma had admittedly been that of rescuing his army intact rather than a spectacular victory, as in Tripoli and here in Tunis. Each task had grown progressively more complex and this, the third, had presented him with a situation that very few commanders could have mastered as he did. Of course, he had been fortunate in having three remarkable subordinates – Slim, Monty and, in a rather different but equally important context, Patton. But no historian, seeking to analyze Alex's performance as a field commander, should underrate the manner in which he sorted out the multi-national tangle of the Tunisian fighting or the way in which he created a new confidence in the forward areas or quietly but immediately assumed absolute control of the ground operations from a bewildered Eisenhower, overwhelmed with political crises and lacking all personal experience of command in battle. That the man upon whom he should have been able to rely to carry a considerable share of the burden was proving something of a broken reed and quite unsuited to handle the Anglo-American situation, particularly as the Americans were in need of so much wise help and guidance, was about the last straw. Yet Alex had held Anderson's hand and had steered him through to ultimate victory. As all these thoughts ran through my mind they were blended with my gratitude for the kindness and good humour he had never failed to show me as I tried to give him the personal support he needed. For all the stresses and strains, dangers and discomforts that we had shared, these had been a wonderfully happy fourteen months with a man whom I was intensely proud to serve.

Now, with the Germans thrown out of Africa, we were about to embark upon new and equally demanding adventures, but the last of the 'Bargos' had been dealt with and any future operations would be conducted from a firm and tidy base.

* * *

On 28 May Winston and Brookie appeared from London to discuss the plans for HUSKY and, in particular, for its exploitation. They had had a rather unsatisfactory visit to America in that a compromise about the conflicting requirements of the Mediterranean and the cross-Channel operation planned for 1944 (OVERLORD) had been reached whereby the decision about the way ahead after HUSKY was to be left to the Joint Chiefs of Staff. After talking with Ike, Alex and Andrew Cunningham, they returned to London convinced that an invasion of Italy must follow directly after the successful conclusion of HUSKY, which was what Winston wanted. He now got his way. Whilst they were in Algiers, the usual round of visits and dinners took place and, after we had given Brookie lunch in the Chief's Camp on 30 May, he and Alex flew to Bougie to inspect the Highland Division. The shadow of St Valery was now well and truly eclipsed by the Division's heroic progress from El Alamein and wherever you went the letters HD announced their presence, so that they soon acquired the perhaps not altogether enviable nickname of 'the Highway Decorators'.

Monty had been in England on leave during the visitation, having extracted a Flying Fortress for his personal use out of the Americans, ostensibly in payment of a light-hearted bet he had had with 'Beetle' Smith which he now insisted should be honoured. Eisenhower was furious and the incident soured relations for some time.

His Majesty the King had long been wishing to get out to Africa to see his troops and now, at last, this had become possible. In great secrecy, he arrived on 12 June to the delight of all concerned. On the 14th we had our first visit from P.J. Grigg, the Secretary of State for War, who had been brought out by Macmillan. Grigg was a powerful figure who, uniquely, had assumed the post from being the Permanent Under-Secretary at the War Office, an appointment he had filled with great distinction. He was devoted to the Army and was delighted by its latest success. Alex invited him to become an Honorary Member of our Mess and to stay in his Camp amidst the pine trees. Grigg loved every minute of it. Alex had made a most valuable ally.

As I said in my Preface, the building we took to house our field headquarters in the outskirts of Tunis was the British Consul's house at La Marsa, now the British Embassy. A good solid building, it had been given to Queen Victoria by the Bey of Tunis in the 1850s. Its great advantage was that on one side of it was a large field, big enough to contain a tented camp for 1,000 men with all the usual military paraphernalia which that involves – a cookhouse, latrines, ablutions and so forth. On the other side it had a large garden and orchard. We gave the left-hand side of the villa to Harold Macmillan and John Wyndham, who also shared our main reception room, and put the Mess on a side verandah. The Chief had a study and bedroom overlooking the garden and orchard. These housed the signals contingent, Ultra terminal and the armoured car, as well as the operations staff and the Defence Platoon. As usual, Bill and I had a room and a verandah which enabled us to protect Alex from unnecessary interruptions as well as making a secure area with a very pleasant outlook. In addition to Harold Macmillan and John Wyndham, Air Marshal 'Maori' Coningham, who commanded the Tactical Air Force, was also an Honorary Member of our Mess. In that most satisfactory set-up we settled down to some very hard work on the planning and preparations for HUSKY.

The British Consul's house at La Marsa on the outskirts of Tunis, Alex's Field Headquarters for 18th and, subsequently, 15th Army Groups. Now the British Embassy, where Alex's portrait hangs.

Chapter Seven

A TIME OF CHANGE: PLANNING AND PREPARATION FOR HUSKY

May – July, 1943

There could be no let-up after the fall of Tunis in May 1943, for Operation HUSKY (the invasion of Sicily) was only two short months away. Inevitably, the complexities and anxieties of the Tunisian campaign and the political wrangling in Algiers had tended to take everyone's eyes off the ball as far as HUSKY was concerned, apart from the planning staff of Task Force 141. Now, when the commanders involved had time to take a proper look at the outline plan agreed at Casablanca, it was clear that it was sadly awry. On Montgomery's insistence it was finally agreed to scrap the old plan and to concentrate both the American and British landings on a strip of twenty-six beaches covering about 105 miles of the south-east corner of the island as offering the best chance of early seizure of the airfields so essential to gaining air superiority. The seaborne assault, the greatest amphibious operation in history, would take place on 10 July, preceded by an airborne operation on the previous day.

The two Armies involved were the new 7th US and Montgomery's British Eighth. George Patton, who had done so well both during TORCH and in command of the 2nd Corps after Kasserine, had deservedly been given command of 7th Army. General Omar Bradley would command the 2nd Corps under Patton. Montgomery had selected 13 Corps (General Miles Dempsey) and 30 Corps (General Oliver Leese). As in Tunisia, the naval and air forces would remain under Cunningham and Tedder. Eisenhower had been unhappy about this continued British dominance across the board, but had been overruled at Casablanca. As Ike's Deputy and as GOC-in-C of what now became the 15th Army Group, Alexander would have overall responsibility.

* * *

Meanwhile, all the signs across the whole face of the war continued to put the writing on the wall for the Axis. In the Pacific the fighting continued to rage to and fro, the Japanese admitting that the situation had become critical, though the pattern was by no means symmetrical, for in Burma the first Arakan campaign had finally been acknowledged to be a failure. In India Wavell had become Viceroy and the Auk was once more C-in-C. In the West the air war against Germany continued to increase in intensity, and the toll of U-Boats sunk was rising in the Atlantic. In Washington and in the meetings of the Heads of Government a long period of controversy had set in, chiefly arising from the relative priorities being given to the various theatres, especially over the provision of landing-craft, a matter that would seriously affect Alex over the months ahead, not least because of American insistence on mounting an operation in southern France soon after the northern invasion. This diversion would involve several divisions and a large number of landing craft. Code-named DRAGOON, it would become a very serious problem at a time when Italy was needing all the manpower it could get. So greatly taken were the Americans and politicians with OVERLORD that it was pretty clear to an experienced mind like Alex's that the Mediterranean was soon going to be fighting tooth and nail for any additional resources they might need – a disquieting thought before the first battle of what might prove a long campaign had been fought.

* * *

It goes without saying that when we became 15th Army Group, an essentially Anglo-American formation, as opposed to a British Army Group with a single American Corps under command, important changes had to take place within the Headquarters, not the least of which was the appearance of an American Deputy Chief of Staff, Major General Clarence L Huebner. The French 19th Corps, commanded by General Juin, with whom Alex was on the best of terms, remained in the new Army Group, to Alex's delight, as he had a high regard for the fighting qualities of the French. Soon after they had first met, Juin had given Alex a 19th Corps emblem, in the form of a shield with an Arabic inscription, to be worn on the right breast pocket of his battle dress. Alex was delighted and proud to wear it for as long as the Corps was under his command. Some time later, when he became the Allied Commander-in-Chief Italy and we became Headquarters Allied Armies Italy (AAI), he designed a similar shield with blue wavy lines on a white ground (to represent the sea) which we all wore.

Few people today will have any understanding of what it meant to meld two such disparate armies into a cohesive fighting organization. It was fortunate for us that Ike had laid down that Alex's headquarters was to be kept as small and mobile as possible and it had been agreed that we should be organized on British staff lines. To have reproduced the vast organization which was Allied Headquarters in Algiers would have been crazy and quite unworkable, so we stayed much as we had been from the outset, but, inevitably, there had to be American officers serving with us. Ike was determined that there should be no national factions within Allied Forces and any officer, regardless of rank, who was offensive in national terms about a member of the other nation was instantly shipped back home. You could call a man a bloody fool but NOT a bloody American or Limey fool! Sadly, General Huebner, who was a fairly robust character, would voice his resentment of British criticism of the US Army during the pre-Kasserine period in Tunisia and simply could not hit it off with the Chief, who, very reluctantly, had to ask for him to be replaced. His replacement was a man who would eventually rise to the top of the Army, Major General Lyman Lemnitzer, soon beloved by us all and known affectionately as 'General Lem'. General Dick McCreery, who had been such a stalwart Chief of Staff to Alex, was rewarded by promotion to Lieutenant General and command of 10th Corps. He was replaced by General Alec Richardson.

Alex's natural ability to get on with people of all nationalities

The planning for HUSKY produced many problems. The GOC-in-C 15th Army Group punches home a point to Ike, his boss and good friend. IWM CNA1074

and from all walks of life, as I had seen so clearly in Burma, was one of his greatest assets and made him the ideal man for this very difficult appointment which he now held and would continue to hold, though under different titles, until the end of the war. He was deeply conscious, as was Ike, of the overriding importance of sustaining the spirit of the Alliance, even though, at times, this made him appear insufficiently ruthless when an officer clearly deserved the sack, and for this he has been criticized, as we shall see later, when both Patton and Mark Clark were seriously at fault and Ike was quite ready to send both men 'back Stateside' and had Marshall's backing for such severity. Yet Alex saved them both, realizing their importance to the Alliance as fighting commanders and the damage that their removal might do to the morale of their soldiers.

Alex recognized only too well what potential trouble lay in the relationship between George Patton and Monty as fellow Army Commanders; if ever two men were born to clash, it was them. Monty did nothing to help.

Not long after the Victory Parade in Tunis Monty planned what one might call a 'Senior Officers' Day' outside Tripoli to which generals from England, the Middle East and Tunisia were invited. Even two Chinese generals were there! The aim was to demonstrate the employment of infantry in desert warfare in the attack, the use of tanks in conjunction with artillery and infantry and the handling of a division in mobile flanking operations, as he had used the New Zealand Division after Mareth. He spoke brilliantly for two hours, having begun the proceedings with his usual homily about 'No smoking, Gentlemen, please'. To General George Patton, a chain smoker if ever there was one, that prohibition was like a red rag to a bull and it was not long before he produced a cigarette. 'Beetle' Bedell Smith, who was beside him, quickly made him put it away, gave him a piece of chewing gum and the day was saved, but Georgie was left fuming. Ion Calvocoressi, Oliver Leese's senior ADC and a very old friend of mine, with whom I had shared a house at Oxford, told me that Patton was staying with his master at 30 Corps Headquarters during this visit and the two men had quickly become firm friends. Oliver Leese asked Patton over lunch what he had thought of the morning. Georgie looked at him, as he puffed on a large cigarette and, with a twinkle in his eye, said, 'Well I may be slow and I may be stupid, but it just didn't mean a durn thing to me!' Unfortunately this was overheard and the story was reported to Monty. This may account for Monty's unpardonable rudeness to Patton and Bradley some time later when, on Alex's instructions, I took them to Monty's Tac HQ in Tunisia. After twenty minutes in his Map Lorry, Monty called for me 'to take the Generals back'; the time was midday and it was patent that no offer of hospitality of any sort had been made. Small wonder that, as we shall see, the two had a blazing row over Army boundaries during the early days of the fighting in Sicily and thereafter were not on speaking terms.

During the feverish reappraisal of the plans for HUSKY which began even before the end of the Tunisian campaign, Monty had instructed his Chief of Staff, Freddy de Guingand, to review the plans for the 13 and 30 Corps landings so that he could discuss them two days later. All were agreed that the Force 141 plan allowed for far too much dispersion between the landing areas of the Seventh and Eighth Armies. Monty decided that an alternative plan must be put forward at the forthcoming conference with Alex and Ike in Algiers. He had a bad cold, so sent Freddy de Guingand to the conference, but Freddy's plane crashed at El Adem (outside Tobruk) and so General Oliver was ordered by Monty to represent him – his first exposure to a conference at this level. Appearing in his normal Eighth Army rig, of shorts and shirt, with no medal ribbons, he was listened to politely, but clearly made no impact. Only Alex supported the new plan from the outset. The rest of those present would not even consider it unless Monty himself was present. The General flew back to report to Monty, who gave him a flea in his ear and told him he was useless as a negotiator. Two days later the two men flew back to Algiers together where Monty sold the plan to Bedell Smith in a few minutes in the lavatory before the start of the conference and the day was won! This was a typical example of how Alex used to run his Army Groups, sending plans to his Army Commanders for consideration and then getting their reactions and amendments; critics might call it command by committee, but in a highly charged international situation Alex knew very well that it was the only way forward. When a command decision was needed he gave it, in the full knowledge that his subordinates had had their say.

* * *

It had already been decided at Casablanca that HUSKY would be followed immediately by an invasion of the Italian mainland and another amphibious assault would be launched at Salerno. To Bill Cunningham's delight, he was instructed to take the plans for this operation, code-named AVALANCHE, to London for consideration by the Chiefs of Staff. Little did he guess what an adventure that trip would turn out to be. He later wrote it up, in his own inimitable style, and kindly allowed me to reproduce his account here:

In the early summer of 1943 I was given the attractive task of taking to England the plans for the Salerno landings to be handed over to the CIGS. For the journey via Gibraltar the US Air Force had provided me with an operational Flying Fortress. I set off from our headquarters in an olive grove near Catania with a heavily sealed package which contained not only maps and plans for the operation but some kind of destructive firework, 'Just in case, old boy.'

The flight, above cloud, to Gibraltar was uneventful until, although the tip of the Rock was clearly visible above the cloud layer, we veered over the Spanish-Moroccan port of Ceuta and were warned off by heavy anti-aircraft fire, not aimed but purely, we assumed, as a 'keep clear' sign. Quite pretty to watch; black puff-balls with orange centres. We duly landed. At the time I thought the pilot was pretty casual about his navigation which had brought us over Spanish territory, for the Spaniards were known to be sensitive over the neutrality of the area.

I spent the night in great comfort with the hospitality of the Governor (how the crew spent their night could be inferred by their part-worn appearance next morning for the 6.30 take off). Staying with the Governor were two persons of distinction waiting for a lift to England, Air Vice-Marshal George Beamish and General Bill Donovan, the chief of all the American Intelligence Services, whose aircraft had broken down. I was happy to offer a lift in 'my' plane, and we set off on time. Because of the danger from German fighters operating over the Bay of Biscay flights to England were normally being made at night at that time; but I was in a hurry, and the plan was to go by day, but to fly a long leg due west to avoid the Bay; then to turn north and eventually east to make a landfall on the coast of Cornwall. My two passengers and I based ourselves in the radio cabin in moderate comfort on parachutes and with blankets in lieu of flying kit. Soon after take-off the radio seemed to be giving trouble and the operator spent the next two hours in exchanging various parts, without effect, and in the end he gave up trying: 'Makes no difference; never mind,' he said. *'The captain is a whizz at dead reckoning; he brought us back from Ploesti the other day on three engines and the radio out. Course we landed in Tobruk instead of Tripoli but he got us there.' The big raid on Ploesti in Rumania had left American bombers spread out between Beirut and Algiers...*

For the next four hours the three passengers read and dozed, the plane too noisy for conversation. About that time I thought the airman became a little edgy and wondered why. Eventually he shouted, 'I hope we come in soon; I reckon we have no more than thirty minutes' fuel left – we should have landed half an hour ago.' I began to feel a little anxious but soon the engine note changed and I glimpsed, out of the window, green land ahead. Then there was the rumble of the undercarriage being lowered and then the sound of the flaps; we were obviously coming straight in to land without circling. My ears popped as the aircraft lost altitude, the next glance through the window and I thought my eyes were deceiving me, for on the edge of the runway on which we were about to land were fighter aircraft with the Luftwaffe's swastikas on their wings. At this moment, there was the sound of machine-gun fire and the rattle of bullets on and through our fuselage. Donovan cried aloud to the junior member of the Trinity, the radio operator did the same and Beamish leapt to his feet and rushed for the passage which led to what later became known on commercial planes as the flight deck. He obviously took command, at once, for we went into a steep circle, then an equally steep bank and dive and my next view through the window was of wave-tops and we were heading for England ventre à mer, *having almost landed in German-held Jersey. The 'whizz at deads reckoning' had missed Cornwall (invisible under clouds) probably because of an unexpected headwind on our northbound course and we were saved by approaching Jersey too low for the heavy anti-aircraft guns to bear on us. If only the machine-gunners hadn't been so wide-awake we would have landed. What a haul! The Salerno plans and Donovan in one go!*

We flew north, close to the sea, expecting every moment to have enemy fighters on our tail. My hand was on the ring which would ignite the destroying firework the moment we hit the water, assuming that we did not reach England or that we did not run out of fuel first. In the end we made our landfall near Plymouth and, after some trouble with the hydraulics, which had been damaged by the shooting over Jersey, we landed just as the outboard engines coughed and died. The station commander arrived in a jeep while we halted on the perimeter track and told us how lucky we had been, for we had been tracked from the Atlantic by radar and it had been assumed that we were a German Focke-Wulf Condor reconnaissance plane on the way home to Jersey after spotting for submarines. Spitfires had been sent up to shoot us down; fortunately they had failed to find us.

I explained the urgency of my mission and was given an RAF Blenheim which fortunately knew the way to the airfield near Dorchester in Oxfordshire which had been my original destination, slightly late, but mightily relieved. I delivered the parcel to the CIGS together with a sack of Sicilian lemons which he regarded of almost equal importance.

* * *

It was an essential element of the plan for HUSKY that additional fighter cover over the invasion beaches should be provided from the island of Malta GC, which lay only about 90 kilometres from Sicily. Equally important had been the decision to establish a forward headquarters area for the senior commanders involved, so that they were within easy reach of the battle during the critical early stages and from where they could visit the beachheads.

Malta, which is virtually a vast limestone rock set in the Mediterranean, was honeycombed with caves and tunnels in which the brave civil population had been sheltering since Italy had entered the war in 1941 and the murderous battering from the air by the Axis air forces had begun. Their courage had been recognized by His Majesty King George VI by the award of the George Cross to the island and its people in 1942.

Although the C-in-C Mediterranean had been forced to move his ships to Alexandria in 1941, the island continued to serve as a vital submarine base, which became a sizeable thorn in the side of the Axis Powers, the better part of fifty per cent of Rommel's supply ships having been sunk. The maintenance of that threat to Axis shipping throughout the Western Desert and North African campaigns had been of critical importance. It will be remembered that at the time of Alam Halfa the sinkings of fuel supplies had produced a logistical crisis for the Afrika Korps. The enemy's failure to knock out Malta had driven Hitler to fury.

By the summer of 1943 the Maltese were at a very low ebb. Very little food could be grown on the island and the running of supply convoys had been extremely costly in terms of men and ships. Somehow they had struggled through. The battered air squadrons had been reinforced, largely by Hurricanes and Spitfires brought in by carriers, and the enemy had been kept at bay.

Now, new fighter strips were built with extraordinary speed and efficiency by American engineers on Gozo, the island just off Malta's north-west corner. These would serve as a base for the 100 extra fighters needed to cover the Sicilian beaches.

* * *

Early in July Alex moved his headquarters to Malta where an operations room and communications centre had been established in what were known as the Lascaris Tunnels, hewn out of the limestone rock. Whilst the sun blazed down outside and the temperatures soared, inside the tunnel it was like working in a cold store and our New Zealand jerseys were very much the rig of the day.

Within that small island fortress, which bore all the marks and scars of two years' relentless Axis air attack, we set up our Tac HQ for HUSKY in some huts just near the tunnels. The two Army Commanders, Monty and George Patton, were also there, together with the commanders of the two assault corps, Oliver Leese and Omar Bradley. Ike would join us later and also have a small headquarters within the tunnels. Admiral Cunningham, very much on home ground, of course had his own naval command arrangements.

How well I remember our first visit to the island in the fast minelayer HMS *Abdiel*. The fastest ship in the Mediterranean Fleet, with a top speed of over 40 knots, she was the only vessel that could make the Malta run during the hours of darkness and that particular visit had to be made by night for security reasons. As we stood in the stern of the ship, as she sailed at top speed, the waves stood six feet above our heads and we seemed to be travelling through a trough in the sea.

Alex was made very welcome by Field Marshal Lord Gort, the Governor, who put him up in the San Anton Palace. His official residence, the Valetta Palace, had been badly damaged by the bombing. The two Guardsmen had so much in common. Like Alex, Lord Gort had been heavily decorated in the First World War, winning not only the VC but also three DSOs. A quiet, intensely modest man, he shared Alex's profound, selfless sense of duty. He had insisted on keeping to the civil ration scale and rode round the little island on a bicycle rather than waste precious petrol which had been brought in at such risk by the Royal Navy. The marks of his self-denial were very evident, for he had lost a lot of weight in consequence. It did not take me long to realize that, as leaders, he and Alex were cast in the same mould. A person he was particularly pleased to see was Oliver Leese, who had been one of his senior staff officers during the 1940 campaign in France when he had commanded the BEF. Oliver and Ion Calvocoressi, his senior ADC, stayed in Monty's house, the Pavilion, Floriana, just outside Valetta, which John Poston and Johnny Henderson had been quick to acquire for their master and his team of liaison officers. General Oliver was lucky to be invited, for Monty would normally never allow senior officers to stay overnight in his Mess.

When Ike joined us just before D-Day (10 July), he was put up in the Verdala Palace.

Whilst General Oliver was still with us, Lord Gort took him to the Valetta Palace to show him the bomb damage to the staircase, library and armoury.

On 4 July the Chief held a high-level coordinating conference before Oliver Leese and Admiral McGrigor, the Naval Commander for the 30 Corps landings, left for Sfax on the following day in HMS *Largs*, the 30 Corps Headquarters ship. At Sfax some forty ships, including four liners, destroyers and tank landing craft, were waiting.

* * *

Monty's revised outline plan for HUSKY had meant a complete re-write of virtually all the work done by Force 141, who had their own camp near Algiers, overlooking the beach. It was inevitable that such an extensive revision would generate its own string of problems, some of which would call for the Chief's decision. We only had short stays there but long enough to enable Alex and I to go for a swim one afternoon. I heard later that the FANY unit, ISSU 6, which did such sterling work in conjunction with various Special Operations teams in the Mediterranean area, who were billeted overlooking the beach, were moved away whilst we swam, to their considerable annoyance. Of course we had no bathing suits, but most of us, who had very suntanned legs, body and arms, looked as if we had white bathing togs on once our shorts were removed! On the same beach I watched a Frenchman snorkelling off the shore. He showed me his mask and breathing tube. This was a brand new method of fishing to me but I soon got the idea and used it with some success after the capture of Sicily to keep the Chief's Mess supplied with fresh fish and give myself a lot of fun.

Chapter Eight

First Footholds in Europe: Sicily, Reggio and Salerno

9 July – 17 September. 1943

The Allied invasion of Sicily (Operation HUSKY) was the prelude to what must be seen as one of the hardest-fought campaigns of the Second World War. As in Burma, the troops would come to feel that they were under-appreciated and that those responsible for the higher direction of the war had no proper understanding of their dire needs. For Alexander, the Italian Campaign would prove one long struggle with Whitehall and the Combined Chiefs of Staff even to hold on to what resources he had, all too often a losing battle at that. Yet, once again, he would emerge the victor on the battlefield.

As we know, HUSKY began on 9 July 1943 with a major airborne operation designed to secure the airfields so necessary for the establishment of air superiority. Carried out by the 1st British Airborne and the 82nd US Airborne Divisions, it was by far the biggest Allied airborne operation to date, but, for reasons far beyond the control of the divisions themselves, was something of a disaster. However, Montgomery's and Patton's seaborne assaults on 10 July were highly successful.

When HUSKY opened, Sicily was garrisoned by the Italian Sixth Army and two German divisions, the Hermann Goering Panzer Division and the 15th Panzer Grenadier Division. Within a few days General der Panzertruppen Hans Valentin Hube's XIV Panzer Corps would have taken these two German divisions under command and brought elements of the 1st Parachute Division with it, assuming control of the German presence in Sicily and of the already planned evacuation scheme across the Straits of Messina. Hube was a fine soldier and he conducted the German withdrawal with considerable skill.

Although Patton would enter Messina, his Seventh Army having made a wide sweep round the western coastline, taking Palermo in its stride on 17 August, the Eighth Army's advance up the eastern coast and through the centre of the island had been a very hard slog. General Hube's last soldier had left Messina at 10 am on the 17th, all his equipment and men having been safely evacuated with

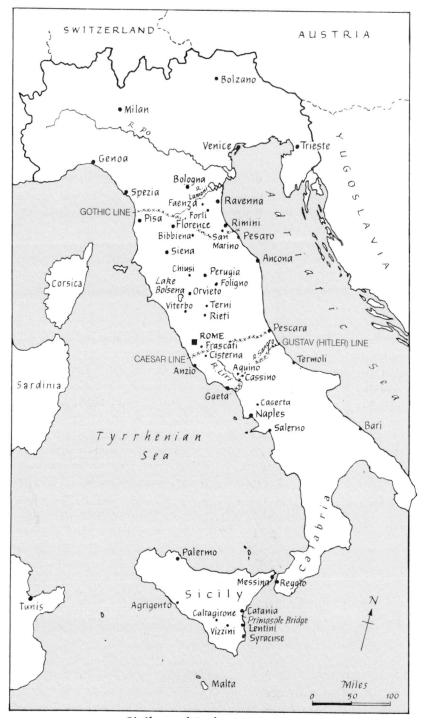

Sicily and Italy 1943-45

remarkably few casualties. That the enemy should have got clean away in this fashion has long been a source of mutual recrimination between the Services out of which no one emerges with any credit.

This short but bitterly-fought campaign was the first in which the Canadian Army had been involved. The brilliant young Major General Guy Simonds' 1st Canadian Division and Brigadier Wyman's 1st Canadian Army Tank Brigade, both serving under Leese in 30 Corps, fought very well and showed no lack of initiative. This was Alexander's first contact in war with the Canadian Army and marked an association of growing mutual respect and trust which lasted to the end of the forthcoming campaign in Italy. This was something that must have influenced his appointment after the war as Governor-General of Canada, where he became one of the best-loved holders of that high office of all time.

For some time, as the Red Army battled grimly on against the German enemy, Stalin had been exhorting his Western allies to start a Second Front in order to ease the fearful pressures faced by his armies. This appeal undoubtedly influenced the Allies into planning to continue the war into the Italian mainland once Sicily had fallen. They hoped thereby not only to make an appropriate gesture to Stalin but also to draw off a number of divisions which might otherwise be available to Hitler when they launched their assault on the Atlantic Wall in the following year. In that context, it is significant that, on hearing of the threat against Sicily and the successful landings which had been made on 10 July, Hitler used this news as an excuse to call off the Battle of Kursk, known now as 'the greatest tank battle in history', in which von Manstein's armies were taking a fearful beating from the massed Russian armour and anti-tank batteries and making very little headway. That within a matter of days German reinforcements under Rommel would be arriving in northern Italy makes it very clear that Hitler was fully expecting the collapse of his Italian allies which would also take place very soon after the fall of Sicily.

✳ ✳ ✳

Once the final arrangements for HUSKY were completed there was nothing further to be done about that operation but wait. However, the commanders and their staffs had a golden opportunity to discuss subsequent operations: BAYTOWN, the Eighth Army's landing at Reggio, on the toe of Italy and across the Straits of Messina, and the Fifth Army's amphibious assault at Salerno, south of Naples (code-named AVALANCHE). For the latter, General Dick McCreery's 10 Corps would be under Fifth Army command.

It was a very useful opportunity during those last days in Malta for Alex to see plenty of Ike with whom his relationship had soon developed into firm friendship. They were ideally matched; Ike, the Chairman, never put a foot wrong; Alex was the natural commander in such a complex international situation for he got on with everyone, was so courteous and yet inspired such confidence and respect, thanks to his considerable experience and record. Just as our two masters worked so well together, so did we of the personal staffs. This would pay a tremendous dividend over the months ahead when the two principals were often far apart and one or the other of us would be sent as a winged Mercury to the other headquarters with top-secret plans or correspondence. There was no standing on dignity and the senior officers were perfectly happy to deal with a young MA or ADC whom they knew and trusted.

At 0800 hours on D-1 (9 July) the fleets set sail from Tunisia and came past us on Malta at 1600 hours in a very strong wind and heavy swell. Four ships were lost on passage, either from the weather or torpedoed by U–boats. However, zero hour (0245 hours 10 July) saw both landings ashore quite unopposed. The Italians had been taken completely by surprise. Presumably they had discounted any possibility of a seaborne attack in such weather. Some of their generals were captured in their pyjamas!

Despite the weather at sea level, the night of 9 July had been clear and starlit so that we had been able to stand outside the tunnels and watch the fleet of C47 Dakotas, some towing gliders, pass overhead on their way to their landing and dropping zones, barely 100 miles away. The parachutists were to seize two very important bridges on the Eighth Army's northbound axis between Syracuse and Catania, the Lentini and Primosole bridges. The rest of the airborne force was primarily targetted on the seizure of vital airfields.

Bit by bit messages began to filter through to the Operations Room that all was far from well with the airborne assault. Very few troops had been delivered to their correct targets and many of the gliders seemed to have been released over the sea, giving no chance to the fifteen to twenty fully armed soldiers they carried who went straight to the bottom. It later transpired that the pilots of the Dakotas had mostly been civilians only a few months earlier and had no experience of anti-aircraft fire and only the most rudimentary knowledge of navigation. As they approached the coast they had been met with heavy flak, much of which had, in fact, come from Allied ships standing off the beaches whose equally inexperienced crews had failed to recognize the C47s. In consequence, the pilots of the tug aircraft released their gliders as described and some aircraft carrying parachutists got shot down. Those paras who were dropped were often some miles from their drop zones and had to walk through the night to rejoin their units. In all these circumstances the airborne forces did remarkably well and fought most gallantly against considerable odds to secure the two bridges, which passed from one side to the other until the relief formations of Eighth Army caught up with them. On 14 July Alex briefed John Gunther, representing the US press, and other journalists on those battles for the bridges. In his book *Flight Into Conflict* Gunther wrote:

> *Monty, the showman, takes the bows, Alexander, the director, hovers in the wings. Even though he* [Monty] *is his junior, Alexander has towards him the attitude of a teacher – proud of a brilliant student.*

Unwittingly, Gunther has painted a very true picture of Alex there, for he never sought the plaudits of the crowd and, as he told General Lem on a later occasion, in his view the role of the Army Group was to make possible the success of the Armies. He was completely sincere in this and never failed to give credit for success to his subordinates. I often think that there were many people who did not fully comprehend this side of his character or appreciate his generosity of spirit, often suggesting that Alex would let men like Monty dominate him, which was very far from being the truth. What he unquestionably did was to handle his difficult subordinates with a masterly touch, as he had at Alamein over the repositioning of SUPERCHARGE.

Alex's first visit to the beaches was to see George Patton shortly after the landings. There he found Patton roaring with delight because his ADC had just shot down a German Messerschmitt ME109 which was strafing the beaches. This he had done with a Browning Automatic Rifle (a BAR) which was not unlike our own Bren gun. George had immediately awarded him a Silver Star for showing a good example and encouraging the soldiers to shoot back and not dive into the sand.

At the same time Major General Joe Cannon, a Mormon from

Utah, who commanded the 12th Tactical Air Force, crashed a fighter on the beach, returning to Alex's Mess in Malta with a broken nose and his face covered with sticking plaster. Under Joe Army-Air cooperation reached a new high and we never had to complain that we lacked air cover. That a fifty-year-old Commanding General should take part in fighter sweeps was something very much out of the ordinary, but that was General Joe. He was a member of our Mess and wonderful company.

On 12 July Monty asked the Chief to move the Army boundary so that the Vizzini-Caltagirone highway, which was essentially the only good route across the centre of Sicily from south to north, was made available to the Eighth Army instead of to Patton's 45th Division. At the same time he urged that the main thrust for Messina should be made by him and that the Americans should assume the role of flank protection to cover his advance. It takes no imagination to guess how George Patton reacted to this typical Montgomery concept. He was livid. Self-centred though he was, Monty was a true professional and there was clearly some merit in giving that route to him. Alex, realizing the damage that this had done to the relations between his two Army Commanders,

On European soil at last! Alex on the steps of his caravan in Sicily. July, 1943. IWM NA3897

visited Patton's Seventh Army Headquarters on the following day, inviting him to come to Tunis on the 17th to discuss a new and major role for his Army. At that meeting a wide westward sweep targetted on Palermo and Messina was agreed. In consequence, whilst the Eighth Army battled steadily northwards against some very tough opposition, Patton swept into Palermo only four days after his meeting with Alex and into Messina on 16 August. It goes without saying that Alex had had a long talk with Ike about this unhappy row. Ike had insisted that the Seventh Army should be given the chance to take Messina so that the *amour propre* of the Army was salved and Patton responded in exactly the way that Alex and Ike had hoped.

Oliver Leese, as the Corps Commander affected by the change, well appreciated how unwelcome it would be to Patton and went across to see Omar Bradley at 2 Corps Headquarters to discuss the problem. Bradley said that the only way was for Oliver to visit Patton at his headquarters in Agrigento and speak to him personally. Although it meant going well outside the 30 Corps area, Leese went over and spent an entertaining night with Patton in his palace, Patton finally agreeing to continue his advance in the same direction as the Eighth Army. Oliver's ADC, Ion Calvocoressi, had to send a signal to Monty saying that they could not be at his Tac HQ for a meeting the next morning as they had a four-hour drive to make, after sleeping on the marble floor of the palace. When they finally got back to 30 Corps Headquarters, they found a signal from Monty saying, 'Don't ever go out of your Corps area without telling me'.

The 7th Army sweep along the Northern Coastal Axis was made by the 3rd Division. Thanks to their excellent four-wheel-drive trucks, which enabled them to bypass the many bridge demolitions carried out by the Germans as they withdrew, the Division made much better speed than had been expected, delighting their Corps and Army Commanders.

On 17 August Alex signalled Churchill:

> By 10 am this morning the last German soldier was flung out of Sicily and the whole island is now in our hands.

The campaign had taken just thirty-seven days of continuous battle.

We had stayed in Malta for a few days after the launch of HUSKY and then moved back to Tunis from where Alex made visits to both Armies. In August Tac HQ was moved to an olive grove in the walled fields of Cassibile, south of Syracuse. Here our 'Commissar', Harold Macmillan, came to stay. Despite the excessive heat, our new resting place was a pleasant spot within a wall and dotted with olive and almond trees. Once more we lived in a tented set-up with the Chief's caravan and armoured car and the Ultra terminal close to the tent which Bill and I shared as usual. We sat at a table under a tree for breakfast or lunch and used the camouflaged mess lorry and tent for the evenings. Alex, needless to say, was constantly on the road, visiting units and places of interest all over Sicily and loved to get back to the peace and quiet of his own mess and caravan. Macmillan always enjoyed his visits to what I think he saw as an oasis of calm in contrast to the political racket from which there was no escape in Algiers. It had already become pretty clear that an Italian collapse could not be far off and General Sir Francis Rodd had been appointed to head the Allied Military Government (AMGOT) in Sicily with Alex as Military Governor and Commander-in-Chief. A conference was held by Macmillan and Rodd, with Alex in attendance. On 26 August he flew back to Tunis and there met General Giraud at dinner. Giraud was the French Commander-in-Chief and High

As ever, at the wheel, Alex accompanied by RC, sets off to visit Headquarters Eighth Army. Sicily, July, 1943. IWMNA 7959

Commissioner. A battle-hardened soldier of the old school, who had little time for de Gaulle, he and Alex were soon firm friends.

* * *

The next day, 27 August, was a very special day for both Alex and me for the Chief visited his beloved 1st Battalion Irish Guards to decorate Sergeant Kenneally with the VC that he had won at the 'Bou' in the battle for Tunis. That award was not only a recognition of the supreme gallantry of a fine NCO but a fitting recognition of the conduct of the whole Battalion in securing and holding that vital position at so high a cost in casualties. It had been an example of the British infantryman at his very best, as the Germans too had found to their great cost. After the ceremony, a Battalion Parade was held and Alex took the salute at the march past. I am sure that it was as emotive a moment for him as it was to me, as comrades of us both came swinging past to the sound of the pipes.

* * *

Unlike Monty, Alex had been given the services of an American aircraft by virtue of his appointment, but the fact that it was known as '*Patches*' was not without significance! In fact it had been bombed twice on the ground before Alex got it and had had no less than 400 repairs to its fabric! We were having lunch after the C-in-C's Meeting at AFHQ in Algiers on 23 August with Ike, the Chief, Monty, Alex Richardson and General 'Lem'. Captain White, the pilot of *Patches*, telephoned Alex's American ADC, Major Lloyd Ramsay, to say that the 500-hour inspection had disclosed that the wings were about to fall off! As Lloyd reported this to Harry Butcher, Ike's principal Aide, who passed the information on to his master, Ike gave immediate orders for a new plane to be issued. It was a very different machine, much more comfortable, safer, fitted with padded seats and a work table, and pressurized, allowing the Chief to work when airborne. Needless to say, Alex was delighted and thanked Ike for his generous gesture. We called the aircraft '*Stardust*'. I have often wondered what was going on in Monty's mind as he sat there that day!

After the capture of Sicily, Bill and I discussed the advantage to German generals of having the use of a Fieseler Storch light aircraft, not unlike the British Auster, with an excellent short take-off capability. Rommel had made constant use of one and we had captured one in the Western Desert. We decided to see if we could 'organize' a Piper Cub, which was very similar to the German machine, for the Chief. The Cub was in general use by US heavy and medium artillery units and, thanks to the US Forces policy on write-off, by which all equipment was automatically written off when it entered a combat zone, the odds looked favourable. The going rate for a jeep was two bottles of Scotch whisky, so we reckoned that four bottles should get us a Cub. Thanks to Major Ramsay, known to us all as 'Feller', they did! A Cub was being re-equipped in Sicily and Feller made friends with its owners, who not only gave us the machine but flying lessons as well in exchange for the four bottles. The junior ADC was left in Sicily learning to fly when we later moved to Bari on the Italian mainland. With a refuelling stop in the toe of Italy, he duly delivered our new toy in Bari where it was almost immediately destroyed in a gale! 'The best laid plans of mice and men...'. I do not think the Chief ever flew in it.

* * *

Alex's handling of his two Army Commanders in Sicily was

Alex chatting with his pilot, Captain Joe White USAAF and the crew of his elderly C47 *Patches* soon to be replaced by the much more sophisticated *Stardust*. IWM NA 1853

typical of the man. Although he gave Monty his way over the switching of the Army boundary, he at once realized how fatal it would be if Monty's suggestion of a flank protection role for Patton had been agreed. As it was, the very fact that that suggestion had been made put a great strain upon relations within the Army Group and angered Ike, who at once insisted that a new striking role for 7th Army should be put in hand. He also insisted that Messina should be a 7th Army objective. Alex acted immediately, as I have described, and got an instant response from Patton who, as we know, captured Palermo almost at once. A measure of Alex's irritation with Monty can be seen in a little story of George Patton's about a visit paid by Alex to the two Army Commanders in Syracuse on 25 July. Patton described Alex's attitude as 'quite angry and brusque' and went on:

> He told Monty to explain his plan. Monty said he and I had already decided what we were going to do, so Alex got madder and told Monty to show him the plan. He did and Alex then asked for mine.

So much for the fable that Alex was clay in Monty's hands.

The story of Patton slapping a soldier in hospital on two separate occasions, because he rated these victims of combat fatigue as cowards, is too well known for me to need to repeat it here. Alex immediately saw the dangers of his getting involved in this purely American row and firmly told Patton that, as far as he was concerned, it was 'a family matter' and the question of Patton's future was handled entirely by Ike. However, I do know that when Eisenhower consulted Alex and asked him if he wanted him replaced, Alex at once responded that Patton was far too valuable a fighting commander for him to be removed in the middle of the campaign, in which he was performing so well. It is of great interest to find that Alex's confidential recommendation became the main plank of Ike's handling of the case as far as Washington was concerned and that General George Marshall backed him to the hilt.

* * *

It is probably not generally understood how intense was the struggle within the Combined Chiefs of Staff over the question of priorities for the conduct of the war. Admiral King, the US Chief of Naval Staff, would never concede that 'the Second Front in Europe' should have priority over the Pacific where the US Navy and Marines were fighting a massive and successful campaign. George Marshall, as

Chairman of the American Joint Chiefs of Staff, was equally determined that priority must go to the destruction of Nazi Germany and so to the invasion of Europe. At the Quebec Conference (QUADRANT) on 19 August 1943 Churchill and Roosevelt and the Combined Chiefs of Staff finally agreed that 'unremitting pressure' was to be maintained against the Germans in Italy and that Operation OVERLORD, the invasion of Europe across the Channel, then planned for 1 May 1944, should be 'the principal United States–British ground and air effort against the Axis in Europe', thereby clearly having priority over Italy, as Alex would find to his cost and concern. At that stage the penetration into Italy was deemed to be limited by the line Pisa-Ancona, clearly reflecting the aim of merely drawing German divisions away from North-West Europe rather than a crushing defeat of all the German forces in Italy, as Alex ultimately achieved. But now, at least, plans for the invasion of the Italian mainland could be finalized and put into effect. The Eighth Army was to cross the Straits of Messina on 3 September (Operation BAYTOWN), General Mark Clark's Fifth US Army would mount an amphibious assault (Operation AVALANCHE) at Salerno, south of Naples, on 9 September (General Dick McCreery's 10th Corps would be under command and targetted on Naples), and on the same day a subsidiary operation by the 1st British Airborne Division would be launched against Taranto.

Meanwhile, the loss of Sicily and the very effective bombing of the marshalling yards outside Rome by the US Air Force had thrown the Italian government into a state of chaos. Powerful political figures who were opposed to Mussolini now saw their chance and he was arrested on 25 July on the orders of the Grand Council. King Victor Emmanuel then invited Marshal Badoglio, a former head of the Italian Armed Forces, to form a new government. Almost at once the Allies began secret negotiations with Badoglio to secure the Italians' unconditional surrender. Some of those negotiations were conducted by Harold Macmillan and his American counterpart, Robert Murphy, in our Tac HQ. At last the negotiators in Washington with Roosevelt and Churchill were given the green light and told that Badoglio had accepted the surrender terms.

* * *

On 2 September the local Italian Delegation reappeared at Cassibile to say that Badoglio had agreed to the dropping of an airborne division on Rome, but, when pressed to do so, said that they had no powers to sign an Armistice. On hearing this, Harold Macmillan sent a message to Alex that the time had come for a showdown. The Chief then arrived in his best service dress, booted and spurred, sporting all his decorations. After telling their leader, General Castellano, that Badoglio had accepted the surrender terms, and simulating a show of anger, he left the conference tent leaving the Delegation talking among themselves.

To our intense amusement, and I think his, Alex had then to crawl round behind a wall to rejoin Macmillan and Murphy so as not to be seen by the Italians who, by now, were gabbling feverishly together. Finally, they asked to see Bedell Smith and stated that they would now seek authority to sign, agreeing to all Alex's demands.

Next day, 3 September, the fourth anniversary of the outbreak of war, even as the Eighth Army was crossing the Straits of Messina to seize Reggio (BAYTOWN), the authority to sign arrived. Ike at once flew to Cassibile and the document was duly signed by Bedell Smith on behalf of the Supreme Allied Commander and General Castellano for the Italian Government. To have knocked Italy out of the war in this way was a great achievement and a complete vindication of Alex's strategy.

BAYTOWN had opened with a typical Montgomery barrage of immense proportions and Reggio had fallen without a shot. However, the Germans were not going to give the rest of Calabria up as easily as that and a series of battle groups, manning demolitions all the way up the 'toe' of Italy, made progress from then on painfully slow.

On 9 September Fifth Army's assault landings on the Bay of Salerno went in and, initially, met little resistance. However, in true German style, some very effective counter-attacks were quickly launched and a tough fight developed, reaching crisis proportions as the German armour very nearly split the beachhead in half on 13 September. On that day Alex and I were on Admiral Hewitt's flagship. Hewitt was the American Commander of the naval forces and Alex asked him to contact Admiral Sir Andrew Cunningham (ABC to all), his Commander-in-Chief, and ask for heavy naval gunfire support. ABC at once despatched HMS *Warspite* and HMS *Valiant* to Salerno, saying that *Nelson* and *Rodney* were also available if needed. The two battleships, with their 12″ and 15″ guns, were on station on the 15th and opened fire at over 21,000 yards, effectively preventing any reinforcements from reaching the enemy. They also engaged the German tanks in the forward area, all other ships in the Bay of Salerno joining in. The air support was tremendous. The whole of the strategic air force in North Africa was diverted to lay a carpet of bombs across the German formations. Joe Cannon's Tactical Air Force put on a programme of continuous strafing and bombing and all the naval aircraft of Admiral Vian's Force 'V', which consisted of five fleet carriers, were also committed. The Germans, who were within a mile of the beaches before this maelstrom hit them, were stopped in their tracks. While all this went on, Alex slipped quickly back to Tunis to arrange for all available reserves from North Africa and Sicily to be sent to Salerno.

It was not all one-sided. On 16 September, just after completing her third bombardment for the day, *Warspite* was hit and badly damaged by a German radio-controlled bomb, our first experience of a stand-off guided weapon. Much to ABC's relief, for she had long been his flagship in the Mediterranean Fleet, *Warspite* was finally taken to Gibraltar for repairs after a rather adventurous passage.

During his first visit to the beaches Alex had been unimpressed by the American Corps Commander, General Dawley, and returned to Salerno on the 15th to check how things were going. On the next day he spoke to Mark Clark and told him that Dawley was not capable of commanding in the present situation and should be replaced. When Ike arrived a little later, Dawley was replaced by General Lucas, of whom we shall hear more later. Alex remained in Salerno until 17 September when patrols from the beachhead made the first contacts with the leading elements of the Eighth Army. Alex had been impressed with Clark's handling of a difficult situation and delighted with Dick McCreery's performance in his first battle in command of a corps.

The battle had indeed been won, but, like Waterloo, it had been a close-run thing and, like the Iron Duke, Alex might justifiably have felt that, had he not been there, it might have gone the other way. However, so modest a man was he and so disinterested in self-glory that I, for one, would have been surprised if that thought had ever crossed his mind.

On 1 October McCreery's armoured cars, the King's Dragoon Guards, entered Naples. There they found the port very seriously damaged. Nevertheless, it would not be long before the Royal Navy and British and American Sappers had got it back into some sort of use, for it was badly needed.

Chapter Nine

THE ADVANCE ON ROME: CRACKING THE GUSTAV LINE. OPERATION DIADEM

September, 1943 – June, 1944

On the evening before the start of Operation AVALANCHE General Eisenhower made a public broadcast announcing the Italian surrender. The German response was immediate. Two days later, on 10 September, all Italian units were disarmed by the Wehrmacht and the Germans occupied Rome.

The Germans had estimated that the Allies would probably not seek to advance further up the 'leg' of Italy beyond Rome and, as we know, had already begun to reinforce the north of the country. However, the Allies quickly discovered that in Field Marshal Kesselring they were faced by a very tough and capable field commander who would make them fight every inch of the way. Although by now a very senior Luftwaffe officer, Albert Kesselring had been a first class artilleryman throughout the First World War and was still, at heart, a soldier, as his brilliant conduct of the Germans' defensive operations would show.

Although the original reinforcement of the enemy's forces in Italy had been in the north, it now became very clear that Kesselring would fight a stiff delaying action from the 'toe' up, based upon a series of planned defensive lines culminating in a very strong position known as the Gustav Line, where they would hold out through the bitter winter. This stronghold ran from Gaeta in the west, through Cassino, up the valley of the Rapido, across the Mariella Mountains and thence along the Sangro Valley to the Adriatic. This was all country which was very different in both terrain and climate to anything the Eighth Army had had to tackle heretofore. All too often, in the mountainous areas, the advance was virtually on a one-tank front. In pouring, freezing rain and glutinous mud, the infantry had to fight and exist in conditions which rivalled the worst days of the Somme.

Rommel's Headquarters, Army Group B, was soon withdrawn from Italy to go north and assume responsibility for the defences of the Atlantic Wall, leaving Kesselring with what was now dubbed Army Group C. This was made up of General von Mackensen's Fourteenth Army and von Vietinghoff's Tenth Army. The Army

Group had some twenty divisions, which was roughly comparable in numbers but not in strength to Alex's Fifteenth Army Group. However, as early as August 1943 General Marshall had warned that the US Army would have to withdraw seven divisions from Italy for OVERLORD and it was patently clear that Whitehall would also be seeking to bleed off some of the cream of the Eighth Army before long. Alex must have spent many a sleepless night over these threats, for he knew only too well what a fight he had on his hands.

He now reinforced Clark's Fifth Army to bring it up to twelve divisions, leaving the Eighth Army with only one British division, the new 1st Canadian Corps and the new Polish Corps, commanded by Generals Crerar and Anders respectively. General Bernard Freyberg's New Zealanders were in Army Group Reserve.

Mark Clark's task was a multiple one. He was to thrust towards Cassino whilst simultaneously breaking through the western end of the Gustav Line and advancing up the Liri Valley towards Frosinone. These two operations were to coincide with Operation SHINGLE, an amphibious assault at Anzio, south of Rome and 60 miles behind the German lines. This was to be carried out by General Lucas's 6th US Corps, which would include General Ronald Penney's 1st British Division. D-day for SHINGLE was 22 January 1944.

The eight months spanning the fall of Naples to the Americans' triumphant entry into Rome on 4 June 1944 must represent the toughest fighting of the whole Italian Campaign. It was also a very tough time for the Allied Commander-in-Chief, for all the reasons that will become apparent.

* * *

The Salerno operation having at last been brought to a successful conclusion, the Chief held a conference in Bizerta on 17 September to discuss the way ahead in Italy. The weather had already begun to deteriorate rapidly and, in the light of the stiff resistance being encountered across the whole front, it had become abundantly clear that the campaign was going to develop into a long, bitter struggle. Alex warned the Prime Minister that he would have to continue attacking throughout the coming winter and expressed his deep concern about the threatened withdrawal of 100 landing craft, the loss of which would deprive him of the initiative and force him into a purely defensive role. The landing craft problem was by no means the only major one that would be landing in the Chief's lap over the coming months, which would be seeing a complete upheaval of the command structure as the demands of OVERLORD for senior commanders came flooding in. All too soon a number of 'the First Eleven' would be leaving the Mediterranean to take up senior appointments in England.

The Chief now decided to move Tac HQ to a village on the Adriatic coast near Bari. Here we moved into a large villa rather than perpetuating our hitherto spartan existence in tents and caravans.

Not long after we moved, Harold Macmillan and Harold Caccia, from the Foreign Office, came to stay with us for talks with Alex about future policy in Italy. This was to be the subject of a meeting in Malta attended by Winston, Brookie and Ike from 17 to 19 November. Lord Gort also came, to Alex's great pleasure. The Malta conference was to be followed by another in Cairo on the 23rd. It was unfortunate that Winston was ill in Malta and that, most unusually, Alex too was taken ill in Cairo, with jaundice. However, the Combined Chiefs of Staff backed his plea over the landing craft and took an important decision to move the northern limit of the Italian Campaign to the Pisa–Rimini line.

Before he went on to his meeting with Stalin and Roosevelt in Teheran, Winston signalled Roosevelt in Washington, pleading:

We must not let this great Italian battle degenerate into a deadlock.
At all costs we must win Rome and the airfields to the north of it.

This did the trick and the landing craft for January's Operation SHINGLE (Anzio) at least were saved.

* * *

The country round Bari was a rest area for Marshal Tito's Yugoslavs. This was Alex's first contact with these tough customers and he arranged support for them, in the shape of arms and ammunition, which were despatched to the island of Vis, where Tito sent his wounded to await onward movement by ship to Italy. Not far down the coast from us was Commander Houldsworth's Special Operations unit, ISSU 6, from Algiers, which deployed the British liaison teams to support Tito and the Italian partisans in the north. The radio communications to these teams were handled by those delightful FANYs who, understandably, had been so miffed when they were moved away from the beach near Algiers when Alex and I were going to have a swim. Each operator acted as the control link with a particular team and was skilled in detecting if the team's operator had been captured and was being used by the Germans. The smallest change in an operator's 'handwriting' on his morse key would alert them. As a check they used personal codes. One, I remember, was 'Mary had a little lamb', the response, of course, being 'Whose fleece was white as snow'. Very simple but effective. Those girls did a wonderful job to which they were absolutely dedicated.

* * *

4 December 1943 was a highly significant day for the Mediterranean Theatre. On that day Winston informed Brookie that Roosevelt wanted Eisenhower as Supreme Allied Commander for OVERLORD. Knowing the vital need to have a commander in Italy who was not only an experienced field soldier but also had the qualities to enable him to command the respect and obedience of a very mixed Army Group of so many different nationalities, each with its own style and sensitivities, Brookie urged that Alex, who had no peer in such a situation, should be left in Italy as Commander-in-Chief, and Jumbo Wilson should take over as Supreme Allied Commander Mediterranean.

A period of great uncertainty and disquiet among all the top commanders and their staffs now followed, for this was patently the trigger for a host of similar changes. Churchill wanted Alex for SAC Mediterranean, to which Brookie was firmly opposed and suspected that Harold Macmillan, who had struck up such a close working relationship with Alex, which they both enjoyed, had his doubts about getting on with the sixty-four-year-old Wilson. On 12 December the Chief had a long talk with both Winston and Brookie in Carthage and said that he was ready to do his duty and serve in any capacity. None of us who served him would have expected him to say anything else, but we knew too that his heart was on the battlefield and with his soldiers.

After that meeting Brookie came back to Bari with Alex and then visited Monty at Termoli. On his return to Bari he noted,

I have an impression that Monty is tired and that Alex has not fully recovered from his jaundice. The offensive is stagnating badly.

Whilst this air of uncertainty was hanging over all our heads, Bill suggested to me that we might play a trick on Monty's staff and send them a signal asking if they would be interested in Alex's two caravans. This really put the cat amongst the pigeons! Bedell Smith had visited Monty on 21 December to tell him about Ike's appointment as Supremo for OVERLORD, leaving Monty saying, 'It seems that Jumbo Wilson, Alexander and myself are in the pool for Supreme C-in-C Med and Army C-in-C Western Europe'. It was known that Ike wanted Alex as his deputy. Monty's ADCs were very worried by Bill's signal and showed it to Monty, who was getting hourly more apprehensive over the delay in announcing the appointments. He sent Freddy de Guingand over to see Alec Richardson, our Chief of Staff, to ask when and if Alex was leaving. All he got was a claim of complete ignorance on the subject. Forty-eight hours later, however, Monty was put out of his misery by Brookie who told him that he was to command 21st Army Group under Ike in OVERLORD. It transpired later that Alex himself had recommended Monty for the appointment. Bill, when commenting to me on the personalities involved, observed that, while Monty would work for Ike, it was doubtful whether he would cooperate with Jumbo. Events would show that Bill was being rather too generous in his assessment! As for Alex, he was quite happy with the outcome, for he wanted to get on with the campaign which he had begun.

On 23 December Winston called for a full-scale conference to discuss Mediterranean affairs on Christmas Day, summoning Jumbo, Ike, Admiral Sir John Cunningham and Tedder. It was in doubt until the last minute whether Alex or Monty would be going home. However, on 30 December, Mary (Maori) Coningham, Alec Richardson and Bill flew to Eighth Army at Vasto to say goodbye to Monty at a buffet lunch which was also attended by Bernard Freyberg and General Miles Dempsey, the 13 Corps Commander. I have often wondered whether both Dempsey and Coningham already knew that they would soon be going home themselves – Dempsey to command Monty's Second Army and Mary to command the 2nd Tactical Air Force. Monty's personal staff were delighted to be off to England the following day. Later, a dinner was given for Mary Coningham, a first-class fighting airman who came originally from New Zealand (hence 'Maori', distorted to 'Mary'). He was a magnificent commander and had led our Tactical Air Force since 1941, but sometimes aroused considerable ill-feeling. He left in General Joe Cannon's Douglas with sufficient brandy, gin and vermouth to see the war out!

It came as no surprise to us that General Oliver Leese had been selected to assume command of the Eighth Army. He was on leave in England when the decision was made and arrived to take over only the night before Monty left. Ion Calvocoressi told me a most amusing story about the speed with which General Oliver, in England at that time, had been rushed out. Apparently he had been telephoned by the War Office on Boxing Day and told to leave immediately to take over from Monty. He at once rang Ion, who was on leave in London, and told him to go and see General Kennedy, the Vice Chief of the Imperial General Staff, and tell him that all his clothes were at the cleaners and he could not get hold of his uniform. General Kennedy replied that, uniform or no uniform, he must leave at once as Monty would be home by 31 December and would certainly want Oliver to command his 2nd Army in North-West Europe. Accordingly, General Oliver left at once and Ion followed with his kit a week later!

As was to be expected, Monty wanted all our best commanders, including Miles Dempsey, now commanding 10 Corps, and the two top Canadians, Generals Crerar and Simonds. Meanwhile, our excellent Chief of Staff, Alec Richardson, had been selected to command a division. To our delight, his replacement was General John Harding, now recovered from the severe wounds he received whilst commanding 7th Armoured Division. Alex held him in high regard both as a staff officer and a commander. He arrived on 2 January. On the same day the Chief and John Grimsley, his American ADC, flew off to a high-level meeting in Tunis at La Marsa. John Harding took off at 7.30 on the morning after his arrival to join them. However, there were still no high-level decisions forthcoming from Allied Force Headquarters – both Ike and Jumbo were away; so different from Alex. The Prime Minister sent a message inviting Alex to stay with him at Marrakesh in Morocco, saying that Lady Margaret could be flown out there in the PM's personal aircraft. Although badly in need of a rest, Alex replied that he could not leave the front at such a critical time. How typical of the Chief. In his unswerving and unshakeable sense of duty lay the key to his success and leadership.

The Chief and his two companions arrived back from Tunis after calling in on Mark Clark in Naples. Winston had asked that his son Randolph and Fitzroy Maclean, his personal representative with Tito and leader of the British Military Mission, should be flown to him in Marrakesh, but the weather was so bad that the Mitchell bomber taking them had to turn back.

As chaos was still reigning on the subject of landing craft for the Allied Armies in Italy (AAI – our new title), the Chief, John Harding and I left for Marrakesh in *Stardust*, our smart new aircraft. Its insulated cabin, heating and oxygen were all very necessary when flying over the mountains and through the storms in Italy. The weather was still frightful and, despite *Stardust's* 'mod cons', the trip was very uncomfortable. However, we got there. As I had nothing much to do, I spent some happy hours with the PM's daughter Mary, easily the best and nicest of his children.

On Sunday 9 January we left after Alex had got some commitments for landing craft and decisions on command. On the way back, flying from Algiers, we visited Fifth Army and I was able to speak to Bill from Naples about our move to Caserta on the 17th. We finally got back to Bari on the evening of the 10th. It had been some trip. After five hours' flying on the first day with a conference in Algiers in the evening, another five hours' flying on day two to Marrakesh and a conference until 2 am, with a 6am take off for Algiers. Day three had seen us in Naples, followed by a visit to Eighth Army where I noticed that there was quite a different atmosphere now that Monty had departed. Everyone was very friendly and helpful, just like it used to be. Perhaps having a Coldstream Guardsman as Commander and two Scots Guards Officers as his personal staff had made a difference. By the time we finally got home to Bari we were all pretty tired. However, it had been well worth while as we had got a decision on the landing craft.

In complete contrast, we next visited the 26 US General Hospital in Bari, something at which the Chief was particularly good. It was housed in a lovely building with lots of equipment and pretty nurses. There were only a few patients, mostly from Jeep crashes. The 14th Combined British and Indian Hospital provided a very different picture. Here we found bomb-shattered wards and hundreds of wounded and uncomplaining Indians, whose faces lit up as Alex spoke to them in Urdu. A few days later we went to see one end of the supply organization which sent arms, ammunition and food to the Yugoslav partisans. In spite of supposed vows of chastity, the hospital was assisting many Yugoslav women soldiers having babies.

On 16 January General Mason-MacFarlane arrived to take over the Control Commission from the American General Joyce. This was a great relief to Alex, in his role as Commander-in-Chief, as Joyce had had no diplomatic experience, unlike Mason-Mac, and had been easy meat for the slick Italians.

We always tried to have the Chief out of the way when moving the Headquarters, so on 17 January I took Alex off to Eighth Army while Bill loaded *Flagstaff*, the Chief's train, with all the office and mess equipment. That train was a godsend in winter. It had accommodation for about twenty officers and fifty soldiers. Bill and I each had a small sleeping cabin and the Chief had a nice bedroom with a bathroom attached. One large coach was divided to make a dining room and ante-room with full-sized furniture, so that we could sit in comfortable chairs and feel a little guilty.

Bill arrived in Caserta by train the following morning. With him were General Lem, John Grimsley and Major Michael Hawkins, 10th Hussars, now PA to John Harding. The task of moving into the Palace at Caserta proved a mammoth undertaking. Our offices were on the fifth floor and everything had to be moved by hand. Our mess was up at the kennels and the Chief's sleeping quarters were about two miles away.

Fortunately Alex and I did not get back from Eighth Army until the evening. On the next day, accompanied by John Harding and John Grimsley, he set off to visit the 1st British and 3rd US Divisions, who would shortly be making the assault on the Anzio beaches, followed by a call on Headquarters 6th US Corps,

Alex looks out over the town of Caserta from his office in our Main Headquarters, May, 1944. IWM NA14520

whose Commander, General Lucas, would command the operation.

This gave Bill and I a chance to sort out the Chief's office and to respond to calls from General Brian Robertson, Alex's brilliant Chief Administrative Officer, General Jake Devers, the Deputy Chief of Staff at AFHQ, and Mark Chapman-Walker, MA to Jumbo Wilson, who wanted to see Alex after he returned. By the time of the 6 o'clock conference we had everything pretty well sorted out and Jumbo and the new Commander of the Mediterranean Allied Air Force (MAAF), General Ira Eaker, USAF, were present.

※ ※ ※

The capture of Rome was obviously our next principal objective but until we could break through the Gustav Line there was no way in which Rome could be reached. Many weeks of bitter fighting under appalling conditions would have to be endured and thousands of lives lost before even that first objective was achieved.

Alex had given much thought to Rome and had planned a massive operation, code-named DIADEM, to begin on 11 May. By the end of December he realized that no further progress could be made on his eastern flank until the weather improved in the spring. To quote that distinguished Grenadier and fine historian, General Sir David Fraser, 'The Eighth Army had been held by the enemy and defeated by the elements' (*And We Shall Shock Them*).

Further west, Mark Clark's Fifth Army had been fighting grimly forward at a heavy cost in lives, many a platoon being reduced to half its strength, particularly during the attempts to cross the Rapido and Garigliano rivers. General Dick McCreery's 10 Corps at last forced a limited crossing of the latter, so the Gustav Line had been breached. On the 2nd US Corps front all attempts to cross had ended in costly failure. Mark Clark therefore shifted his main point of emphasis to an area north of Cassino where General Juin's French Expeditionary Corps had overwhelmed the German positions in the mountains and the 2nd US Corps was now brought north to fight through the German defences north-west of Cassino itself.

Alex very much hoped that Operation SHINGLE, at Anzio, would ease the pressure on the Fifth Army. Cassino, the key to the Liri Valley, the doorway to Rome, remained to be tackled.

As at Salerno the initial landings at Anzio on 22 January 1944 achieved complete surprise. The aim of SHINGLE, as given by Alex to Clark, was 'To cut enemy communications and threaten the rear of Fourteenth Army'. Clark's version of this to General Lucas, which one is bound to feel was heavily influenced by his own burning desire to capture Rome for the American Army, was 'To form a bridgehead and then advance to occupy the Alban Hills'. These hills are the high ground just south of Rome across which run the Appian and Castillian Ways, at that time the lifelines of the Germans holding the Gustav Line. As Alex would explain to Brookie in a later letter, Clark's plan would have called for a much larger force than the four divisions that Lucas had at his disposal, which were, in any case, about the limit of what the Navy could support across the beaches.

In the event it would be about 1 March before the Germans were finally defeated at Anzio after six weeks' tough, bloody fighting.

*　*　*

On 21 January the Chief, Jumbo Wilson and Admiral John Cunningham went out in a destroyer to see the assault convoys for SHINGLE set sail, having decided that the weather was favourable. Next morning the landings began and by 0700 hours the leading troops were five miles inland with little opposition. The Allied air forces were bombing the roads but the main counter-attack was not expected until the following day.

On the 22nd the Chief and I landed from a motor torpedo boat (MTB) and visited all the battalions ashore. For part of the time Alex travelled in an armoured car and I had an uncomfortable ride on the back, behind the turret. The beaches were bad. They were steep and with a sandbar approach, so that the vehicles had to be towed through six feet of water from the landing craft. By the following day the two divisions (1st British and 3rd US) were ashore with their guns and some of their tanks.

Meanwhile the Germans were attacking both the 2nd US and 10th British Corps. These attacks, which were clearly intended to frustrate any link-up with 6 Corps in the beachhead, were beaten off but did have the intended effect in the short term. It would be over a month before that link-up was finally effected.

On 25 January the Chief and John Grimsley left for Anzio in the destroyer *Kempenfeldt* at 0630 hours. They visited 6 Corps and both Divisional Headquarters. On the face of it all was going well and the forecast was that the Appian Way would be cut on the morrow. When they got back to Tac HQ Alex found Harold Macmillan and Brigadier Terence Airey (our BGS (Intelligence)) waiting with a draft signal to the PM saying: 'Bridgehead established – fighting within 5 miles of Cisterna'.

The enemy's strength against the SHINGLE beachhead had now begun to build up and was estimated at about 30,000, most of whom were Panzer Grenadiers, with many more expected soon. Lucas's main attack was not due to begin until 30 January but Alex was already getting worried about his fitness to command. His failure to report was seriously inhibiting the use of our overwhelming air superiority and Alex accordingly instructed Mark Clark to set up a small Tac HQ at Anzio in order to put some ginger into Lucas, who was no George Patton.

Clark's own attack against the Rapido river line had failed and Kesselring now switched a further five divisions to Anzio. This produced an imbalance in favour of the enemy of about 95,000 to 75,000 and when Lucas's attack went in on 30 January, as planned, it failed. True to form, the Germans now began to counter-attack vigorously. On 1 February two US Ranger

The Chief, accompanied by RC, walking through the shattered streets of Anzio. February, 1944. IWM NA11883

battalions were heavily attacked at Cisterna and on the 4th more heavy attacks came in against General Penney's 1st British Division, forcing him to withdraw his salient in the area of Campoleone. To make matters worse, the weather had deteriorated so much that the provision of desperately needed air support became impossible. The situation was reaching crisis proportions and Penney is reputed to have said, 'Replace Lucas or we shall lose the bridgehead.'

Alex now put it to Mark Clark that Lucas must go and signalled Winston to say that neither he nor Mark Clark were happy about the way things were going and that Clark was returning to the beachhead to get a grip of things. Alex then joined Clark there. He took the opportunity to inspect 24 Guards Brigade who were theoretically at rest in a wooded area but still subject to shellfire. The Brigade had suffered fifty per cent casualties, sixty-two officers and sixteen hundred other ranks. He visited his old battalion and talked and joked with the soldiers, warmly greeting some old hands who had served with him.

16 February was an eventful day. The Germans launched their main attack against the beachhead and Lucas was temporarily replaced by the dynamic General Lucian Truscott, the Commanding General of the 3rd US Division. Alex signalled Brookie that morning to ask him to get Eisenhower to release Patton to come and take over 6 Corps. This was agreed and the necessary aircraft were put on stand-by to fly Patton in. However, the impact of the new hand on the tiller was such that Truscott was confirmed in command. Not surprisingly, when Mark Clark took over 15th Army Group from Alex some months later, it was Truscott who succeeded him in command of the Fifth Army.

The main enemy attack on the 16th against the 45th US Division was comprehensively defeated after several days' intensive fighting. On the left, where the British 56th Division had relieved the 1st, the Germans fared no better. On 19 February the German armour had another try and advanced about a mile, only to be checked by a most gallant and resolute defence and heavy artillery fire delivered with considerable accuracy.

Alex had been reluctant to replace Lucas, despite his shortcomings. However, even Mark Clark's efforts to spur him on had failed and it was plain that there was nothing for it but to make a change. The man had no presence or charisma and was the very antithesis of a successful fighting commander. He was known to us all as 'Father Christmas', for when he made one of his rare sorties from his underground headquarters he would invariably be wearing a mackintosh strung around with haversacks and a musette bag and smoking his corn cob pipe. As we have already seen, Alex felt very deeply about the importance of having a close relationship and mutual confidence with his fighting generals and the replacement of US generals who failed in battle was always a matter of great concern to him. The case of Lucas was a particularly difficult one. The man had been pulled out to take over at Salerno from Dawley and then picked again for SHINGLE. He had the highest political connections in the United States and his removal in the middle of a critically important operation was bound to cause resentment within the US Army. Alex's last wish was to cause any upset within the Alliance. It had been fortunate that a man of Truscott's calibre had been available, for the impact of the change was not unlike that when Patton had relieved Fredendall in Tunisia. Within a fortnight or so the losses inflicted upon the enemy had effectively brought them to a halt. On 29 February the Germans made one last attempt but this failed as completely as the earlier attacks. They had shot their bolt and the battle had been won.

And what a battle it had been. No man who fought at Anzio or even visited the beachhead when the fighting was at its height will ever forget it.

While the battle at Anzio was raging one of the most controversial operations of the war was launched at Cassino – the bombing of the ancient monastery. World opinion of this action was very adverse and, needless to say, the Germans did all they could to ensure that this was so. Alex came in for heavy criticism but he remained unmoved. He would simply quote the well-understood principle that no Commander could hesitate between destroying a building, no matter how famous or even holy, if it was occupied by the enemy and the lives of his soldiers were thereby put at risk. As I shall show, there were grounds for believing that the monastery was occupied by the Germans, despite the fact that both sides had given an undertaking to the Pope to keep out of it and to spare it. The local German Corps Commander, General Frido von Senger und Etterlin, was a very devout Catholic and would never have breached such an

St Patrick's Day, 1944. Alex presents shamrock to officers of the 1st Battalion Irish Guards. IWM NA12943

Major D. M. Kennedy, Irish Guards, receives the ribbon of the Military Cross during the St Patrick's Day Parade. IWM NA12945

Alex takes the Salute as the Parade marches off. IWM NA12947

undertaking. However, General 'Gertie' Tuker, the GOC of the 4th Indian Division, whose troops were tasked with the capture of the monastery, refused to accept that the Germans would stick to the agreement; he knew nothing of von Senger. General Bernard Freyberg, now commanding the New Zealand Corps, consisting of his own New Zealand Division and 4th Indian, supported Tuker's demand that the monastery should be bombed flat before the Indians attacked.

I later learned from Colonel David Hunt (later Sir David and Private Secretary to the Prime Minister) who was our GSO I (Intelligence) that the monastery was indeed not occupied by the German parachutists who were holding the Cassino feature. However, a radio intercept of the German command net reported that a parachute commander had been heard to ask, '*Ist Abt in Kloster?*' and was answered, '*Ja in Kloster mit Mönchen.*' The Intelligence Officer who received the intercept only recorded the answer 'Yes' from the enemy. The translation then produced was 'Is the HQ in the Abbey?' the word '*Abt*' being taken as an abbreviation for '*Abteil*' (a battalion or unit) rather than Abbot. It was only when Colonel Hunt questioned the translation and the whole intercept that it transpired that the correct reply to the question was, in fact '*Ja, Abt ist mit Mönchen in Kloster*', i.e. 'Yes. The Abbot is with the monks in the monastery'. Tragically, this discovery was made too late and the bombers were already approaching. Alex and I were lying out on the ground about

Cassino. Bomb damage to Tac Headquarters Eighth Army by aircraft well short of the target, 15 March 1944. Luckily these bombs were armour-piercing ones, so damage was limited and there were no fatalities. This Nissen hut was the Army Commander's Mess!
IWM NA13004

Repairs in progress. Note the crater in the foreground and the range of mountains in the background, giving some idea of the terrain upon which the Gustav Line was based.
IWM NA13005

3,000 yards from Cassino. As I watched the bombers, I saw the bomb doors open and bombs began to fall well short of the target. I said to the Chief, who was watching the forward area, 'Some of them have dropped their bombs even before reaching us'. Some fell on 5th Army Headquarters and the medium gun lines. Others fell on General Oliver Leese's Tac HQ and Eighth Army Headquarters, destroying the General's Mess, where the ADCs took refuge under the table. Luckily, the General was out visiting the troops.

Of course a high percentage did fall on the monastery itself and reduced much of it to rubble, thereby providing the enemy with a first-class defensive position, of which they took full advantage. Rather than saving lives, that bombing would lead to savage losses and the deaths of many refugees who had been sheltering in the monastery. The German defence of Cassino must rate as one of the classic defensive battles of history. Both sides fought heroically for several months and it would be 18 May before the defenders silently slipped away just before a brigade of the 4th Division entered Cassino.

* * *

Whilst the battles raged round Cassino, Alex had been preparing his appreciation and outline plan for the way ahead. When finished, copies were to go to Jumbo, Joe Cannon and Admiral John Cunningham. The Chief also signalled Brookie saying, 'I shall send this home to you by special messenger'. On seeing the draft, Bill said, 'This looks like a good trip home for Rupert'. The Chief grinned and agreed. Bill added, 'I hope the navigation is better than my experience of dead reckoning, as this time the Boche might shoot straighter and Rupert would have to eat the plan – all fifteen pages of it!' But it was not to be. Some weeks later, in April, I would accompany Alex and Terence Airey to London for a general discussion on future policy on Italy.

On 3 April Alex went to Benevento to present the ribbon of the Victoria Cross to Major Bill Sidney (later Lord De L'Isle and Dudley and Governor General of Australia from 1961–65). The

An unforgettable occasion, 3 April 1944. The Chief presented the ribbon of the Victoria Cross to Major Bill Sidney, 5th Battalion Grenadier Guards. Standing beside Alex on the Saluting Base is Field Marshal Viscount Gort, the Governor of Malta. Lord Gort was Bill Sidney's father-in-law and it was the ribbon of his own VC which was pinned on Bill that day, to Lord Gort's great pride and delight. RC stands behind the Saluting Base. IWM NA13548

presentation was made at a parade of the 5th Battalion Grenadier Guards, attended by Bill's father-in-law, Lord Gort VC.

We had considerable difficulty in obtaining the ribbon and, in particular, the small cross that is worn on it. We had sent a request to General Freyberg's ADC for the loan of his ribbon. However, Lord Gort, on hearing of the problem, insisted that his ribbon should be used. Meanwhile, the Royal Army Ordnance

Oliver Leese, in a very typical pose, 'ribbing' General Juin, who clearly enjoys a joke, which seems to be lost on Alex. IWM NA13509

Corps had made a cross from a copper coin. Lord Gort's offer was, of course, accepted and Alex had the pleasant experience of decorating Bill with his father-in-law's ribbon, to the great pleasure of the Governor of Malta. This must surely have been a unique occasion. It was certainly a memorable and happy one.

Two days later, accompanied by Terence Airey, we flew to Algiers on the first leg of our trip to London. There we were picked up by the Prime Minister's York for the onward journey. US General Jake Devers, Jumbo's Deputy, was to act as locum tenens for the Chief during his absence of an expected ten days. Unfortunately, and most annoyingly, we were held up at Gibraltar by the weather until 10 April. This meant that poor Alex, who so richly deserved a few days at home, had only eight working days in England, all at the War Office, and just a couple of days, at the weekend, at home – and even those were only made possible by getting out of an invitation to Chequers. We finally returned on *Stardust* on 20 April with a very tired Chief and myself with a temperature of 101 degrees and a raging throat infection which sent me straight to hospital. There I was joined by Captain Wright, now co-pilot of *Stardust*, who had a broken ankle. He, poor man, faced two months there, as opposed to my expected fortnight with tonsillitis.

Still pretty weary after his demanding trip to England, Alex now began a round of visits, starting with one, accompanied by Harold Macmillan, to General Juin and his French Expeditionary Corps, who had been fighting magnificently in the mountains. At Tac HQ Eighth Army he met Oliver Leese and his three Corps Commanders – Dick McCreery (10 Corps), Sidney Kirkman (13 Corps) and Lieutenant General E.L.M. Burns, commanding the 1st Canadian Corps. After a quick trip to Algiers, where, after a very bumpy flight in *Stardust*, he stayed with Harold Macmillan and met Jumbo Wilson, Field Marshal Smuts, Air Marshal John Slessor and the Prime Minister of Rhodesia, Mr Huggins, he was back in time to prepare for his conference with all his senior Commanders and their Chiefs of Staff on 1 May at which there was a presentation of plans followed by lunch on *Flagstaff*, his invaluable train. The Meeting went well and Alex was very pleased with the way things were progressing. His major battle for the Liri Valley, Operation DIADEM, was due to begin on the 11th. Somehow he had fitted in visits to both Armies and to the

Anzio beachhead before this conference and was poised to visit both Clark and Leese on the morning of the 12th to gauge the progress being made.

* * *

General Sir David Fraser (*And We Shall Shock Them*) reminds us that Alex had no less than twenty-five divisions under command for DIADEM – seven US, five British, four French, three Indian, two Canadian, two Polish, one South African and one New Zealand. One is driven to wonder how many people today have any conception of the complexity of such a situation or of the diplomatic skill and powers of leadership it demanded of a man in Alex's position. It was not just a matter of deploying formations in ethnic groups. For example, the Eighth Army now had two British Corps,

Major General G F Vanier, the Canadian Minister to the French Committee of National Liberation, visits General Juin's Corps Expéditionaire Française (generally referred to as the French 19th Corps - part of the 5th US Army). General Juin has his back to the camera. IWM NA14436

one Canadian and one Polish, with the 6th South African Armoured Division in Army Reserve. The Fifth Army had an even more patchwork make-up and, just to complicate matters further, Lucian Truscott's mixed American and British 6th Corps holding the beachhead at Anzio.

The general outline of DIADEM was that the line of the Adriatic coast should be held whilst the Eighth Army made the principal effort towards Rome. After taking Cassino and crossing the Rapido, they were to break through the Gustav Line into the Liri Valley astride the Via Casilina (Highway 6) which ran from Cassino to Rome. The Fifth Army was to attack on the left through the mountains, developing the shallow bridgehead established by General Juin and held by his French troops throughout the winter. At a moment to be decided by the Chief, Truscott would break out from the Anzio beachhead with a view to cutting off the Germans who were withdrawing into the Caesar Line, immediately south of Rome. Von Vietinghoff's Tenth Army, with six divisions, was facing the two Allied Armies on the main Gustav Line. Von Mackensen's Fourteenth Army, with five divisions, was covering Rome and Anzio.

The week which followed the opening of DIADEM was one of intense battle and much bloodshed. All attempts to outflank the German withdrawal operation or to smash it by head-on attacks failed. On 23 May, on Alex's orders, Lucian Truscott broke out of Anzio. It was a brilliantly planned and executed operation and, in two days, he was through the Fourteenth Army and far behind the Tenth, which was embroiled with Leese's Eighth.

What now occurred became as great a source of controversy as the bombing of Cassino. Mark Clark, utterly determined that Rome should be seized by the American Army and not the British, switched Truscott's line of advance so that it no longer aimed at cutting off the German withdrawal but was directed towards the Caesar Line and so towards Rome itself, in absolute defiance of Alex's orders. Clark realized that the Caesar Line was a formidable position and would require a full-blown assault to breach it. However, quite against the odds, the Fifth Army found a gap in the defences and an American division was quickly passed through it on to the Alban Hills. By 4 June the Army was marching triumphantly through Rome.

It was an extraordinary affair, for what had transpired was in fact a tactical triumph and there had been nothing that the Eighth Army, pushing doggedly forward, often on a one-tank front, could have done to emulate it.

A commander who loved publicity no less than Monty, Clark's

<u>Soldiers of the Allied Armies in Italy</u>

Throughout the past winter you have fought hard and valiantly and killed many Germans. Perhaps you are disappointed that we have not been able to advance faster and farther, but I and those who know, realize full well how magnificently you have fought amongst these almost insurmountable obstacles of rocky, trackless mountains, deep in snow, and in valleys blocked by rivers and mud, against a stubborn foe.

The results of these past months may not appear spectacular, but you have drawn into Italy and mauled many of the enemy's best divisions which he badly needed to stem the advance of the Russian Armies in the East. Hitler has admitted that his defeats in the East were largely due to the bitterness of the fighting and his losses in Italy. This, in itself, is a great achievement and you may well be as proud of yourselves as I am of you. You have gained the admiration of the world and the gratitude of our Russian Allies.

Today the bad times are behind us and tomorrow we can see victory ahead. Under the ever increasing blows of the air forces of the United Nations, which are mounting every day in intensity, the German war machine is beginning to crumble. The Allied armed forces are now assembling for the final battles on sea, on land, and in the air to crush the enemy once and for all. From the East and the West, from the North and the South, blows are about to fall which will result in the final destruction of the Nazis and bring freedom once again to Europe, and hasten peace for us all. To us in Italy, has been given the honour to strike the first blow.

We are going to destroy the German Armies in Italy. The fighting will be hard, bitter, and perhaps long, but you are warriors and soldiers of the highest order, who for more than a year have known only victory. You have courage, determination and skill. You will be supported by overwhelming air forces, and in guns and tanks we far outnumber the Germans. No Armies have ever entered battle before with a more just and righteous cause.

So with God's help and blessing, we take the field - confident of victory.

H.R. Alexander

General,
Commander - in - Chief.
Allied Armies in Italy

May, 1944

The Chief's Order of the Day before Operation DIADEM which was to break through the Gustav Line and end with the capture of Rome by Mark Clark's 5th US Army on 4 June 1944. IWM NAM142 dash for Rome was, as General Fraser puts it, 'unabashedly nationalistic'. It is even held that he issued orders that the British advance on Rome was to be prevented, by force if necessary!

Whatever the rights and wrongs of the case may have been, it is indisputable that Mark Clark and the Fifth Army pulled off a remarkable coup and that by driving the Germans out of Rome they had struck a formidable blow for the Allied cause.

* * *

At 2300 hours on Thursday 11 May Operation DIADEM opened with a barrage from 2,000 guns along the whole of the Eighth and Fifth Army fronts, from Monte Cairo to the sea. After a slow start, the 5th British Division got a bridge over the Rapido on 13 May enabling tanks to pour across. The French then advanced, after capturing Monte Maio, to the line of the Liri River. In all, three bridges were constructed by the Sappers over the Rapido for the Canadian Corps' advance.

Alex and his Chief of Staff, Lieutenant General John Harding, arriving at Headquarters Eighth Army to discuss the progress of Operation DIADEM, which had begun five days earlier. Note that John Harding wears two bars on his DSO ribbon, a rare tribute to his courage and skill as a fighting commander. IWM NA14949

As he leaves the Headquarters later in the day, Alex has a farewell word with Oliver Leese, the Army Commander. He is travelling in his open desert car which gave such yeoman service for so many thousands of miles across the battlefronts from 1942-45.
IWM NA14947

Alex visited both Armies during the critical opening days of the operation on two occasions. On 15 May he took Jake Devers to see Oliver Leese at Eighth Army and then went on to the Polish Corps to encourage General Anders, whose soldiers had been having a tough time, held up by very determined counter-attacks in the mountains approaching the monastery. Three days later, as the 4th British Division entered the town of Cassino, the Poles proudly raised their flag over the monastery. Writing to Brookie at that time to describe the intensity of the fighting, Alex said, 'I do not think any other troops could have stood up to it, perhaps, except these para boys.' Oliver Leese had visited General Anders at Polish Corps Headquarters at 7 am that morning to drink champagne with them in celebration of their great achievement, which, in this his first major battle as Army Commander, he described as a magnificent contribution to the success of the Eighth Army.

On another day the Chief and Jumbo Wilson went to see Mark Clark and then on to the French Corps to see Generals Juin and de Gaulle. De Gaulle, never a popular figure with the High Command, was castigated for breaching the agreement by which the French were allowed a direct radio link to him. He had ordered Juin to send him direct news of the battle, something which only emerged when de Gaulle, in Algiers, announced the capture of San Georgio four hours before it was officially released.

The success of Cassino allowed the Derbyshire Yeomanry and a squadron of tanks from the 17th/21st Lancers to penetrate the Adolf Hitler Line near Aquino. Unfortunately, they could not be supported and, in the face of heavy counter-attacks, they were forced to withdraw. It had by then become clear that a major attack would be needed to break through this new position, a task allotted to General Burns's Canadians. Supported by 800 guns and 400 tanks, of which 150 were Churchills from 25th Army Tank Brigade, they pierced the Adolf Hitler Line in a single day.

A few days earlier Alex had signalled the CIGS asking that the King should approve the award of the CB to General Keyes (now commanding the 2nd US Corps), Anders, Juin and Sidney Kirkman. The front had been advanced 38 miles towards Rome and over 10,000 prisoners had been taken. The request was approved in two days. On 24 May Alex visited Anders in the field and presented him with his well-earned CB ribbon, a tribute not only to his leadership but to the magnificent performance of his soldiers.

On the 25th we heard the good news that Keyes's 2nd Corps had contacted 36 US Division near Littorio, the first link-up with the Anzio beachhead, from which Truscott had begun to break out two days earlier. Alex visited Fifth Army, accompanied by Oliver Leese and John Grimsley, next morning and then, on the

26th, went to Anzio, taking General Joe Cannon and our BGS, Hugh Mainwaring. It was very obvious to Alex that General Lucian Truscott had produced a master plan for his break-out and that it had been brilliantly executed. Under his management 6 US Corps had moved into a new league and the dismal days of poor old Father Christmas were now but shadows in the past. We, the personal staff, had dinner with the Chief on our own that night and had a tremendous discussion about OVERLORD, now less than a fortnight away.

The Eighth Army had been having a very difficult time forcing its way up the eastern flank of the Liri Valley and it was as plain

Presenting the ribbon of a Knight Commander of the British Empire to Lieutenant General Mark Clark, Commanding General 5th US Army, 29 April 1944. IWM NA14288

as a pikestaff that any idea of a pincer movement to cut off the withdrawing enemy before they reached the security of the Caesar Line in front of Rome was a dead duck. When the Chief and I went to Eighth Army on the 28th Alex asked Oliver Leese to let the Fifth Army use the main road heading for Rome, as, from their present position and with 6 Corps now coming rapidly more and more into the battle picture, they should be able to clear the way into Rome more quickly than he. Oliver agreed to check the Eighth Army in the Liri Valley beyond Ferentino and said he would bring the 6th South African Armoured Division into the line, ready to carry on the pursuit and cross over the Tiber when it was clear. As I listened to this conversation, I suddenly realized that Mark Clark had made a switch from the planned operation that Alex had spelled out to us all before the start of DIADEM and that he was now heading for Rome, hell-bent to get the great prize for his own Army. This must have emerged when Alex spoke with him on the 26th. The Chief must have been very angry that this should have happened in defiance of his orders but he was far too good a soldier not to realize that, in view of the way the battle up the Valley had gone, Eighth Army would not have been in any position to push through the Caesar Line for some days at least and that, in truth, the Fifth Army was better poised for Rome. No good purpose would have been served in making a major issue of Clark's action now. What mattered was to get into Rome and Clark was all set to do so. In the event he had a very lucky break, for his patrols found a gap in the Caesar Line through which he was able to push a division on to the Alban Hills and the battle then was as good as won.

On 4 June, just two days before the landings in Normandy, the US Fifth Army marched triumphantly into Rome, giving Churchill our promised contribution to OVERLORD in the nick of time.

Knowing Mark Clark as we did, a lover of personal publicity and a man of burning ambition, Bill and I were well aware that this had been no lucky break which had enabled Clark to turn the tactical situation to his own advantage but a coldly calculated act of planned disobedience. Nobody's fool and knowing Alex as he did, Clark had clearly gambled that, providing his ploy came off, he would get away with it and bring great kudos to the American Army – and himself.

When Alex was asked about Clark's disregard for his orders, the Chief replied, 'I am for any line which the Army Commander believes will offer a chance to continue his present success'. It was so much in line with his selfless approach to his position, in which he believed that his job was to enable his Army Commanders to win their victories.

He now gripped the new situation and ordered both Armies to continue their advance. As he wrote in his despatches, his intention now was, 'To pursue the classical manoeuvre of parallel pursuit' with his two Armies.

His orders to Oliver Leese were to pursue the following objectives:

1. Terni and Rieti, and to gain contact with Fifth Army at Orvieto.
2. Perugia, Foligno–Chiusi.
3. Bibbiena–Florence.

All the bridges in Rome were intact but those to the east of the city had been destroyed. Accordingly, arrangements were made to pass the South Africans through Rome in order to advance west of the Tiber. It was a complicated move but very well handled by the Military Police of both Armies.

As for us, with the expectation of a move of Tac HQ, the Chief decided to have one of his caravans rebuilt and Bill had designed and ordered an office caravan on a 3-ton Bedford chassis for the personal staff, including Michael Hawkins.

Chapter Ten

ON TO FLORENCE

June – August, 1944

Pressing on hard with Alex's parallel pursuit, the two Allied Armies pushed the Germans back steadily towards the formidable Gothic Line which ran across Italy from a point near Pesaro on the Adriatic, along the line of the Apennines, just north of Florence, and on to the Ligurian Sea just south of La Spezia. As they had done in the south, the Germans continued to offer dogged resistance at various intermediate positions and progress was often painfully slow and expensive in terms of lives lost.

The period from June–August, 1944, was overshadowed by the effects of Operation DRAGOON, the invasion of Southern France by the US Sixth Army Group for which the four French Divisions and three American, all from Clark's Fifth Army, would be required. The operation would be commanded by Jumbo's current Deputy, General Jake Devers, who was a capable but self-centred officer whom Ike had once described as 'obstinate'. It calls for little imagination to realize how drastic a measure the loss of those seven divisions represented to 15th Army Group. At times Alex was in despair and fought bitterly to try and persuade both the Prime Minister and the Combined Chiefs of Staff (CCOS) that, given the strength he already had under command, he could not only put paid to Kesselring's Army Group C but could then exploit northwards and take Austria in his stride. But it was all to no avail. The CCOS and their two political masters had given OVERLORD absolute priority. Ike was already calling for any operation that would take the pressure off his two Army Groups fighting so grimly in Normandy. DRAGOON was just such an operation. Furthermore, it was deemed to be of the first importance to get the French actually fighting in their own country.

Throughout June and July the fighting in Normandy swung to and fro. Both the British and the Americans were taking very heavy casualties – the loss rates among the infantry were comparable to those on the Somme nearly thirty years earlier. The Battle of the Atlantic had now, to all intents and purposes, been won. In the air the arrival of the Mustang long-range fighter had enabled the

Americans to carry out heavy daylight raids on strategic targets at a fraction of the cost of the losses suffered earlier, when no escorts were available. In India Bill Slim's Fourteenth Army had begun to take revenge for the 'hell of a licking' they had suffered at the hands of the Japanese in 1942. After the great battles of Imphal and Kohima all Japanese hopes of invading India had gone. Slim had inflicted fifty per cent casualties on Mutaguchi's troops and the reconquest of Burma was about to begin. In Russia the Red Army, with 146 infantry divisions and 43 tank brigades, had opened its summer offensive on a 300–mile front. In Tokyo the Emperor was discussing the worsening military situation with his senior officers and advisers. The achievement of an Allied victory was no longer a question of 'If' but 'When?'

Only in Italy was there a growing feeling of despair amongst Commanders. Despite the dogged determination and courage shown by all the troops under Alex's command, fighting under appalling conditions, and the successes won as they strove to create a situation which would enable him to sweep Kesselring's armies out of the country, the robbing of troops, landing craft and aircraft for OVERLORD was making them feel 'a forgotten army'. It seemed that all the loss of life and suffering involved as they began to reach the point at which they had every hope of crushing the enemy would now be wasted.

For all his own disappointment and anger, Alex was determined to make the best of a bad job and to win through with the resources left available to him – as indeed he would.

* * *

Arrangements were now put in hand to move our Tac HQ up to an area just south of Rome and on 8 June I flew up there in an Auster piloted by a young Spitfire pilot who was having a rest. I asked him to land on a golf course near the spot we had decided to recce. Most unfortunately he failed to see the high tension wires which crossed the fairway he had selected to land on. As we were on final approach, he suddenly realized that we were in trouble and tried to lift over the wires, a normal reaction for a fighter pilot. However, we hadn't the necessary engine power and the light aircraft stalled and crashed in a bunker. During the afternoon Bill had a telephone call to say that the Chief's aircraft had crashed near Rome, although Eighth Army could not say whether it was *Stardust*, in which Marshal Badoglio and the Prime Minister of New Zealand were being flown up to the city or the Chief's Piper Club, in which they were expecting him. They then discovered that the answer was 'neither' – the victim was his ADC in an Auster! Everyone heaved sighs of relief and all were happy once more – except me, with a large bump on my head, a headache and nothing left of my aeroplane!

The parallel pursuit of the enemy continued, with the Germans split into two, with only four divisions withdrawing north, parallel to the west coast and being pushed back by the Fifth Army at Orvieto. Oliver Leese got immediate permission to follow up and take advantage of the situation, but Mark Clark would not cooperate until he had written instructions from Alex. Clearly the rocket he had had over his dash for Rome had had its effect! Luckily, Alex was with him on the following morning and gave him the go-ahead, but the delay had allowed the Germans to bring troops through Orvieto to check the Eighth Army's advance about Viterbo.

The enemy's rearguards fought stubbornly to hold up 13 Corps at the southern end of Lake Trasimene and 10 Corps, who were east of the lake and around Perugia. There was nothing for it but to lay on a formal break-in attack by three divisions and this was planned for 24 June. When the day came, a series of violent thunderstorms turned the area into a quagmire and this enabled the enemy to seal off the penetration which Eighth Army had achieved.

Some days earlier Alex and Oliver Leese had visited General Anders at Headquarters Polish Corps. They were greeted with a guard of honour and taken to the stadium at Ancona where a large number of Polish officers had assembled in the grandstand to see them both invested with a prestigious Polish honour, the Virtuti Militari by General Sosnkowski, the Polish Commander-in-Chief. Alex had greatly admired the superb gallantry of the Poles at Cassino, as had General Oliver.

On 12 June I went off in advance to pave the way for the move of Headquarters, Allied Armies in Italy (as we had now been called for some time). The site was the Pope's presently unused summer residence. The new Headquarters was due to open at 0800 hours on 14 June in the Park Hotel. The Germans had occupied it and all the drains were blocked, the lavatories being full of filth and the water supply out of order, none of which seems to have bothered the Germans. It certainly bothered us and the Sappers were soon at work. We put the Chief's mess in a small villa, but there, too, we had drain problems!

As I had known ever since those far-off days in Wilton, Alex loved to play truant and go off on 'a bit of a lark'. He was every inch the schoolboy at heart, so we packed him off with Air Vice Marshal John D'Albiac for the day whilst we moved in. They went to Capri and then sailed to Ravello, getting to Frascati at about 9 pm. By this time we had got the place sorted out a bit and looking rather more like the C-in-C's headquarters.

We were all so delighted when John Harding's KCB was gazetted on the 13th. He wanted to be 'Sir John' but his baptismal name was Allan. We were all pretty sure that this would not be a real difficulty and that the Military Secretary's staff would soon be able to untangle it.

17 June was an unforgettable day. Alex and I visited the Vatican for an audience with His Holiness Pope Pius XII, there to pay our respects to the Holy Father, the spiritual leader of all Roman Catholics. After about an hour's talk, with the Pope speaking faultless English, His Holiness expressed a desire to have a personal line of communication to the Allied Commander-in-Chief of the Allied Armies in Italy. Alex had anticipated this and said he would be sending Father 'Dolly' Brooks, our fighting priest from the 1st Battalion Irish Guards, explaining how he had been decorated with the Military Cross for gallantry as a platoon commander in the First World War and had then been a master at Downside between the wars. On the outbreak of the present war he had pestered his Bishop until he got permission to rejoin the Regiment. As we left, the Pope said, 'Goodbye, Major Clarke'. Alex said immediately, 'He is Captain Clarke, not a Major,' to which His Holiness came back at once to say, 'He soon will be, after the capture of Rome'. And, of course, he was right! When, in due course, Alex became a Field Marshal (of which more anon), I became his PA and was duly promoted.

Two days later we had our first visit by General George Marshall, Chief of Staff of the US Army and Chairman of their Joint Chiefs of Staff, a man of immense power and influence. He and Alex had a long and important talk, discussing the vital decisions to be taken regarding future operations in Italy and the strategic direction of the AAI. Alex was bitterly opposed to the concept of DRAGOON, the planned invasion of southern France by the 6th US Army Group under Jake Devers. The removal of seven of our divisions for this operation, including our best mountain warfare troops, the French, hardly bore thinking about.

Alex had long since made his own appreciation and plans, which he would present to Winston and the Combined Chiefs of Staff. Accordingly Bill flew down to Caserta with the Chief, spending the night in their comfortable quarters on Alex's train. General Eaker gave a big dinner for the US Joint Chiefs of Staff which was attended by both Jumbo and Alex. A very concerned and thoughtful Alex returned to us at Frascati and then went off to visit Fifth Army, taking John Grimsley with him. This gave Bill and I a chance to go to St Peter's with John de Salis of the Irish Guards who was a Count of the Holy Roman Empire and so *persona grata* with the Vatican. Our tour included a special visit to the underground crypt containing the sarcophagi of all the Popes, which John had very kindly arranged as a special favour, but I have to own that Bill and I found it rather boring!

Alex and Harold Macmillan were the closest of allies and firm friends. As he could not go to London himself to present his plans to Winston and then the Combined Chiefs of Staff, Alex was very keen that Harold should fly home with General Gammell, Jumbo's Chief of Staff, to explain his (Alex's) plans to the Prime Minister, to whom Alex sent a strongly worded signal:

> *Kesselring's 10th and 14th Armies are a beaten force, but not yet eliminated. It is clear that the Germans will try to hold the Apennines position with ten to twelve divisions, for a front of 180 miles. Against this, I can, provided I have left to me intact my present forces, amass a powerful force of fresh divisions, tanks and artillery as will split the German forces in Italy. I shall then have nothing to prevent me marching on Vienna.*

Macmillan flew to England as planned and, on 22 June, presented Alex's plan to the Combined Chiefs of Staff, with Winston in attendance.

On 21 June, naturally very anxious about the success of the Chiefs of Staff meeting and impatient to hear the outcome, Alex decided to ease the tension by having a day 'on the swan', i.e. wandering at will looking for something to see or do. In Ostia he and I were looking at the ruins of what had clearly once been a fine old house when, being a lot heavier than he, I fell through an upstairs floor, badly bruising my back, which rather marred our outing. So back we went to our headquarters and got on with the preparation of an Army Commander's Conference which Alex had called for the following day. Field Marshal Jan Smuts was going to attend. He was, of course, a member of Winston's War Cabinet and his views carried a lot of weight, so Alex was hoping that something might come of his presence. Both Army Commanders were present and so was Brigadier George Walsh, the BGS Eighth Army. Alex was not disappointed, the Field Marshal later sent a very fine signal to the Prime Minister, urging his case against the Combined Chiefs of Staff.

On 28 June General de Gaulle brought General Juin and his Chief of Staff, General Béthouart, to see the Chief. As Commander of the French Expeditionary Corps, we were inclined to view Juin more as an Army Commander. We, of course, knew him well for he and Alex were good friends and had great mutual respect for each other. Juin was a top-class professional soldier and had already done excellent work with his mountain-trained divisions. Sadly, we got the impression that de Gaulle might be turning against him on political grounds.

There was still no decision about the future for Allied Armies in Italy and Alex was getting visibly restless. How well we understood his feelings. His troops had fought so magnificently and the enemy were on the verge of defeat. How terrible it was going to be if all that had been achieved at such a high cost of life and human suffering was now to be thrown out of the window. But, being Alex, he was standing up under the strain remarkably calmly.

Meanwhile, the Chief and John Harding went off on 30 June to visit the Fifth Army and the Polish Corps. While they were away Bill and I managed to acquire a motor boat with a Ford V8 engine for Alex to use on Lake Bolsena. It had a top speed of about 12 knots and we tried it out by going out to the island in the middle of the lake. There a middle-aged Italian had a nice house with an attractive cousin as his housekeeper. His wife lived in Rome.

On our return to Tac HQ we found that a considerable flap was on as the RAF had heard that the landing strip which the Chief was to use when visiting the Poles was under shellfire. A Spitfire had been scrambled to intercept them and divert them to another airfield. The Spit had failed to find the Fairchild they were flying in and the party duly landed quite safely to be met by

General Anders.

Black Saturday, 1 July. A signal was received from Brookie saying that he was sorry to have to inform Alex that the decision was likely to go against him and suggesting that he should fly home to discuss future plans for what would be left of AAI. At about the same time Harold Macmillan and General Gammell arrived back from London. Harold told the Chief that he felt that there was nothing for it but to reconcile himself to the fact that DRAGOON would take place and the loss to his forces not only of the seven divisions but also of Joe Cannon and his 12th Tactical Air Force. The latter was indeed a grievous blow.

A signal arrived from Winston on 2 July confirming that DRAGOON was on and that the Chief should return at once in the PM's York. It was Bill's turn to accompany Alex and they set off on the following day with John Harding and Michael Hawkins, taking off from Viterbo. In Rome they transshipped into the PM's York and flew briefly to Algiers for a quick meeting with Jumbo Wilson before going on to Gibraltar for dinner with the Governor, General Eastwood. After dinner they left for Northolt and arrived at 0630 hours next morning, having had a comfortable flight in bed.

The party was met by General Weekes, the Deputy CIGS, and my old friend Barney Charlesworth, Brookie's PA, who had been so kind to me before we went to Burma in March 1942. Alex was whisked straight off to have breakfast with Brookie in his flat. That evening he was able to go down to the country for a couple of days before attending a War Cabinet meeting on 7 July where he gave an account of operations in Italy.

After a meeting of the Chiefs of Staff on 8 July Brookie drove Alex down to Virginia Water and they had a long talk in the car. Although outwardly a rather severe character, Brookie had a deep sympathy for the fighting man and was a soldier himself through and through. He well understood what Alex was going through in his hopeless fight to keep his command intact.

After another day at home Alex took off at 2300 hours on the 9th. That Winston himself came to see him off was a measure of the sympathy he had for the plight of his favourite Commander.

The Chief landed at Algiers on 10 July and went straight to see Jumbo Wilson and report to him on the unsatisfactory outcome of his journey. It appeared that only an American black unit and a Brazilian division were available as reinforcements for AAI. A very disappointed Commander-in-Chief and CGS went off to Eighth Army to start planning further advances with the emasculated armies in Italy. At Eighth Army they found Oliver Leese as sure as they were that had the AAI been allowed to continue their offensive at full strength it would have been possible to get into Austria and Germany in the Autumn. That they did drive the Germans out and force them into surrender and did occupy Austria was an achievement for which nothing like enough credit has ever been given.

* * *

For all its bitter disappointments, life had its lighter moments. Eve Curie arrived to stay briefly on 20 July. Alex and Air Vice

14 July 1944. Bastille Day in Siena. General Juin, Alex and Mark Clark take the salute at the Bastille Day Commemorative Parade. Note that General Juin salutes with his left hand, the right having been severely damaged when he was wounded in 1940. IWM NA16808

Marshal John D'Albiac took her out on the lake in the motorboat to visit the island and showed her all over the palazzo, including the bedrooms. John D'Albiac, very much the ladies' man, was in his element. However, on their return it was revealed that the palazzo had been used as a brothel by the Germans, which Eve Curie knew and had presumed that her hosts also knew and had been a little curious as to why they had shown so much interest in the bedrooms!

* * *

For some days all had been hustle and bustle around the Headquarters, for the King was due to arrive for a visit on 24 July and would be with us until the 31st.

We met His Majesty at Viterbo on the Monday afternoon and then drove straight to Alex's Tac HQ in the olive grove on the banks of Lake Bolsena. As there were no baths in camp and only some rather inadequate showers, Alex and I used to walk down to the water's edge before breakfast for a wash. So now I had a problem: I had to liberate a bath for our royal visitor. As I will reveal later, this particular project also landed me in hot water!

Alex's two caravans were made over to His Majesty. Piers Leigh, the King's senior Equerry, had a tent next to Bill, the rest of the equerries, including Mouse Fielden and Eric Miéville, were in the visitors' camp.

The King was in very good form and laughed and joked a great deal. Next day the Chief showed him round the camp and introduced a number of Brian Robertson's staff from Main Headquarters 15 Army

Alex meets His Majesty the King at Viterbo on 24 July 1944. The King stayed with us at Frascati until the 31st. Author's collection

159

Group. For us the highlight of the day was John Harding receiving the accolade of his KCB and being knighted in the field.

I had handed over the running of the Chief's mess to John Grimsley, who was considerably miffed when the BBC announced, 'Last night His Majesty dined with General Alexander on ordinary Army rations'. Bill observed that this was just a little inaccurate. The menu had been caviar, soup, fish, breast of chicken, savoury, ice cream and peaches. 'Though,' he added, 'you could say that the peaches were Italian Army rations, the ice cream US Army and the caviar was Russian Army issue.'

After lunch on the 25th the King and his staff went off to Eighth Army, the Chief and I following later by air.

Sir John Harding shakes hands with His Majesty after being knighted. IWM NA17253

After visiting the troops, His Majesty knighted Oliver Leese who, like John Harding, had been awarded a KCB. Oliver was deeply impressed by the fact that the King had brought a stool with him upon which Oliver, who was very tall, could kneel – and not only a stool but a cushion too! After spending the night at Eighth Army and attending a dinner, to which Alex and I had also been invited, His Majesty left early on the morning of the 26th to visit 13 Corps, where he stayed the night. Once more he had an early start on the 27th, fortunately blissfully unaware of a little upset which caused many of us not a little laughter. Air Vice Marshal Dickson had a captured Fieseler Storch. Unbeknownst to Eighth Army, he had decided that His Majesty should fly with the RAF and was about to suggest a change from the Army Commander's Auster, flown by a superb Gunner pilot, Vic Cowley. On landing at Tac Army HQ, Dickson turned his aircraft

Sir Oliver Leese is knighted. IWM NA17215

over, having kept his footbrake locked on, and was hanging by his straps. Vic Cowley was a particularly good friend of ours and it was he who said that Alex was the only General he had ever flown who would swing his propeller for him when starting. Vic flew the King down to our Tac HQ at Lake Bolsena. He arrived half an hour early, but fortunately Bill was there to meet him, His Majesty having sent Alex a kind message: 'No need to be present'. Meanwhile, Alex and I had gone off on a visit. Apparently the King was not best pleased when we were found to be away; perhaps the midsummer heat was proving trying.

The New Zealanders were now within 2 miles of Florence but were then counter-attacked by Tiger tanks and pushed back half a mile or so. The King said he would stay on an extra day if he could go and see Florence, a considerable problem for us. However, he stayed in camp on the following day awaiting a most important letter which Admiral Dundas had warned us to expect from England by hand of special officer courier. The officer duly appeared, but the vital letter was, in fact, one from the Queen to His Majesty! The New Zealand troops were still outside Florence.

Sunday 30 July brought a very pleasant surprise. The King had visited the 1st and 36th Divisions and 1st Armoured whilst Alex got on with some very necessary paperwork, which the visit had interrupted.

Driving away from a visit to General Anders' Polish Corps. IWM NA17253

Not long before dinner Piers Leigh asked Bill to assemble some of the Chief's staff at the King's caravan at 1945 hours. At a charming little ceremony, Brian Robertson received a KCVO, Brigadier Dickson a CVO and Bill the MVO, a very nice present for him on his thirtieth birthday.

On 31 July the Chief took the King to the top of Monte Trocchio where he described the Cassino battles to him before seeing him off from Viterbo. His Majesty had also visited the Canadian Corps at Vanafro that morning, so had had a busy day.

I have never been allowed to forget the incident of the bath! When the King came back from staying with Oliver Leese, he described how he had been sitting in a bath (which Oliver had liberated) behind a screen whilst the band of the Coldstream Guards was playing music from *The White Horse Inn* on the other side and he was watching the flashes of the German guns in the distance, the shells falling in a valley about a mile away. This meant, of course, that Clarke had to acquire a bath for His Majesty. This done, with some considerable difficulty, I put it near his caravan under the olive trees. When I had got enough hot water from the cookhouse, I knocked on the door and said, 'Your Majesty, the bath is ready'. I thought I had done rather well, so was a bit hurt to get a rocket from the King in the Mess because there had been olive leaves floating in the bath! After the war, whenever I met the Queen Mother, she would remind me of the King's complaint.

When the King left us he went to stay with the C-in-C Mediterranean near Naples from where we heard an amusing story. A naval picquet boat patrolling outside the Admiral's Villa Emma at dawn had encountered a tiny boat with two people in it, fishing. A fine upstanding woman was busily throwing lines over the side whilst a tiny, wizened man was baiting the hooks. The woman was furious at the approach of the picquet boat, shouting that she was the Queen of Italy and the little man, of course, was King Victor Emmanuel. A figure appeared on one of the Villa Emma's balconies and shouted, 'What the hell is all this bloody row? I want to sleep.' It was the King of England!

* * *

Needless to say, visitors to our camp were never-ending. In contrast with the charms of Eve Curie, we had one from the

Russian Ambassador in Rome, who had come for dinner and was to stay the night. He refused to sleep in a separate tent from his very tough-looking bodyguard and insisted that the beds for the whole of his entourage should be put in one tent. Despite all the fuss, we discovered in the morning that the beds had not been slept in and that the whole party had left during the night.

* * *

In accordance with the Chief's new plan, Eighth Army had taken over the front of the French Corps on its left. This further slowed the progress of 13 Corps who had encountered very stubborn resistance from some parachute troops and SS Divisions which had brought Eighth Army's advance to a halt some 5,000 yards south of Florence. All the bridges in the old city had been destroyed except the Ponte Vecchio, which had been spared, following an agreement made with the Germans over the radio to save this historic bridge.

At the end of July Mark Clark was understandably furious to learn that further withdrawals from Fifth Army for the benefit of Seventh Army had been advised. Alex had a very serious discussion with Jumbo on the subject of emasculating Fifth Army. He was convinced that Devers, who would command DRAGOON, and was currently Jumbo's deputy, was controlling Jumbo and doing what he liked in the interests of Seventh Army. Fortunately, Churchill would be arriving soon for a visit and that might improve matters.

The motorboat was a great attraction for many of our visitors and, with Winston and his entourage due in mid-August, I thought I ought to take it out to make sure that it was in good order. It was as well that I did for it broke down in the middle of the lake. As my passenger, Michael Hawkins, had lost an arm in the Desert, there was nothing for it but for me to swim the 1½ miles to the shore for help, which gave Alex a good laugh when he heard about it.

* * *

I was always very impressed with the consideration which Alex showed to his subordinate Commanders, listening carefully to their views and being perfectly ready to make changes to his plans if persuaded by those views. The story of how General Sidney

Kirkman was able to voice his concern about some of the planning for operations after the fall of Florence was a perfect example of this.

Preparation for the advance north of Florence to Bologna was put in hand in early August 1944. Taking Oliver Leese to the higher ground at San Casciano, south of Florence, which his Corps had recently captured, General Kirkman led him to the top of the church tower, from where they could see the city, the foothills beyond and the mountains behind them which marked the Gothic Line, our next major obstacle. He suggested to Oliver that, as the German reinforcements had come into this sector, a switch to the Adriatic flank could obtain a valuable measure of surprise. Leese agreed that he certainly had a point and on the following day, 4 August, he brought some of his staff across to our camp at Lake Bolsena where discussions lasted all day.

On 8 August John Harding went off early to Main Headquarters Eighth Army for further talks and Alex joined him by air later in the day. Sidney Kirkman had asked for a chance to put his views on some recent Eighth Army planning to the Army Commander and had been asked to wait until John Harding arrived. After a long discussion with Oliver and John, Kirkman went back to 13 Corps feeling that John had come round to his point of view.

The Chief and CGS stayed in the Chief's Camp near Tac HQ Eighth Army that night and went across to 13 Corps in the morning to have a long talk with Kirkman about future policy, by the end of which Kirkman felt that the Chief too had come round to his ideas. So it was that Kirkman was called to Tac HQ Eighth Army near Siena to see the Army Commander. Just before Alex left, he took Kirkman to one side and gave him details of the whole situation, with the plan in accordance with his (Kirkman's) suggestion.

On the following day, 9 August, the AAI Headquarters at Lake Bolsena closed and moved to Siena in a much cooler and more European atmosphere. Alex had his caravan and the rest of us were spread around the woods in tents. However, this was no place for Winston when he arrived on 17 August. A comfortable house near our Camp had to be found. We discovered just the place, owned by a well-known Fascist. His family were still living in the house but were told that they must move out for the visitor.

The Countess was charming. Her lovely sixteen-year-old daughter was bewailing the fact that the Germans had stolen all her tennis balls!

* * *

Alex had worked hard to achieve a happy rapport with the American Air Force and General Joe Cannon was very much a friend, providing the Army Group with the most superb air support with his 12th Tactical Air Force. It was therefore particularly regrettable that, thanks to a careless mistake, a confidential signal, sent personally from Alex to Brookie, with a copy marked 'Personal' to Jumbo, had also been copied in error to General Ira Eaker, the Commanding General of the Allied Air Forces Mediterranean. Alex's signal had asked for details of the close air-to-ground cooperation which had been working so well in France. It was taken by Eaker as criticism of himself, the MAAF and Joe Cannon, and he wrote a very rude letter to Alex on the subject. Alex refused to rise to the fly and sent a very dignified reply, but we all thought less of Eaker in consequence.

* * *

On 13 August we entered Florence, though bands of partisans and *Fascisti* were still fighting in the streets. Now for the sternest task of all – the Gothic Line. If he could crack that, Alex knew that the end was indeed in sight.

Chapter Eleven

THROUGH THE GOTHIC LINE

15 August – 6 December, 1944

It was now mid-August and General Jake Devers' 6th Army Group was about to invade the South of France in Operation DRAGOON. In Normandy the closure of the Falaise Gap was nearly completed and those of the enemy who had escaped were streaming eastwards across the Seine. The massive Allied surge forward across France, Belgium and Holland would soon begin. By September the front would be closing up to the German border in places, but the enemy would show remarkable skill and resilience in re-establishing a western defence line. Much very hard fighting lay ahead.

For all his achievements in the battle of the beachhead, Montgomery was deeply resentful of the fact that Eisenhower had taken over personal control of the land battle and was proving a very difficult subordinate. His tiresomeness and arrogance infuriated both Bradley and Patton, who had never forgotten his rudeness to them in North Africa. Ike was very much regretting that he no longer had Alex at his side to act as his Deputy and, of course, to control the tiresome Monty.

On the Eastern Front the Red Army was now on the borders of East Prussia and so had at last set foot on German soil. In the Far East the Japanese had finally been driven out of India and the recapture of Burma by Bill Slim's Fourteenth Army was now well in hand.

At home Hitler's two 'V' weapons, the V–1 Flying Bomb and the V2 ballistic rocket, were inflicting new casualties on the civil population and high priority had been given to the 21st Army Group and the RAF to locate and destroy the launch sites.

* * *

DRAGOON was launched on 15 August and General Juin's French troops spearheaded the advance against very little resistance. We were all glad to hear of Juin's success, for he had been a great favourite of Alex's and his troops had fought so well for us in Italy, but it was impossible not to feel bitter about the loss of the seven divisions we had sent to 6th Army Group and the threatened loss of Joe Cannon's 12th Tactical Air Force, which, fortunately would not occur for some months, so that we were able to count on them for the tough battles ahead. However, all concerned were determined that we would continue to push the Germans back and out of Italy.

* * *

Earlier in the month we had had a visit from Marshal Tito. He had been accompanied by Brigadier Fitzroy Maclean, Winston's personal representative to the Marshal and Head of the British Military Mission in Yugoslavia. The party had had a very rough flight over the Adriatic and Tito had been very sick, so needed time to recover. On arrival at the Chief's Camp, he lay down on a bed in John Harding's caravan and did not reappear until 4 pm. On being invited to get back into the aircraft to fly to Rome, he firmly announced that he would go by car! The Marshal had two officers with him and, to our amusement, a very tough interpreter, Olga, a female Partisan, complete with pistol and two hand grenades in her belt. Woe betide any soldier who tried to get fresh with her! Although Bill and I were disappointed by the man whom we had expected to look the part of the Brigand Chief, he and Alex hit it off at once and soon became friends, a fact that would prove of some importance at the end of the war.

* * *

We had begun our move from Bolsena to the lovely old walled city of Siena, famous for its annual horse race round the cobbled streets, as soon as we could get the Chief and John Harding off on a visit to Eighth Army and out of our way. The new camp was in a pine wood just outside the city. There for the first time we were able to leaguer our splendid new office caravan alongside the Chief's. The Headquarters opened in Siena on 9 August, just eight days before Winston was due for a visit.

Over the move Bill had been very busy getting in supplies for the Prime Minister's entertainment. These included two bottles of Veuve Clicquot champagne. They were strictly for the Grand Old Man himself; everyone else would have the local Spumanti. When the time came to consume it, we left Winston's two bottles uncovered for all to see but wrapped the bogus stuff, well-iced, in napkins. To our intense amusement the deception worked!

Everyone thought that they were getting the genuine article and there was much appreciative smacking of lips! Which just shows how little the average Briton knows about wine.

* * *

All minds were now bent upon the problem of cracking the Gothic Line with our much reduced forces. It seemed clear that the original plan, based upon our full strength, which envisaged an attack in the centre, through the mountains, where our brilliant French mountain-trained troops would have been in their element, was no longer a starter.

As he always did, Alex sat down at a table with his CGS and two Army Commanders and thrashed the problem out, taking full cognisance of their views.

Oliver Leese later described that meeting in these words:

I went to see General Alex and his Chief of Staff, John Harding, who listened most sympathetically to my appreciation of the situation. We then discussed the problem from all points of view in a most candid and thorough talk. To me it was always a great privilege to serve under General Alexander as he was always so ready to hear your views and to discuss future plans with one. It gave one great confidence.

As Sidney Kirkman had already suggested, the most suitable country over which to deploy our great advantage in guns, tanks and aircraft was along the Adriatic coast. The Chief therefore decided to transfer the main Eighth Army thrust to that sector. Mark Clark agreed with this plan and to subordinate his Fifth Army operations to Leese's coastal thrust. He would concentrate his efforts on the Florence area with a view to advancing north upon his own axis towards Bologna. Owing to the shortage of American divisions, Leese had to leave Kirkman's 13 Corps in the line, east of Florence, separated from the rest of Eighth Army by a range of mountains. Clark immediately asked the Chief to place 13 Corps under Fifth Army, so that all operations in the Florence area could be coordinated and directed by a single headquarters. The Chief asked Oliver if he was agreeable to this and, after some thought about the consequences of splitting up his Army, he agreed. Alex then issued his orders. Initially Fifth Army was to create the impression of a major build-up in the area of Florence and of an impending large-scale operation. For as long as possible the enemy must be led to think that the Eighth Army's attack on the Adriatic flank was a feint. Meanwhile, a plan was to be prepared to break through the Gothic Line in the Florence sector. US 2nd Corps was to thin out between Florence and Pisa so that General Geoffrey Keyes could concentrate his four divisions for the attack. 13 Corps was to seize the high ground north of Florence as a start line for 2nd Corps and would then operate east of the 2nd Corps thrustline. The timing of this attack was critical and would be decided by the Chief himself.

Eighth Army was to concentrate on the Adriatic flank, the bulk of the Army having to move across the Apennines. That concentration was achieved in two weeks and, thanks to the air superiority exercised by the RAF, the move was achieved quite unbeknownst to the enemy. At the same time the Poles had gained the line of the Metauro River, enabling the Canadians and the 5th Corps to deploy on their left. The aim of the Eighth Army operation was to gatecrash the Gothic Line and break out into the good tank country beyond Rimini, joining up with the Fifth Army around Bologna. The easternmost elements of the Eighth Army were to force the River Po and capture Venice. The operation would begin on 25 August.

It was fortunate that the problems Hitler was now facing in France had led to the switch of four German divisions from Italy just before the Eighth Army attack was launched.

* * *

The Prime Minister duly arrived at Venafro on 17 August and drove to the villa which we had prepared for him. There a series of petty irritations began. Two additional staff had appeared unannounced – a marine orderly and a warrant officer stenographer. The Detective Inspector refused to feed with the male staff – all much more trouble than the King's visit, not from Winston himself, of course, but from the stooges travelling with him.

On the 19th Winston went to see the Fifth Army and fired off a large gun in a counter-battery shoot. Like Alex, in so many ways, Winston had a strong streak of the schoolboy in him!

The PM visited 13 Corps and had seen Florence from an OP before he left for a day in Rome. The CIGS arrived at this time and attended Alex's nine o'clock conference. He found Alex very upset and it was at once apparent that relations with Jumbo were at a low ebb. Alex liked Jumbo but at times found him interfering and inclined to get in the way. After only a short stay, Brookie went back to London while Winston returned to our headquarters in Siena.

The Eighth Army's battle was due to start at 2300 hours on 25 August. For two days before D–day Winston and Alex visited

The Prime Minister visited Italy in August, 1944. Here he watches an Eighth Army convoy moving up the Line before an attack. IWM NA18047

Winston walks through a recently captured, shell-torn village. IWM NA18047

Alex describes the lie of the land in the forward area. IWM NA18035

Headquarters Eighth Army and a number of units who would be taking part, giving great encouragement to the troops.

Precisely on time, the Eighth Army attack across the River Metauro was opened one hour before midnight on the 25th.

The PM, with Alex, had spent the 24th behind the wall of a farmhouse about 3,000 yards from the river, with the odd shell bursting close to us. The Chief and I had reconnoitred a spot out of range of small-arms fire from the enemy but close enough for Winston to hear the rattle of machine-gun fire and see shellfire at quite close quarters. Wearing his solar topi and his famous 'zoot suit', he was in his element and loving every minute of it. In his war memoirs he wrote, 'This was the nearest I got to the enemy and the time I heard most bullets in the Second World War'.

Winston, accompanied by Alex, RC and John Stimpson, a liaison officer from Headquarters Eighth Army, gets a sight of an Eighth Army attack from an Observation Post established in a ruined house which, only two days earlier, had been occupied by the enemy. IWM NA18031

By nightfall on the 26th the line was 6,000 yards over the Metauro and by last light on 29 August the Canadian divisions were overlooking the Gothic Line from the high ground round Ginestro, while the Polish armoured cars were entering Pesaro. The enemy had been taken by surprise and by the time they realized the extent of the danger their tanks and infantry were two or three hours too late and had been defeated in detail. The Line was found to be stronger than forecast: for example, we found the turrets of Panther tanks concreted into positions a mile or two behind the main position. Their very powerful L/70 7.5 cm guns represented a very serious threat to our tanks as they began to break through the forward areas of the Line. To have penetrated the Gothic Line as they did was a great triumph for the Eighth Army. A series of very tough battles now took place and casualties mounted alarmingly. Thanks to DRAGOON, there were very few men available, let alone complete units or formations, to fill the gaps. All too soon, the torrential autumn rains came to flood the battlefields and before long the whole front had degenerated into a morass. Military activity was reduced to patrolling by the end of September.

* * *

One might have thought that Alex had had enough to put up with from the War Lords and little enough recognition of his achievements in Italy, but the announcement on 1 September 1944 that Monty had been promoted Field Marshal was about the last straw as far as we who served Alex were concerned. Alex, who sought nothing for himself and was the epitome of modesty, seemed unmoved, but his personal staff and the staff of Headquarters AAI were in a fury that their beloved Chief should have apparently been 'passed over' in this way. So too, it soon became clear, were the officers and soldiers of the Eighth Army. On 5 September Alex had a letter from an unknown Gunner officer, Captain Kirby, which simply said, 'Sir: Just one of many who wish that you were a Field Marshal. Sincere wishes from us all – W. Kirby. Captain RA.' Alex at once replied, 'My dear Kirby: Thank you very much for your letter – it was very nice of you, and I am very touched that you should wish for my promotion – but, you see, I must earn it first. All good wishes to you and your chaps – Yours sincerely, H.R. Alexander'. Monty's immediate promotion 'on the field of battle' was, of course, a highly political move. We now know from Brookie's diaries that Winston, clearly very conscious of the implications of that promotion as far as Alex and his Command were concerned, had been constantly on the telephone to ensure that it would be possible to ante-date Alex's promotion when the time came, so restoring his seniority over Monty.

Eighth Army's battle was slowing up a bit at this time and Alex went up to see Oliver Leese with a view to gingering things up. By the 11th the battle was still bogged down, so Alex and John Harding went up to 13 Corps in a couple of Austers. John came back that evening looking rather depressed by 13 Corps' outlook on life. The Corps had been fighting continuously since December 1940, when the Headquarters was formed. John had been its first BGS. Inevitably, everyone was tired and despondent in this sixth year of war and the Corps Commander, Sidney Kirkman, seemed to have lost a great deal of his former punch.

On 13 September Bill went to Ravello on the Sorrento Peninsula for a week's local leave, which he richly deserved. Alex too was feeling the strain. When Harold Macmillan came to stay with us in the camp outside Siena, he noted in his diary:

> *General Alexander looked, however, rather tired, even strained. He feels rather bitterly the neglect of the powers-that-be of this campaign and the lack of support he has received... As it is, the Germans [now] have twenty-six divisions against his twenty.*

No one should underestimate the immensity of the task facing the emasculated Army Group as the divisions battled against that immensely strong Gothic Line, manned by very determined and efficient soldiers.

After the morning conference on the 16th, Harold accompanied us in the Chief's open car to review the progress being made by Fifth Army up the Florence–Bologna road and the Futa Pass front and then across the Apennines to see Eighth Army on the Rimini front, where they were up against strong German resistance.

Headquarters Fifth Army was in Florence. From there we went north to a village called La Trellia where, for two hours, we watched the battle taking place, with a lot of smoke being used.

No bombing or shelling of Florence had been allowed, on Alex's personal orders. Macmillan commented, 'Alex is very proud of saving Rome, Pisa, Florence, Siena and Perugia from all except minor damage. However, these continuous five years of command, almost always in conditions of great anxiety, have left their mark on him.' How right Macmillan was. They had indeed been years of great anxiety, arguably an experience shared by no other field commander in the Second World War, though the heavy burden of responsibility borne by Brookie, though different in nature, was certainly comparable and must have been crushing at times.

To my great relief Bill returned to the fold on 21 September. I had been wrestling with the Chief's accumulation of papers in addition to accompanying him on tour and it was with some relief that I was able to place them quietly in Bill's 'In' tray! His return allowed me to go off with Alex and Harold Macmillan to Eighth Army where Alex left Harold with Oliver Leese. There the good news was that Fifth Army had taken the Futa Pass.

By the following day, 23 September, we were through the Gothic Line in two places after heavier fighting than we had experienced even at Cassino and the Adolf Hitler Line in the Liri Valley. The casualties, too, had been heavier. Yet the

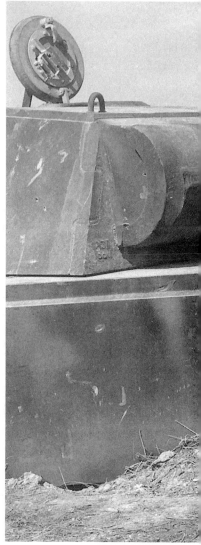

world press had ignored Italy in favour of France, despite the fact that the AAI was fighting more Germans than they were in France and were pushing the enemy back with only a rough parity in strengths, as opposed to the great Allied superiority in North-West Europe.

Before leaving Harold with Oliver Leese, the three of them drove to San Marino, a tiny state near Rimini, there to accept the homage of the Civil Authorities. The Head of State had at first said he would not receive the party, but fortunately reason

In the Gothic Line. The German defences proved stronger than had been expected and included a number of turrets from Panther tanks mounted on concrete emplacements. Oliver Leese, John Harding and Alex stand by one of these and discuss the layout of the enemy's strongpoints. IWM NA18349

prevailed and a picturesque little ceremony was held on a terrace of the hilltop palace, overlooking the whole battlefield. After an excellent lunch each member of the party was presented with some decorative stamps of the State. At this time the news had come through that Oliver was to go off as Commander-in-Chief

Land Forces South-East Asia Command. Dick McCreery would assume command of the Eighth Army.

* * *

During September the Government's demobilization scheme was announced. For some days there was no other topic of conversation. Calculations were to be based upon actual age plus one year for every two months' service. This gave Bill and Ralph Snagge 60 and 63 years respectively, against my 45, which would effectively guarantee me another two years in the Army. The scheme also introduced another, called PYTHON, which enabled all who had served overseas for five years to go home for three months' leave at the risk of then having to serve in the Far East rather than back with their former regiment, wherever it might be. As far as I was concerned, that was all a bit academic, for nothing would have induced me to leave Alex while he still needed me.

* * *

In consequence of our taking a Brazilian division under command, the Brazilian Commander-in-Chief, General Dutra, arrived at our camp on 26 September to invest the Chief with the Insignia of a Grand Commander of the Order of Military Merit, with its green and white ribbon. This probably made Alex the most highly decorated serving soldier, with a top row of three ribbons and five rows of four. Of course, by the time our own campaign medals appeared and the usual round of additional awards from allies at the end of a war, the whole scene was going to change out of all recognition!

When General Dutra had departed, having been duly entertained, we left for Eighth Army, taking General Joe Cannon and General Lem with us. The weather deteriorated and the Chief stayed for two days at Eighth Army, during which time the signal from Brookie confirming the various command changes arrived. We also learned the Air Vice Marshal John D'Albiac was to return to England and that Dick McCreery was to go back to London for a couple of days before taking over from Oliver Leese. This suited us well as it enabled me and Ralph Snagge, the CGS's PA, to go along too. Alex had invited Ted Seago to come out to paint, so we were to bring him back with us.

We took off at 0530 hours on 2 October in really bad weather. Happily, Joe White, now back from hospital, and his crew were experts at this rather dangerous flying through the Apennines. Next day Bernard Freyberg, just out of hospital, came to stay with Alex, having suffered another quite severe wound. His Auster had crashed in a gale as he was landing at Tac HQ Eighth Army and hit the Army Commander's plane, the broken wing-tip of which came through the side of his aircraft and into his stomach. The Chief was keen for Bernard to go home and join Lady Freyberg for a rest but there was no way in which he could persuade him to leave while the New Zealand Division was engaged in battle. That was just what Alex himself would have said in such circumstances, as he had shown over Winston's offer to fly Lady Margaret out to Marrakesh.

We picked up Ted Seago and got him out safely, despite him having forgotten his paints and having to go back for them! He was soon comfortably ensconced in the Visitors' Mess and started to paint the lovely Tuscan countryside. As he explained to me, these were just colour sketches in oils which he would work up into proper landscapes when he got back to his studio again. Ted stayed on for some weeks and, despite falling victim to dysentery and a touch of heart trouble, which was why he had been invalided out of the Army, produced a whole range of superb war sketches as well as his landscapes. These have been on exhibition again in London as recently as the summer of 1999.

Soon after I got back, Alex had to fly down to Caserta where Joe Cannon's parade for his investiture with his KBE was being held. He then visited the hospitals in the Naples area while he awaited the arrival of Winston, Brookie and Anthony Eden who were on their way to Moscow. After a short conference with them, he drove to Rome and spent the night on *Flagstaff* as the weather was too bad for him to fly back to us in Siena.

With all that wind and rain, the roads and tracks in the forward area had turned into quagmires. The Fifth Army had now secured all the high ground, but had to get back to the lower levels before winter arrived and the passes became snowbound.

On 21 October Alex flew down to Naples to meet Winston and Brookie on their way back from Moscow. The conference before and after dinner was most disappointing and was not a very satisfactory affair, but the Chief did get a chance to put his point of view across. I fear he sometimes felt that he might as well save his breath, for little or no help was coming from England, despite our heavy casualties, and the 'forgotten army' feeling would not go away. Alex saw the PM's party off in the morning and then came back to Siena, only to find the camp nearly flooded. Fortunately we had found a nice country house for him outside the city, while we had our offices in Siena in former Fascist buildings. The staff had gone into billets. Life in the swamp was not only unpleasant but thoroughly unproductive and depressing. But things would look up again.

Harold Macmillan had come up again and he and Alex discussed the problem of the whole command set-up in the Mediterranean. Harold noted in his diary:

> There is really no room for AFHQ and AAI (Generals Wilson and Alexander) and there needs to be tighter and more efficient control at the Centre. Alex likes Jumbo Wilson and is very unwilling to take any action which might be construed as a personal intrigue against him.

Meanwhile preparations were in hand for an Army Commanders' conference to be held on 29 October and Alex spent some time with Ted Seago who was painting his portrait. The meeting went off very well and, to quote John Harding, 'There were no complaints', which in the circumstances of the campaign said much for the good relationships which existed between the various headquarters. It had been Dick McCreery's first appearance as Eighth Army Commander. Mark Clark and Joe Cannon were also there and all had their Chiefs of Staff with them, so it had been an excellent chance to get down to brass tacks. The Chief and John Harding had each presented outline plans so that all present were well into the overall picture and aware of what it was hoped to persuade the Combined Chiefs of Staff to agree. They all then took what they had been given back to their own staffs so that work on planning at Army level could go ahead. The results of that work would be presented to the Chief at a further meeting and he would either approve or suggest amendments. It was an excellent way of doing business and gave the Army Commanders great confidence in their Commander-in-Chief.

There was still no indication by the beginning of November as to whether the Combined Chiefs of Staff would consider our plans for 1945 with favour. Brian Robertson would be going to England to agree administrative and logistical arrangements.

On 5 November, whilst Alex and John Grimsley were away at Fifth Army, Bill very kindly organized a dinner party for my birthday and had invited three or four of the brightest and loveliest ATS. John Harding also came and thoroughly enjoyed himself. A great birthday present was my promotion to Major which came through that day.

Taking advantage of the Chief's absence at Fifth Army, we moved the headquarters into the former Fascist building in Siena. We had done this exercise so often that it was a cut and dried operation with everyone knowing what had to be done.

The rainfall for October, which had just been reported, had risen from a monthly average of 2½ inches to 11½. On 1 November we had had a deluge with 4 inches falling in eight hours. Bridges all over Italy had been washed away. Our local Bailey bridge, just by the camp, was washed from its foundations and ended up 100 yards downstream. There had been quite a number of drownings when trucks had been driven into flood water and drivers had been washed away when trying to escape from their vehicles.

Jake Devers had been replaced as Jumbo's Deputy by a General McNarney. We heard that he had said at a recent meeting in AFHQ that the main effort should continue in Italy, unfortunately too late to have any influence over the Combined Chiefs of Staff, who were irrevocably committed to the support of Ike and Supreme Headquarters Allied Expeditionary Force (SHAEF).

Alex and John Grimsley were back with us on the evening of 7 November and in time for Alex's first visit to the Brazilian Division on the 8th. He took General Lem with him and Major Vernon Walters, Mark Clark's former Aide, to act as interpreter. The party was met by General Mascarenhas, who had recently assumed command of all Brazilian units in the line, with an impressive parade and Guard of Honour. German shelling was continuous. During lunch twenty-one shells burst near the hotel, hitting the terrace and killing a sentry.

In a short speech Alex said that 8 November 1944 would always live in his memory, being the dual anniversary of the Allied landings in North Africa in 1942 and his first visit to the

Brazilian Division in 1944, an opener that was well received by his hosts. He ended by thanking Mascarenhas for his 21-gun salute, but said, with a typically charming Alex smile, that he only rated 18 guns! After lunch he visited the 6th Infantry Regiment, commanded by Colonel Costello. There was a supply of steel helmets for visitors and Major Walters offered one to General Lem who replied, 'Christ yes, but he won't wear one and if he doesn't, I can't either'. Alex was never, ever seen to wear a steel helmet. When C.L. Sulzberg visited Anzio with Alex on the destroyer USS *Kempenfeldt*, he noted how some American officers and men, when visited by the Chief, complained that his red hatband seemed to draw enemy fire. When questioned by Sulzberg about this, Alex admitted that this might have been so but he wanted his troops to see that their Commander-in-Chief went right up into the front line.

* * *

Although, by tradition, we seldom spoke politics in the Chief's Mess, things changed a bit when senior politicians came to stay. At about this time both Winston and then his Deputy, Clem Attlee, dined with us and Alex asked Winston to explain his policy for the forthcoming election, due in 1945. Only about three days later he put the same question to Clem Attlee. At that time we could not see much difference between the two answers – Conservative and Labour. After hearing Attlee's response, Alex said to me, 'It looked like most of the same policy'. When the time came, just after the end of the war, we looked back on those evenings and realized how wrong we had been. The Army had voted ninety per cent against the current political leadership and Attlee had won on a very different policy from the one he had put forward in Alex's villa in Siena.

* * *

At last Alex's promotion was promulgated on 27 November, his seniority as a Field Marshal having been ante-dated to the fall of Rome, thus correcting the nonsense which had made Monty senior to him.

Earlier in the month there had been a number of question marks hanging over Alex's head. After the sad death of Sir John Dill in Washington, there seemed to be two possibilities: either

Alex would replace him or would become CIGS. He would have hated both those appointments and so would Bill and I. We all three had to just cross our fingers and hope for the best. Fortunately, common sense prevailed. There was only one man who fitted the Supreme Commander slot and who really understood the Italian Campaign. To have moved Alex at that time would have been madness. Furthermore, to have taken their Commander from them would have been the last straw for the troops, who would thereby have been finally convinced that Italy now counted for nothing and that all they had gone through and all the lives of their comrades which had been lost had been sacrificed for nothing.

The decision was made that Jumbo would replace Dill in Washington and that Alex would become Supreme Allied Commander as well as remaining Commander-in-Chief Allied Armies in Italy. On 23 November he had been to Caserta to discuss the problems of handover with Jumbo. The latter was to be promoted Field Marshal on taking over his new post in December.

* * *

By early December the Eighth Army was making good progress on the Adriatic front. Alex and I went off in *Flagstaff* to see them, coming back in the train to Anzio from where it was only just over two hours' drive to Siena. Whilst we were at Eighth Army, the good news came through that Juin and his Frenchmen, who had fought so magnificently in both Tunisia and Italy, had pushed through the Belfort Gap and reached the Rhine.

Brian Robertson sent a signal from London, where he was pleading our case for more logistic support, to say that some appalling facts and figures have emerged regarding supplies for future operations. That signal confirmed our view that the War Office and Chiefs of Staff could not adjust their plans to the realization that the war was not about to end and that it would not do so before the coming summer, if then.

After his talk with Jumbo, Alex had sent his outline proposals for the new set-up in the Mediterranean to London for Brookie to consider, but had had an immediate reply that nothing could be agreed without full discussions. On 2 December Jumbo, who had been in London, appeared with Mark Chapman-Walker, his MA, and Fitzroy Maclean for more discussions about future plans.

It was then Alex's turn to go to London and he left on 4 December in the PM's York, accompanied by Bill. They were met at Northolt by Archie Nye, the Deputy CIGS, who whisked Alex straight off to the War Office. Bill meanwhile took the Chief's car and dropped Ted Seago, laden with those marvellous sketches of his and the portrait of Alex, at his flat in Grosvenor Square.

After all the fuss and bother, the Chief's proposals were well received by the War Office and he was free to return to Italy. As so often happened, the weather had gone sour in the meantime and his return had to be delayed. But 'It's an ill wind...', for the delay gave him two days at home at The Vale.

Whilst in London, Alex had had a short talk with Harold Macmillan who told him that there were serious problems afoot in Greece where revolution had broken out. The situation was to be debated in the House of Commons on 8 December and Winston had instructed him to return to Italy to give Alex all the help he could with it.

Harold arranged to fly back with the Chief and they were also joined by Brian Robertson, who would now be the Chief Administrative Officer at AFHQ. Despite his dismal signal about supplies, he and Alex must have done some pretty persuasive talking for a mass of brand new equipment for the Eighth Army was already on its way, equipment which would be of immense help during the later battles and the advance to the Po.

Chapter Twelve

REVOLUTION IN GREECE

10 December, 1944-16 January, 1945

Despite the weather and extreme cold, the Eighth Army had advanced up the road towards Bologna during November and by 7 December had driven the Germans out of Forli and Faenza, having crossed the River Lamone. Meanwhile the Canadians, driving up the coast road, had taken Ravenna on the 5th. From then on it was hard pounding all the way, but by 4 January the Army was on the banks of the River Senio. There they dug in and prepared for a renewal of the advance when the spring weather would make this possible. They rested, trained and refurbished, absorbing considerable quantities of new equipment. On the Fifth Army front, to the West, the line along the Apennines was firmly held and, as General Fraser puts it so succinctly, the troops 'kept watch, froze, patrolled and endured' (*And We Shall Shock Them*). The two Armies had fought magnificently and, over the past eighteen months or so, had been through as tough an experience as any endured in any theatre in the Second World War.

Further north, in Belgium and the Rhineland, Hitler had made his last desperate throw to split Monty and Bradley before cutting through to the Belgian coast. Despite the experience of 1940, which had shown so clearly that the Ardennes could be penetrated by armour, the Americans were caught on the hop and for a few days it looked very much as if Hitler would pull it off. Thanks to the fighting qualities of the American troops and some fairly nifty footwork by Monty, who quickly redeployed the bulk of the Second Army to shield Brussels and to assist Omar Bradley on the northern shoulders of what had now become known as 'the Bulge', the day was saved and the advance checked just short of the River Meuse. The cost to the German Army was very heavy and there was now nothing in reserve to replace their losses, whilst the Americans had replaced all their losses and equipment within a matter of weeks. One thing was certain, there was no longer any question of the Wehrmacht being able to reinforce Kesselring's Army Group 'C'. The Tenth and Fourteenth Armies were on their own and the writing was very much on the wall for both.

* * *

It would be difficult to imagine a more trying situation than that which faced Alex on his return to Italy from London on 10 December. Just as he should have been handing over the Army Group to Mark Clark and the latter should have been doing his own handover to Lucian Truscott, Alex was given no alternative but to get himself to Athens without delay, for the Greek Communist Party had revolted against the government of George Papandreou and, for about a week, had been trying to seize power. In his new role as Commander-in-Chief Allied Forces Mediterranean, the ball was fair and square in Alex's court and urgent action to repair a very dangerous situation was called for. On 11 December the Chief and I, accompanied by Harold Macmillan, with his PA, John Wyndham, and our own BGS, Hugh Mainwaring, flew to Athens, landing at Kalamaki airfield, as the main aerodrome, Tatoi, was in the hands of the insurgents.

By the end of August the German forces in Greece had begun to withdraw to a line running along the borders of Yugoslavia and Bulgaria, leaving a very dangerous internal situation in the country, with a relatively weak government headed by a liberal democrat, George Papandreou, and a very strong Communist Party in opposition, backed by some tens of thousands of armed guerrillas (ELAS), who worked in conjunction with the Liberation Committee of Communists (EAM). British troops and a Greek Brigade were put into Greece to provide support for the Government. Initially, the British element consisted of the 2nd Parachute Brigade and Brigadier Harry Arkwright's 23rd Armoured Brigade, which was acting dismounted with the exception of a single squadron of tanks. Lieutenant General Ronald Scobie was appointed GOC-in-C Greece.

Papandreou had warned the British Ambassador (Rex Leeper, an Australian) in November that he was having difficulty with his Communist ministers in the Cabinet. A plan had been issued in early November containing a timetable for the disbandment of the guerrillas who had been harassing the Germans. The existing gendarmerie would be replaced by a new National Guard and a new police force would take the place of the ELAS police. All this was to have been completed by 10 December, but on 30 November the Communist ministers had refused to sign the demobilization decree unless it contained some totally unacceptable amendments. Meanwhile Scobie had been given authority to publish the disbandment dates, outlawing all guerrillas bearing arms after 20 December.

On 3 December ELAS called for a mass meeting in Constitution Square and for a general strike to start on 4 December. The demonstrations on 3 December led to violence and the government forces opened fire on the mob. This gave rise to hostile press reports of eleven civilians dead and sixty-four wounded. Scobie declared martial law on 4 December and Winston sent a signal to Jumbo Wilson, who was still Supreme Allied Commander Mediterranean, instructing him that victory in Athens was of paramount importance. On the 5th he wrote to Scobie giving him his full personal support for firm military action and accepting the need for some civilian casualties. Most unfortunately, that letter was leaked to the *Washington Post*, thereby creating a wave of adverse reaction throughout the United States. On the 4th and 5th ELAS overran the remaining police stations in the Piraeus, thereby acquiring considerable quantities of arms and ammunition.

On 6 December Scobie ordered Brigadier Harry Arkwright to clear ELAS from Athens and the Piraeus. With only the equivalent of some six infantry battalions, a single squadron of Sherman tanks and a field battery facing over 20,000 armed ELAS troops, this was a pretty tall order. Fortunately the 2nd Parachute Brigade had the 5th Parachute Battalion holding the Acropolis; even so the situation was not good.

Tatoi, the principal airfield, had been captured by the insurgents and some 700 RAF men of Air Rear Headquarters taken prisoner. Kalamaki was the only airfield now available to the British and 23rd Armoured Brigade had had to establish an armoured 'taxi service' with scout cars and command vehicles between it and Scobie's 3 Corps Headquarters in the centre of the city. Sniper fire was heavy, making that journey very unpleasant. ELAS now had a profusion of arms for, as was revealed in 1967, the Germans had done a deal with them to provide them with arms in exchange for immunity from interference with their withdrawal.

* * *

Such was the incipient major disaster into which we were plunged on 11 December. The Chief, Harold Macmillan, Hugh Mainwaring and I were each ferried in an armoured car to Scobie's Headquarters, the rest of the party travelling by the 'armoured taxi service', a fairly hairy experience!

Alex immediately took command of the situation and, having realized how things were developing under Scobie, ordered Lieutenant General Hawkesworth and Headquarters 10 Corps to come to Athens to take over control of the battle, Scobie remaining as GOC-in-C Greece.

At this time the Embassy was under seige, the Government still occupying only a small part of central Athens, and the insurgents were firing 75mm shells into the Hotel Grande Bretagne. There was food and ammunition for seven days. Quite apart from any military action which could be taken, it was clear that dramatic political action was also called for if the situation was to be brought under control. There was one man who had the personal standing within the country to enable him to restore order, Archbishop Damaskinos. Harold and Alex sent a cable to Winston urging that the King of Greece, then in England, should be persuaded to appoint the Archbishop as Regent and the insurgents be given an ultimatum to withdraw. That done, Alex left a British Liaison Officer with Damaskinos and we all returned to Caserta on the following day to arrange for reinforcements, ammunition and supplies for our beleaguered troops.

By the time we got back Bill had handed over our Siena office to some of Mark Clark's staff and had taken over a going concern from Mark Chapman-Walker at Caserta, which included the

Athens, 11 December 1944. Alex climbs into a Staghound armoured car in which he was transported from the airfield at Kalamaki to Lieutenant General Scobie's headquarters in the middle of the city. IWM ROM145

Mountain Lodge, the Kennels Mess, where the personnel staff lived, and the Villa Revalta in Naples. He had done wonders in the short time available and Alex was able to get straight down to work in his own office without further ado after flying down to Caserta on the morning following our return.

The decision to send the 4th British Division was very much at the expense of our Italian operations and caused John Harding to exclaim that it was 'the biggest disaster since Tobruk'.

As always Alex was as calm and unfussed as if this was all routine stuff, but he did not leave the office until Harold Macmillan and Harold Caccia returned from Athens for a conference at Caserta, where all the principal players gathered to sort the problems out under Alex's chairmanship.

The bad news now was that Winston replied to the joint signal sent from Athens to say that he would not approach the King of Greece on the subject of getting the Archbishop appointed Regent. Winston was, of course, a true royalist at heart and a great supporter of minor kings. Neither he nor the King trusted the Archbishop. Alex remembered how he had said at the Marrakesh Conference that, 'Only Kings have the dignity to represent small countries in conferences'. Winston reinforced his views in a signal on 19 December saying that the Cabinet considered that military operations to clear Attica and Athens should continue. Military success was an essential prerequisite to negotiation. According to Harold Macmillan, Papandreou shared these views.

After consulting with Air Marshal Slessor and representatives of Field Marshal Smuts, as well as, of course, with Harold Macmillan, Alex returned to the attack with what Churchill later called 'a grave reply', outlining his confidence in his ability to clear Athens and the surrounding area, but emphasizing the difficulties of defeating ELAS in mainland Greece and forcing them to surrender, something which the Germans had failed to do with six or seven divisions and for which he would probably need the same number, adding:

It is my opinion that the Greek problem cannot be solved by military measures. The answer must be in the political field. Finally, I think you know that you can always rely on me to do everything in my power to carry out your wishes, but I earnestly hope that you will be able to find a political solution to the Greek problem, as I am convinced that further military action after we

189

have cleared the Athens–Piraeus area is beyond our present strength.

Not best pleased, Winston came back at him on 22 December saying, 'The political field can only be entered by the gate of success.'

Grave that signal of Alex's may have been, but it was to bear golden fruit and might well be seen as the lynch-pin of our ultimate success in Greece.

On the following day Alex and I set out for Athens once more. The weather was so appalling that we had to drive for eight hours by car to get to Taranto, where we boarded a destroyer. Our overnight trip to Greece was through some of the roughest seas I have ever encountered.

We arrived in Athens late in the morning of Christmas Day to find a welcome Christmas present awaiting us – the situation there was much improved and we had avoided the frightful military disaster which had faced us when Alex took control.

Meanwhile, back at Caserta, Bill had had warnings of VIPs arriving at half past eight in the morning. Thinking that this must be Anthony Eden, the Foreign Secretary, he, John Harding and Ralph Snagge had gone to the airfield to meet him. However, the face they saw at the window of the aircraft was that of Tommy Thompson, Winston's Personal Private Secretary, which could only mean one thing. The Prime Minister, despite the views he had expressed about political solutions, had clearly decided that Alex and Harold were right and had now made this magnificent gesture of coming out to lend his own formidable weight to our efforts to resolve the crisis in Athens.

We met the Prime Minister's plane at Kalamaki after lunch and took him at once to his headquarters for the visit, the cruiser *Ajax*. There he was fully briefed during the afternoon and received a visit from the Archbishop in the evening. This was a great success and was a decisive factor in Winston's 'conversion'. All his doubts about him were dispelled and he became persuaded that he was 'Shrewd, able and forthcoming'. It was agreed that a conference would be called for 4 pm the next day (the 26th) to be attended by all the parties involved. It was to be kept small with no more than four or five people representing each faction.

The Archbishop came to the Embassy for talks next morning and at 3 pm Winston arrived. We then all repaired to the Greek

Ministry of Foreign Affairs where the conference was to be held.

Like every other principal building in Athens, the Ministry was without light or power, so we had, perforce, to have hurricane lamps spaced out along the table, producing a rather eerie, conspiratorial atmosphere. The Archbishop sat in the middle of one side, flanked by Winston, Anthony Eden, Alex and Harold Macmillan. Damaskinos was a very imposing figure and, in his robes, was taller than me (six feet four inches). The various Greek factions faced him. The Chief was deeply suspicious of both ELAS

Archbishop Damaskinos making the opening address at the historic meeting between the British and Greek Governments and the representatives of the Greek insurgents (who had not by then actually arrived). RC stands with his back to the window 'riding shotgun'. At the table (L to R) Anthony Eden, Winston (busily lighting a new cigar!), the Archbishop, Alex and Harold Macmillan. IWM NAM164

and the EAM and had asked Scobie's staff to provide an ante-room where their arms could be deposited. There was some opposition from the insurgents about this, but they finally complied when allowed to put their own guard on the door. In order to provide complete protection, I was ordered to stand in the curtained window at the end of the table in semi-darkness. Feeling rather like Al Capone, I stood with my arms crossed with an automatic pistol, loaded with sixteen rounds, under each armpit. (The *Illustrated London News* published a picture of the conference with a shadowy figure at the end of the room!)

ELAS were late and Winston was already speaking when their delegation arrived – the most fearful-looking brigands you could

From the 'tower' at the eastern end of the Acropolis (the vast rock which was formerly the citadel of Ancient Athens), Alex looks down on enemy movement in the city. As a tribute to the fighting qualities of the Airborne Forces, which they were demonstrating to such effect in the fight against the ELAS, he is wearing their maroon beret. Note that he is also wearing the formation sign of the Allied Armies in Italy, which he had designed himself. The NCO manning the machine-gun is Sergeant S. R. Anderson of the Parachute Regiment. IWM NA21086

From a point west of the Erechtheum, which, together with the Parthenon, was one of the two major religious buildings of the Acropolis, Alex scans the embattled area of Athens which the Airborne officer beside him is describing. Left: RC with the map. Right: a Greek National Guardsman. IWM NA21090

ever imagine. Winston's opener lasted some twenty minutes. He was followed by Anthony Eden and then by Alex who, in a short, soldierly speech, ended by saying, 'Instead of me having to put my brigades into Greece, I should like to see Greek brigades coming to help me in Italy in the war against the common enemy.' After short contributions from the Greeks, the Allied party left the room, leaving the Greeks at the table to sort out their problems. I learned some time later that during the routine security check on the building on the previous evening no less than a ton of dynamite had been found in the sewer below it. Happily, even had the charge been fired, Winston would have come to no harm, tucked away as he was in *Ajax*.

Knowing Winston's earnest desire to see some of the fighting, Alex took him to an observation post from where he could see right over the city and explained the operations to him. It was an ideal viewpoint on top of the Acropolis, where 5 Para were still very much in evidence, complete with machine guns and mortars. Winston was in his element. I quickly saw the truth of the old saying that 'He who holds the Acropolis holds Athens'.

Before leaving Greece with Winston, on the following morning Alex visited the troops. Meanwhile, John Wyndham and I had left for Caserta in *Stardust*. When they got back to Italy that afternoon, Winston, Anthony Eden and Harold stayed in our VIP guest house, the Villa Revalta in Naples, where a dinner had been arranged to which Air Marshal John Slessor and Admiral John Cunningham had also been invited.

Winston's visit had been an outstanding success. The report on the conference which the Archbishop had chaired and a major press conference marked the turning points in obtaining American support in influencing the King of the Hellenes to appoint Archbishop Damaskinos as the sole Regent on 30 December. The Archbishop was a completely selfless man and utterly sincere. He believed that Greece was even more in need of a spiritual rebirth than a political one, so was clearly starting out on the right lines. He announced that he would take no action as Regent until he had taken the vow of consecration, probably on the following day. So far, so good. Disaster had been avoided. Now it had all got to be made to work and peace terms with ELAS completed.

✻ ✻ ✻

30 December was a fortunate day upon which the news about the King's capitulation over the Archbishop should be announced as the Chief was holding his first Supreme Allied Commander's political conference. The conference dealt with, he drove by car to Rome where he picked up *Flagstaff* and left to meet Mark Clark and visit 15th Army Group Headquarters in Florence. There was talk in the air at this time about the appointment of a new Chief of Staff. If John Harding was to become an Army Commander, which was surely a certainty, he had to have some time in command of a corps. His departure would be a sad time for many of us, for the Headquarters had been a very happy place under his jurisdiction and we were all devoted to him. His going would certainly be a very severe loss for the Chief who must have been the first person who realized that the change must be made and

would never have stood in John's way, whatever the cost to himself.

* * *

Poor Alex never had a moment's peace in which to come to terms with his new responsibilities as Supreme Allied Commander. With the war in Italy having reached a critically important stage and the crisis in Greece making ceaseless demands upon him, he scarcely had time to draw breath between visits. Fortunately, he had always ensured that his key staff officers were 'first eleven' men and, with John Harding and Brian Robertson and an outstanding MA in Bill Cunningham, the ship not only stayed afloat but steered a very good course.

On 4 January he flew back to Athens once more, accompanied by Bill and Brigadier Hugh Mainwaring, who was to become Chief of Staff to Scobie. On the previous day the Archbishop had appointed the former Minister of Defence, General Plastiras, an acceptable republican, as Prime Minister. The Chief and Harold Macmillan set about drawing up terms for a truce with ELAS; just in time, for on 7 January General Hawkesworth, whom Alex had put in command of all operations for the clearance of ELAS forces from Athens, the Piraeus and the Peloponnese, recaptured the Piraeus, inducing a delegation of ELAS fighters to approach Scobie and offer to establish a cease-fire, admitting defeat and offering to withdraw their forces 150 kilometres from Athens and to evacuate Salonika, the Peloponnese and most of the islands. By mid-January British forces had ejected the Communists from Attica and a truce actually came into effect on 15 January 1945. By this time the Greek affair had cost the British Army just over 1,500 casualties.

Alex and Harold had returned to Caserta on 8 January and on the 16th we went back once more to Athens. The Chief at once went round the Athens garrison and on to see the 4th Division at Eleusis and Megara with Hawkesworth. Returning to Athens, he and Harold Macmillan called upon the Archbishop where they explained the need to reduce British commitments in Greece as soon as this became possible. Harold also raised the question of an amnesty. That done, they called upon General Plastiras, and then returned to Caserta. The affair was by no means over, for martial law still reigned in Athens, but the situation had

195

changed out of all recognition.

For five weeks Alex had given a most brilliant demonstration of the art of command and another 'Bargo' had been demolished. It is not easy to realize over such a span of time just what the Chief had had to face. To arrive back from London on 10 December, ready to take over his new appointment, to hand over his Army Group to Mark Clark and resume control of a very tough and difficult campaign and to find himself pitchforked into a military/political crisis little better than the one he had been dropped into in Rangoon in 1942 was a situation demanding the most outstanding capacity for command and few people could honestly suggest today the name of any man who could have handled it better. Alex would have been the first to admit that, without Harold Macmillan's wise council and stalwart support and Winston's brilliant and gallant gesture, the battle could not have been won, yet it was he, aided by Macmillan, who had persuaded an obdurate Prime Minister that this was first and foremost a political affair.

* * *

EAM and ELAS continued to control northern and central Greece, imposing a reign of terror on the people. Supported with arms and ammunition by the Communist regimes in Yugoslavia and Bulgaria, who also provided refuge for the guerrillas, the Communists' war intensified after the British left Greece in 1947. Nevertheless, thanks to Alex and his soldiers, Greece remains the only country in south-eastern Europe where a Communist take-over attempt was foiled.

Chapter Thirteen

'THE PATH OF DUTY': QUIS SEPARABIT

D uring January 1945, while Alex and I were still shuttling between Athens and Caserta, we learned that the two Irish Guards battalions in the Guards Armoured Division had suffered heavy officer casualties during the Ardennes battle and were desperate for reinforcements. The 2nd Battalion was an armoured regiment, for which I had no training, but the 3rd were Lorried Infantry and, furthermore, had a number of former 1st Battalion officers serving with them, including some of my old friends. So that was clearly the place for me should I respond to the call for volunteers. I had no doubt that, hard as it would be to leave the Chief I had served for so long under such varied circumstances, it was my duty to go back to regimental service. Alex at once agreed and the Hon Desmond Chichester MC, Coldstream Guards, was appointed to take my place.

I thought I was lucky when General Joe Cannon offered me a lift to France in his personal B-26 Bomber, one of the fastest bomber aircraft in the USAAF, known to us all as 'The Flying Prostitute', as its small, high-speed wings made it look as if it had no visible means of support. We took off with all my kit, gathered over two years campaigning in Africa and Italy. Apart from General Joe, there were two Colonels and myself – a mere Major.

Unhappily, as we crossed the Mediterranean to Marseilles, we lost one engine. The pilot, a Colonel, told me to help with the business of throwing everything we could from the aircraft – the guns, ammunition, our kit, even the parachutes – as the machine was now down to a few hundred feet and we were still 50 miles from land. I was beginning to wonder whether, as the junior officer on board, it would soon be my turn to jump and bitterly regretted those parachutes! By the greatest of good fortune the aircraft just skimmed over the beach and landed on the airfield.

Lady Luck was with me and I managed to get a seat on a courier plane to England where I landed without a stitch, except the clothes I stood up in, but at least I was in one piece and unharmed, for which mercy I was duly grateful.

I now entered the reinforcement sausage machine and began to see the war from ground level rather than through the bird's eye view I had been enjoying for so long. Although I was sent to the Senior Officers' Battle School at Barnard Castle, where I was supposed to learn the mysteries of how war was fought in North-West Europe, the urgency of the 3rd Battalion's needs was such that after three days I found myself with four officers and a draft of some forty guardsmen on my way to France on 13 April. We followed the Battalion through Holland and joined it in Germany where I was at once given command of No 2 Company, though having to revert to the rank of Captain.

I always flew the Irish tricolour at Company Headquarters, making us easy to find. Just before the war ended, a German regiment came to us to surrender, saying that they wanted to fight the Russians, obviously hoping that we too had the same idea in mind. Having disarmed them, I told the officers to surrender their own pistols but to stuff the holsters so that they looked as if they had been allowed to retain personal weapons and to enable them to maintain discipline.

We were at Bremervörde when all fighting ceased at 0800 hours on 8 May. We had had a grand *feu de joie* with all our weapons on the previous evening and celebrated with French champagne, captured from the Germans, which resulted in a number of sore heads the following morning.

The experience of liberating the concentration camp at Bremervörde has left an impression on my mind that will never disappear. It was surprising how little most of us had known about the Holocaust and the sight of these poor dead and dying figures in their blue-striped pyjamas filled us all with a burning anger against the Germans and a heart-rending pity for their victims. The smell of death was all-pervading throughout the camp and the surrounding area.

We were all glad when we moved from Bremervörde to a new deployment area around Bonn and Cologne. Divisional Headquarters was in Bonn and my company was on the Rhine at Hoffnungstahl, halfway between the two cities. We now formed part of the occupation force of the British Army of the Rhine.

An important duty for the Company at that time was to maintain security in the area, which contained a number of

Displaced Persons (DP) camps, housing about 3,000 DPs, mostly former prisoners of war and mostly Russians. A large number of them would break out of their camps at night, collect buried arms and create mayhem, robbing and raping the Germans who lived in the farms and houses in the area. At that time, the summer of 1945, the occupants were mostly women, children and old men, for few of their menfolk had yet returned home. As one means of curbing these activities, we imposed a curfew at night and manned a number of roadblocks.

To help me deal with this thorny problem, I had a Russian Liaison Officer with the Company, a Guards Captain, accompanied by a burly Cossack sergeant. The Captain, who had been sent by Marshal Timoshenko, had been given absolute authority over all Russians in the camps, regardless of rank, as all were deemed to have forfeited their rank on being taken prisoner. The Captain had been severely wounded at Stalingrad. As a Guards officer and an interpreter he received double pay. He wore large gold epaulettes and would be saluted by soldiers at least fifty yards away!

Discipline in the DP Camps improved dramatically, for the Captain had three levels of punishment, which he dealt out remorselessly. The first was six lashes with a cat o'nine tails, laid on with considerable vigour across his victim's back by the burly Cossack, his victim being spread-eagled, stripped to the waist. The second level required the prisoner to dig a hole six feet deep and about three feet wide in which he was then confined, in total darkness with an iron plate over the top of the hole, for twenty-four hours. When I asked about the third level, he gave me a knowing wink and tapped his pistol. I at once replied that in such circumstances I would need a receipt for one soldier, corporal or Captain, as the case might be, for I had no wish to end up facing a war crimes tribunal, something Alex used to joke about, saying that if we were on the losing side, that would be our fate, as befell the luckless Field Marshal Kesselring.

On 10 October 1945, as I was taking my Company to my old haunts in Bavaria and showing them the Schloss at Murnau-am-Staffelsee, the home of General Jürgen von Arnim, who, it will be remembered, gave me his field glasses and Leica camera after he had surrendered Tunis, I had a message to tell me that I had been promoted and my majority restored. However, my new-found seniority was short-lived for, on the 28th of that month, I was posted back to England to join the 1st Battalion. There I learned that I was one of seventeen Australian officers serving in the British Army for whom General Sir Thomas Blamey had asked to have sent back to Australia. Full of joy at the thought of returning home, I was quickly demobilized and on board the aircraft carrier HMS *Victorious* bound for Sydney, where she would collect British WRNS serving in the Headquarters of the British Pacific Fleet for repatriation. As she had no air squadrons embarked, I was able to travel in great comfort in the Wing Commander's cabin, allocated to me as the senior British officer on board. Two good friends travelling with me were John Young, Scots Guards, a future Chief Justice of Victoria, and Malcolm Morris, who would later become an Ambassador.

So ended my days as an Irish Guardsman. I had been intensely proud to serve in the Regiment and had enjoyed experiences beyond my wildest dreams on leaving Sandhurst. I was proudest of all of my privilege to serve the finest master and best friend that I could ever have hoped to meet.

Chapter Fourteen

FINALE

January – May, 1945

Although five months were to elapse between my leaving Alex for my return to regimental duty and the final German surrender in Italy, this book would be incomplete without at least a brief survey of the events which were to lead up to Alex's remarkable victory, achieved two days before Monty's great surrender ceremony on Lüneburg Heath, which has come to be regarded as the end of the war in Europe.

On 29 January the Combined Chiefs of Staff opened their final conference (ARGONAUT) in readiness for their meeting with Stalin at Yalta from 5–9 February. Winston and Brookie arrived in Malta, where ARGONAUT was being held, on the 29th and Alex saw Winston on the following day. Alex reported his intention to go on the defensive in Italy while he built up his strength for a major offensive in April and rested those formations who had borne the brunt of the recent fighting. To his dismay, he now learned that he must part with five British and Canadian divisions which were needed to reinforce Monty's 21st Army Group for the coming assault on the Rhine. Three divisions from the Eighth Army were to move at once and two from Greece to go later. A plan to rob the Fifth Army of two divisions was fortunately dropped. Worst of all, the 12th US Tactical Air Force (Joe Cannon's command) was also to be sent to support the Seventh Army. Obviously, if the troops on the ground were to be so drastically reduced, the availability of tactical air support, always a vital factor in Italy, became more important than ever. Finally, a rather half-baked compromise was reached with the possibility of some light and medium bombers being left in Italy. Alex was more successful when it came to obtaining equipment for the Greeks, as the Chiefs of Staff in London wanted to end the Greek affair as soon as possible.

Bill Cunningham accompanied Alex to Yalta where, of course, the post-war fate of Europe was settled and the scene was set for the Iron Curtain to be brought down across the Continent.

It was a very unhappy experience for the British delegation, as Roosevelt, by then a desperately sick man, propped up by massive doses of drugs, had decided that he would no longer play second fiddle to Winston, who normally carried so much weight at these meetings. Not only was there a general feeling in America that the

Yalta, 5-9 February 1945. Winston Churchill, Roosevelt and Stalin sit in front of their military staffs. The British delegation is grouped behind Winston, (L to R) Alex, Jumbo Wilson, Brookie, Andrew Cunningham (now First Sea Lord), 'Pug' Ismay (Winston's Chief of Staff) and Charles Portal. Admiral William Leahy, Chairman of the American Joint Chiefs of Staff, is beside Portal and General George Marshall, Chief of the US Army Staff is behind him. IWM NAM235

massive contribution made by the United States had won the war for the Allies but also a strong feeling of resentment against traditional British colonialism. Winston, who was also unwell, had a wretched conference.

Bill Cunningham, who was convinced at the time of Roosevelt's ganging up with Stalin against Winston, described the return from Yalta like this:

> *We took a lift in Winston's plane as far as Athens, where our own Dakota picked us up; baggage was transferred and we set off on what was always rather a tricky flight. Navigational aids were primitive then (the Americans had just landed a whole planeload of nurses in Yugoslavia having missed Italy on the way from Algiers). Our headquarters was at Caserta, near Naples on the west side of the peninsula, which we had to somehow get across. We tried the Straits of Messina – cloud was too low to get through; then we tried several of the river valleys which ran east–west, flying up the river till cloud blocked the way, then backtracked with an almost vertical turn with mountains at our wingtips. Rough, rough air with bumps and sudden drops, but in the end we struck an easier valley, got a bearing on Vesuvius and came into our own airstrip in pitch dark by the faint glimmer of the paraffin landing lights. A car arrived to fetch us and half an hour later we were back at the Hunting Lodge and I was looking forward to my camp bed in my American tent with a red hot stove for comfort.*
>
> *I said goodnight to my master, but bed was not to be, not yet. 'Tell my batman to get out my best uniform and my best boots. Ring the Polish Corps and tell them that I'm coming up to see General Anders now; we should be there in a couple of hours if you can find the way.' The Poles were on the mountain slopes in front of Cassino, in a maze of jeep tracks and shell-shattered countryside. I sent for my favourite jeep and the latest situation map and arranged for a guide to meet us close to Anders' headquarters and we left in rain and sleet; two hours later we were led into the warmth of Anders' mess tent. Anders was looking grave, but not as grave as Alex, who when he had shaken hands said directly, 'I'm afraid I have bad news for you, General; your country has been given away to the Russians.' I thought Anders was going to cry, but after a moment or two he drew himself up and replied, 'In that case how can you expect my men to go on fighting in this awful place?' Alex said quietly, 'General, you and I are both soldiers; we are obliged to go on fighting until the end, whatever the end may be. Goodnight; I shall come and see you again tomorrow.'*

As we left I saw that poor Anders and his staff were actually in tears. Two hours later we were 'home', it was four in the morning, soaking wet and exhausted. Alex was in his office by eight and dealing with the pile of papers which had accumulated while we were in the Crimea.

Meanwhile, in Germany, Monty had opened his offensive to close up to the Rhine and clear the Reichswald Forest in preparation for the major assault he planned to make on the river which would, in fact, be 'bounced' by the 9th US Armoured Division on 7 March, to Patton's huge delight, at Remagen, where the Ludendorff rail bridge had been found damaged but usable.

As for the Germans, the Red Army had overrun Upper Silesia and were within 50 miles of Berlin. In Hungary, Budapest had been encircled. One helpful consequence of all this, as far as Alex was concerned, was that three divisions were withdrawn from Italy to go to the aid of the Fatherland, matching the three that he was about to send to Monty.

In the circumstances it was a source of amazement that the enemy had not withdrawn across the Po to the Adige or even the Alps. Had they done so, they could have released many more formations to the Eastern and Western Fronts. In fact, Kesselring had proposed just that, but the idea had been flatly rejected by OKW (*Oberkommando der Wehrmacht*). The Field Marshal himself was transferred to the West to relieve von Rundstedt as a result of the Ardennes failure. Von Vietinghoff took over the Army Group in March but did not challenge his orders and the fate of Army Group C was sealed.

Alex had been ordered by Brookie during ARGONAUT to put an end to the commitment in Greece as quickly as possible so that the troops tied up there could be released. Peace terms were finally settled on 12 February, enabling Alex, accompanied by Desmond Chichester, to visit Belgrade for talks with Tito and Marshal Tolbukhin, the Soviet Army Group Commander in the Balkans. Alex was already on terms of personal friendship with Tito and got on well with the Marshal, so the arrangements for Allied support for Tito's planned offensive up the Adriatic coast were soon settled. Although the staff at AFHQ had grave doubts about the likely success of this operation, it would prove successful, due, in some measure, to the withdrawal of four German divisions from Dalmatia and the support of the fighter bombers of the Balkan Air Force.

On 6 March John Harding finally left AFHQ to take command of 13 Corps of which he had been the first BGS in 1941. His place as Chief of Staff was taken by Lieutenant General W.D. (Monkey) Morgan.

It will be remembered that 15 Army Group had devoted much time during the months of winter stalemate getting ready for the spring. Their new equipment was the by-product of the strenuous efforts made in England to prepare for the assault on the Normandy beaches and would also stand Eighth Army in very good stead. There were now armoured engineer units for breaching and gap-crossing, DD swimming tanks, Landing Vehicles Tracked (LVT, known as Buffaloes, which had played a leading role in the operations in the estuary of the Scheldt, of which the Canadian Corps Commander, General Charles Foulkes, had had experience), flail tanks for minefield-breaching, Crocodile flame-throwing tanks and Kangaroo armoured

Alex paid a visit to Belgrade for talks with Marshal Tito in late February. Here he is being greeted by Brigadier Fitzroy Maclean and Yugoslav General Arsa Iojanovic. General 'Lem' Lemnitzer, who accompanied Alex, stands behind him. IWM NAM235

Alex with Marshal Tito and 'Tiger' on the steps of the White Palace in Belgrade. IWM NA22641

Walking in the Palace grounds. IWM NA22640

personnel carriers (APCs). The latter were, in fact, turretless Canadian Ram tanks and very popular with the infantry.

So this was a very different army from the one that went ashore at Salerno, for example.

The Army Group's new offensive was code-named GRAPESHOT. In the light of its massive re-equipment and greatly enhanced battlefield effectiveness, the Eighth Army was surprised to find that its role was in subordination to the Fifth Army's attack, with no plan to destroy the enemy south of the Po but rather to cross that river and to exploit up to the Adige and the foothills of the Alps. However, Clark's plan was amended by Alex so that the final version issued on 18 March took account of Alex's intention to destroy the German divisions south of the Po,

On leaving Belgrade Alex had a secret meeting in Hungary with Marshal Fyodor Tolbukhin, the senior Soviet Commander in the Balkans. In 1943 he had been in command of the defence of Stalingrad. In October 1944, in conjunction with Tito's partisans, he had recaptured Belgrade for the Yugoslavs. He is seen here, right, in lambskin hat, being introduced by Alex to the British party. IWM NA 22645

After the talks. Alex with the Marshal and General Kiselev, Head of the Soviet Military Mission in Belgrade. IWM22646

to form a bridgehead and advance to Verona.

Eighth Army was to open the attack in order to draw the German reserves and to give Fifth Army's main attack the element of surprise. To help Fifth Army's deception plan, Alex had asked Ike to create a diversion in the South of France to hold the 5th Mountain and 34th Infantry Divisions on the Franco-Italian border and forestall their use as reserve formations for Army Group C.

Eighth Army was directed on the Argenta Gap with the possibility of Ferrara becoming the main objective, depending on the success of the amphibious operation, using 200 LVTs. Pursuit by mobile formations of armour and infantry would then follow with the intention of linking up with Fifth Army after securing crossings over the Reno and Po. Meanwhile, Fifth Army would cut off Army Group C south of the Po before linking up with Eighth Army. If all this was achieved, both Armies would establish bridgeheads over the Po and exploit to Verona.

D-Day was 10 April. The initial attacks across the Senio and then the Santerno began with a massive programme of carpet bombing by heavy bombers in the early afternoon. This was followed by final attacks by fighter bombers at 1930 hours, just before last light, the last sorties being dummy runs to keep the Germans in their dugouts whilst the assaulting infantry crossed the start line. The two Eighth Army formations involved were the 5th and Polish Corps, the latter now being commanded by General Bohosz-Szyszko, General Anders having been promoted to act as Commander-in-Chief of all Polish forces, though he still kept in close touch with the Corps he had been so proud to command and with which he had achieved so much.

GRAPESHOT was spectacularly successful, although it involved some very hard fighting for both Armies. As they had throughout the campaign, the enemy were fighting with great determination. As planned, Army Group C was cut off south of the Po and on 23 April it collapsed, enabling Alex to report the capture of 54,000 prisoners. Some formations continued to fight on grimly, notably 26 Panzer and 29 Panzer Grenadier Divisions, but by 25 April they too had been mopped up.

On the 23rd Alex visited both Armies, finally going to Bologna for discussions on planning for Austria and Vienna. He also attended 15 Army Group's Order Group at which Eighth Army were ordered to take Padua and then exploit to Trieste, while Fifth Army took Vicenza before making its final advance to Bergamo and Como to block all German escape routes in North-West Italy.

On 28 April a German delegation appeared at Caserta to discuss surrender terms. They were given three hours to consider them. The capitulation was timed for 12 noon on 2 May. Despite some difficulty in contacting Von Vietinghoff and persuading Kesselring that there was no alternative but surrender, final agreement was reached in the small hours of 2 May. Alex informed Churchill that the German Headquarters in Bolzano was broadcasting orders in clear that the terms of the surrender were to be carried out and that he would issue public confirmation of the surrender terms at 1830 hours that day. Winston had already sent a typical piece of Churchilliana to Alex on 29 April:

> *I rejoice in the magnificently planned and executed operations of the 15th Group of Armies which are resulting in the complete destruction or capture of all the enemy forces south of the Alps... This great final battle in Italy will long stand out in history as one*

Ravenna. 6 April 1945. Alex, on a visit to the Eighth Army, is met by Dick McCreery, his former Chief of Staff and now the Army Commander. The great battle of the Argenta Gap, in which the Army so distinguished itself, was just four days away. IWM23714

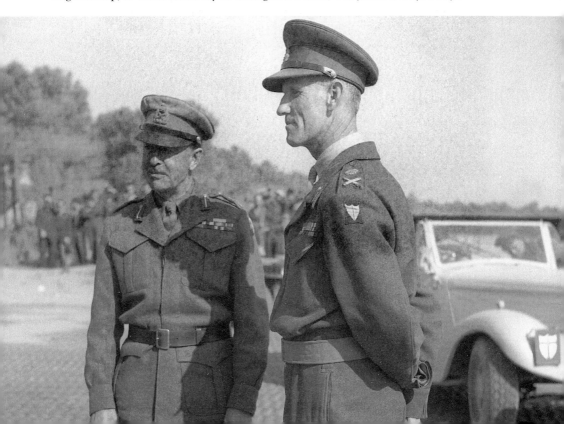

of the most famous episodes in this Second World War.

The message ended, of course, on a congratulatory note to all the Commanders and troops involved.

* * *

So ended Alex's Italian Campaign, his second total defeat of the German Army in the field. As in every phase of that campaign, the cost of GRAPESHOT had been heavy, but only about half the price paid by the enemy who had suffered some 30,000 casualties. In addition some 200,000 prisoners were taken.

May, 1945. Alex and Bill Cunningham leaving the War Office. IWM H82798

EPILOGUE

It had been a notable victory and Alex had once again shown himself to be a master of the operational art. However, his problems in Italy were by no means over for, on the very day of the German surrender, 2 May, when the New Zealand Division entered Trieste, they encountered a considerable number of Yugoslav troops and Partisans who had no business to be there and showed no inclination to go away. It then transpired that they had also invaded Dalmatia. Tito had long coveted Trieste and the Italian province of Venezia Giulia, both being well outside the internationally agreed demarcation line. This situation was completely unacceptable to Alex who needed a secure line of communication to Austria. With the full support of Churchill and President Truman (who had succeeded Roosevelt) and all the nations involved in Allied Armies Italy, he mustered eighteen divisions to evict the Yugoslavs, should it come to that pitch. Nobody knew exactly how Stalin stood on the matter but Russian support for Tito was implicit. Fortunately, under the weight of international political opinion, Tito suddenly backed down and the Yugoslavs were withdrawn and the world breathed again.

Alex was also greatly bothered over the thorny question of what should happen to the Russian and Yugoslav prisoners of war who were now in Austria and who had all served in or alongside the German Army. The problem escalated to crisis proportions and its solution still remains a matter of controversy.

Alex had laid down the heavy burden of Supreme Allied Commander Mediterranean on 1 October, 1945, having commanded troops in battle for four and a half years without a break. In the New Year's Honours, 1946, he was created Viscount Alexander of Tunis. When he first entered the House of Lords the House cheered him to the echo. It must have been with considerable relief that he had found himself summoned home to become Governor General of Canada, a post he filled with great distinction until 1952.

Not long after he had arrived in Ottawa, Field Marshal Kesselring was put on trial for war crimes and conduct contrary to the Rules of War. He was convicted and sentenced to death.

FIELD MARSHAL THE EARL
ALEXANDER OF TUNIS
1891 – 1969
COLONEL IRISH GUARDS

The Statue in Wellington Barracks.

Frau Kesselring appealed to Alex for help. With Mackenzie King's agreement, he sent a strongly worded representation to the Italian authorities stating that the Field Marshal had always abided scrupulously by the Rules of War. The sentence was commuted to life imprisonment. In 1952 Kesselring was released on grounds of ill-health.

Meanwhile, back in Australia I had married and, to our pride and delight, Alex consented to become Godfather to our eldest son, Rupert Grant Alexander.

In 1951 my wife and I visited Alex in Ottawa. It was just like old times. A Yugoslav military mission of generals and colonels visited Ottawa and attended a dinner at Government House. Few of them spoke English so Alex took the Russian speakers to the head of the table and I had the German speakers at the bottom! Whilst we were there, Alex took us in his train to Toronto where he opened the football season with a magnificent kick.

We saw him again when, as Minister of Defence, he visited Australia. That was a position he only accepted because Winston urged him to do so. Sadly, it was not a success.

It was with great sadness that I learned of Alex's death on 16 June 1969. Nothing can ever erase my memories of those long years through which we shared so many adventures and stood at the forefront of history in the making. He had honoured me not only with his complete trust and confidence but also his unwavering friendship.

A magnificent statue was erected in Wellington Barracks in memory of the Chief and was unveiled by the Queen. On the evening before the ceremony I gave a dinner at my Club for the former members of Alex's staff and Harold Macmillan came as Guest of Honour. Next day I helped him, because of his failing eyesight, by telling him the colours of the dresses worn by Her Majesty and Princess Margaret, both of whom came over to talk to him. Alex and Harold had made a splendid team and each owed much to the other.

Appendix I

ALEX: FAMILY MAN

The Family Man with Margaret.

Alex was a deeply devoted husband and father and, while he was in North Africa and Italy, sorely missed his family life. His sense of duty was such that he would never take advantage of his position to give himself more time at home than his very occasional duty trips to England made possible. Thus he never had more than two or, at most, three days with his wife and children at any one time from his arrival in Cairo in 1942 to the end of the war in 1945. He told me one day, with a laugh, just after he had returned from one of those short trips home, that Nanny Turner had said to him, 'You may be able to control your troops, but you cannot control your sons'.

At the end of February and in early March 1944, when the weather in Italy had virtually brought operations to a standstill, Alex took the opportunity to write to his two sons, Shane and Brian, and his daughter Rose, illustrating his letters with the most delightful little drawings and cartoons. His sons have very kindly allowed me to reproduce five of those enchanting letters, which of course were most jealously kept over the years. They tell you more about Alex the human being than any words of mine could hope to express.

At the time the letters were written, Brian, the youngest boy, was four and living at home. Shane, eight, and his elder sister Rose, eleven, were both at boarding school.

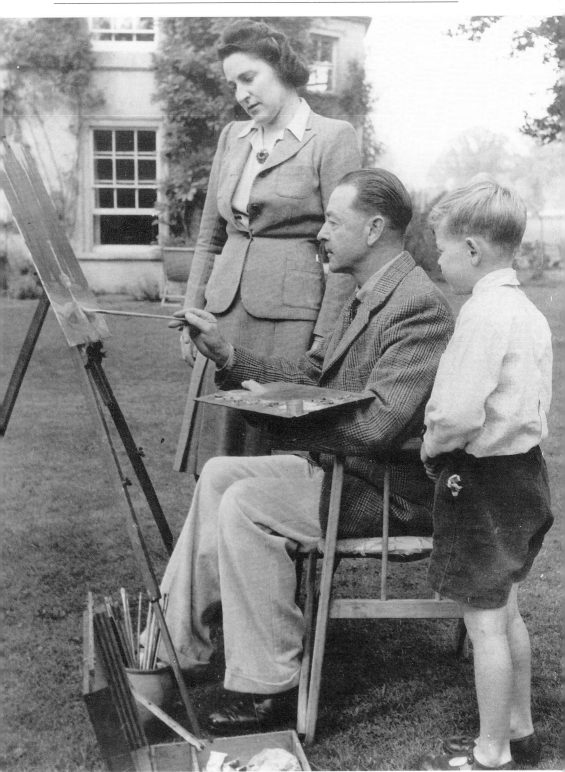

At The Vale with Margaret and six-year-old Brian, not long before the family left for Canada.

HEADQUARTERS ₀
Allied Central Mediterranean Force

Feb. 12ᵗʰ 1944.

My dear Brian — " Hello! what a dear little house — they must be nice people who live there! "—.

Well I wonder where it can be?
How is the Pony and the Chickens and the Ducks? What about having a Dog?
I hear you had a lovely time at Xmas.
I had a good Christmas too, but father Xmas took most of my presents to the Vale because he forgot I was out here.
Love to Mummy and Nanny and Rose and Shane and to you too.

From your affectionate

Daddy.

Letter 1. 12th February 1944.

Letter 2. 8th March 1944.

HEADQUARTERS o
Allied Central Mediterranean Force

Italy...

march. 10th
1944

GO A-WAY YOU
NASTY RABBIT.

hull! Children, here we are again. I had no
idea Kitty was so smart, or clever. I wonder who
she is knitting that sweater for? Whose birthday
is it next? Please thank Rose for her letter
and Shane too for his, and for Brian's also.
Do you know they all arrived on march 9th
which was only 3 days after you posted them.
I hear that Rose is now a hoarder at School,
like Shane, so I suppose Brian has the whole
of the tale to himself. I have got a
special Train all fitted out with a dining car,
a sleeping car and a bathroom — and whenever
I want to go somewhere which is along way away

I get into it — sleep all night and arrive there next morning. And I can drive the engine myself, if I want to. Then you know I have my own aeroplane which is a big one and can carry at least a dozen passengers. It has 2 engines and I fly it myself sometimes, especially when we go high over the tops of the mountains or above the clouds. I also have 2 caravans, 2 open motor cars, a shut motor car and a jeep. I should like to bring them all back to the Vale, but I am afraid we should not have enough room for them.

Well you naughty ones, I must stop now as the post will be going shortly.

Love to you all from your affectionate

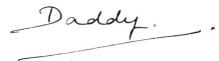

Daddy.

Letter 3. 10th March 1944.

"So there are witches after all!"

HEADQUARTERS •
Allied Central Mediterranean Force

Italy.

March 10ᵗʰ 1944

My darling Rose.
Thank you so much
for your letter giving
me all your news —
And so Henrietta Scott
is going to Heathfield
with you which will
be nice — I suppose
you are great friends. I think Mummy misses
you alot being away from the vale — and Shane
away too. Brian must have a high old time all
to himself. How do you like LAC:? — are
you good at it? — I hear you are leader in
the Gym: which shames me an awful lot —

That is good and I do congratulate you — but I remember that you were always good at Gym: How is John's baby? — and what is it like? — is it dark or fair — blue eyes or brown eyes?

You know I have never seen your honey kitty yet.— so I don't know if the pictures of her I drew are like or not — anyway it was what I imagined her to be.

Well my darling — au revoir pour le moment, j'écrirai encore.

Best love from your affectionate

Daddy.

Letter 4. 10th March 1944.

Letter 5. 14th March 1944.

Appendix II

RELATIONS WITH ALLIED COMMANDERS

One of Alex's greatest gifts was his ability to bring men of different nationalities together to work in amity and a common commitment to the Allied cause. His natural charm, the charisma of his good looks and soldierly bearing, his gift for languages all contributed to the instillation of that confidence in his powers as a fighting Commander without which the control of the polyglot force which Allied Armies Italy eventually became would have been impossible; no less than twelve nations were represented in it. To have created the strength of unity and purpose of which Gregory Blaxland wrote in his *Alexander's Generals* (see Appendix III) was an achievement almost beyond credibility and to have defeated the German Army in the field with that force compels us to rate him as one of the outstanding Commanders of the Second World War. As we know, Stalin had no doubts on that score when he greeted Alex at Yalta.

Alex's personal philosophy for command was that it was his job to serve those who served him. He sought no personal glory and made sure that his subordinate commanders received full credit for their successes. He made it clear to all national contingents that he was proud to have them under his command. Small wonder that, as Omar Bradley put it, he won the adulation of those who fought under him. Captain Kirby's letter to Alex, regretting that he had not been made a Field Marshal when Monty's promotion was announced, was a clear example of the affection in which he was held by the ordinary soldier in the line (see page 174). His gentle correction of General Lem when the latter wanted to get the media to give more prominence to the Army Group was also typical of the man.

Within the Alliance, of all Alex's military relationships none was of greater importance than that with Eisenhower. Ike, like Alex, was a humble man with no sense of his own importance and very conscious of his own lack of experience of field command. He had the humility to ask for a man as his Deputy who had the battle experience to handle his campaign for him on the ground. He had fallen under Alex's spell when they met over lunch in London (see p.38) and knew that if there was a man who could meld the various nationalities in his command into a single effective fighting force, it was he. When Alex arrived in Tunisia at the time of Kasserine, things were about as black as they could be. Yet within weeks the scene had changed completely. Within a few months complete victory had been assured and the confidence of the American Army in Tunisia had begun to burgeon once more. In George Patton and Omar Bradley, both outstanding men, he had gained staunch supporters. In Ike he had made a friend for life.

Despite his seniority and great experience, Alex was prepared to play second fiddle to Ike because that was what the Alliance demanded of him and it was his duty to do as he had been ordered. It would never have crossed his mind to do anything else. He treated Ike as his Chairman, and a most able Chairman at that, and responded immediately to Ike's every request, such as giving Patton's Corps the opportunity to take Bizerta, a badly needed prize to help boost the morale of a Corps which had taken a severe beating at Kasserine and undergone a change of Corps Commanders. All this Alex understood so well, for he was, above all things, a fighting Commander, deeply conscious of the needs of each and every formation in his Army Group.

The two men had implicit trust and confidence in each other, so it was hardly surprising that, when Ike was appointed to command OVERLORD, he wanted to take Alex with him as his Deputy and, once more, ground force commander. However, he was denied this. On the second occasion, in December 1944, Ike applied *again* for Alex's services in place of Air Chief Marshal Tedder and for some weeks it looked as if the move would in fact take place. Alex was quite happy to go to SHAEF but the idea was then vetoed by Roosevelt and Marshall, who took the view that it might be seen to inflict some loss of face on the Americans after the near disaster of the Ardennes. Doubtless, Monty's thoroughly unfortunate Press Conference after that battle, in which he implied that he had saved the day, had something to do with this, for it caused great resentment, particularly with Bradley and Patton. It is interesting to speculate what effect the move might have had upon the length of the war, for Alex was liked and respected throughout Bradley's 12th Army Group and might well have been able to make some major operational moves, as he had done in Tunis and Italy, to achieve surprise and bring about an earlier collapse of German resistance, thereby probably saving thousands of lives and the worst consequences of Yalta, as far as the future of Europe was concerned.

Alex had the experience to identify at once the shortcomings of senior commanders, as he showed in Tunisia, at Salerno and at Anzio, where, although he was reluctant to ask for American generals to be removed, he did so in the best interests of the Alliance and was fully supported by both Ike and Marshall. But he would also show, as he did with Mark Clark over the latter's disobedience in taking Rome, that he would stay his hand if, in his view, the impact of a removal would have an adverse effect upon the Alliance. Clark respected Alex, but they were never close friends. Eisenhower once described Clark as 'the best organizer, planner and trainer of troops I ever met', but he was also very conscious of Clark's vaulting ambition and chauvinism, something to which Ike himself was bitterly opposed. Clark was a good soldier and a brave one and the fact that Alex supported his appointment to command 15th Army Group, when he himself became Supreme Allied Commander, reflects his confidence in him.

Alex handled the proud General Giraud with great respect and dignity in a very tricky situation and was well repaid by receiving Giraud's respect and trust in return. De Gaulle was a different problem. As he did with all Allied personnages and senior officers, Alex treated him with courtesy, but, it will be remembered, did not hesitate to have him rebuked when he broke confidence over his personal radio link with General Juin, which Alex had agreed to on the strict understanding that confidentiality was observed. Juin himself, whom de Gaulle seemed to distrust on political grounds, was a great favourite of Alex's. As fighting generals the two had much in common; both were professionals and battle-hardened, both had been wounded more than once. Juin had to salute with his left hand as his right had been so badly injured. Alex loved to visit the splendid French 19th Corps, which Juin commanded, and to meet his fine *goumiers*, who fought so well in mountainous country. The loss of Juin and his Corps to DRAGOON had been a serious blow.

The Corps would have been invaluable in the fighting for the Gothic Line.

In General Anders and his Polish Corps Alex possessed another invaluable asset. Anders was, like Juin, a professional soldier *par excellence*. It must have been heartrending for Alex to have to relay to him the awful decision made at Yalta surrendering Poland to Russia. Alex handled that very moving and difficult situation to perfection and, in consequence, kept one of his best formations in the battle.

Alex was indeed fortunate in his Commonwealth Commanders, Bernard Freyberg of New Zealand and Leslie Morshead of Australia, both of whom led some of the finest fighting troops in the world. Alex was always very close to the New Zealanders and had a young New Zealand Gunner, Dick Simpson, as one of his ADCs in Tunisia. Before Dick, he had had Peter Francis, from the South Africans, who would go on to win an MC and, before the war's end, would command his regiment in Italy. As for Leslie Morshead's 'Diggers' of the 9th Australian Division, he made no bones about the fact that he considered them the finest division under his command. (See Appendix IV for his farewell speech to them in December 1942). The Canadians arrived for Sicily, their first major operation, and Alex showed great understanding of their three generals, Crerar, Burns and Simonds. Indeed, it may well be that it was that relationship which influenced the Canadian Prime Minister, Mackenzie King, to ask for Alex as Governor General after the war.

The absorption of Italian formations into the Allied Armies was inevitably a tricky business, but, thanks to Alex's understanding of the imperative need to make them feel welcome as partners in the fight to restore their homeland, it was achieved successfully and the Cremona Division fought with distinction in the final battles in Italy. It was Alex himself who had issued the necessary orders to ensure that they were fully equipped with British weapons, an essential part of making them feel that they were wanted and were welcome.

He was equally conscious of the need to instil confidence in the Brazilian Division which, with no previous experience of war, had arrived at a time when the going in Italy was pretty tough. His soldierly bearing and address to them and his unruffled calm when their headquarters was shelled during his visit quickly convinced them that they were now commanded by a soldier of real distinction.

It goes without saying that Alex took endless pains to develop as close and warm a relationship as he could with the Americans; for example the inimitable General Joe Cannon, who commanded our Tactical Air Force, was a member of the Chief's Mess. Alex's two American ADCs, Lloyd Ramsey (who went on to command a battalion) and John Grimsley, were both devoted to him, as was his long-serving Deputy Chief of Staff, General 'Lem' Lemnitzer, a great soldier who would later rise to the top of the Army.

Appendix III

ALEX: AS OTHERS SAW HIM

Alex had been subjected to a good deal of criticism by historians, few of whom seem to have understood the nature of the man or his philosophy of command. No man is without fault and Alex would have been the last to deny that, with hindsight, there were things done and decisions taken which might have been handled differently, but the plain fact remains that the armies under his command drove the troops of the Axis out of North Africa and Italy, utterly vanquished.

Here was a man who commanded the respect of all who served under him and was widely regarded with affection; a man who knew no fear and whose calm, unshakeable presence in the forward area instilled that confidence without which no army can fight for long; a man with the rare gift of being able to command a polyglot group of corps and divisions and to win his battles with them under the most adverse conditions; a civilized man, who spoke several languages, loved to paint, with an almost boyish sense of fun and a profound love of his family. He was that rare being, a man of absolute integrity, and had an iron sense of duty. Above all, he was a man of great humanity and humility – no seeker of personal glory but devoted to the service of those who served him.

There will be those who have read this book who will have accused me of 'sheer hagiography'. No word of it is untrue and the quotations I have chosen from a variety of distinguished and less distinguished pens may be thought to bear me out. All have one thing in common, they saw Alex as one of the truly outstanding Allied leaders of the Second World War. Comparisons are odious and none have been drawn.

Sir David Hunt (Alex's GSO I and, later, Private Secretary to two Prime Ministers.)

Alex, as he was called by his friends, was both intelligent and good-looking, which scarcely seems fair... He really was the only man I know who had all the characteristics of Aristotle's 'great-hearted man' except for the self-esteem which (some) consider an indispensable part of greatness. Much of Lord Chesterfield's famous passage describing Marlborough is applicable to Alexander: 'Of all the men I ever knew he possessed the graces in the highest degree, not to say engrossed them... his manner was irresistible...' It was by this engaging, graceful manner that he was enabled, during all the war, to connect the various jarring Powers of the Grand Alliance and to carry them on to the main object of the war, notwithstanding their private and separate views, jealousies and wrong-headedness.

General Omar Bradley US Army (in his autobiography *A Soldier's Story*)

In each successive campaign, Alexander had won the adulation of his American subordinates.

Lord Longford
(Historian, diplomat and politician, in his autobiography *The Grain of Wheat*)

If anyone asks me whether one of the highest persons in the land is truly great, I begin to apply this test to them... Wellington's 'I am but a man' is a classic example of a humble attitude in circumstances of earthly glory.

Lord Attlee and Field Marshal Lord Alexander of Tunis can be cited as outstanding examples of humility... Only the humble man, as I see it, is capable of treating every human being as of equal and infinite worth...

Ronald McKie (Australian correspondent in his *Echoes of Forgotten Wars*).

Alexander was that rarest of combinations, a fighting soldier as well as a thinking soldier. There was a distinction... From his record and from men who had served under him, I knew enough about his career and personal life...to feel that of all the British and American service leaders he stood out as probably the most distinguished military leader of the Second World War.

Edward Seago (Landscape artist and personal friend of Alex's, who served under him as Camouflage Officer at Southern Command. Taken from a biography of the painter)

Seago respected Alexander more than any man he had ever met. He responded to the soldier's simplicity, humility and utter integrity...Both had charm, loved to laugh and had a great sense of fun and an eye for the ludicrous.

Anthony Eden (Politician and future Prime Minister. He was Foreign Secretary at the time in question. From his Memoirs, *The Reckoning*)

A torrential downpour of rain which lasted several days almost immobilized us and destroyed my hopes of seeing the battle front [the Gothic Line], but at least I understood the conditions in which the Army and Air Force had to fight. My host's [Alex's] company, impervious alike to the weather or enemy action, redeemed the chagrin I must otherwise have felt.

Major General Vernon Walters US Army (In his Memoirs, *Silent Missions*)

Alexander was an impressive soldier. He was completely unflappable, forceful, intelligent and gracious in a non-pompous way...I had come to admire him greatly when I was General Clark's Aide. His behaviour during his first contact with the Brazilians and his calm soldierly conduct during the shelling only served to increase my respect and admiration for this truly great British soldier.

Gregory Blaxland (Historian. In his *Alexander's Generals*)

It is to be doubted that anyone but Alexander could have kept the ardour of these divers contingents [i.e. from French Equatorial Africa, India, Canada, Poland, New Zealand, South Africa, Brazil, Greece, Palestine and even some from Italy] alive and channelled in unison – except for the one divergence caused by the magnetism of Rome. Few would again experience such sense of unity and purpose.

Lieutenant General John Coates (Australian Army)

To those who knew him well, Alexander was the epitome of the born leader. Neither ruthless nor remorseless, he was a soldier's general, always close to the sharp end...Many officers of the 9th Australian Division who fought in North Africa found him much more naturally impressive and captivating than Montgomery, who worked harder at it.

Appendix IV

GENERAL ALEXANDER'S FAREWELL SPEECH TO THE 9TH AUSTRALIAN DIVISION, 22 DECEMBER, 1942

The 9th Australian Division, the 'Rats of Tobruk' and 'The Men of the Match' at El Alamein, were due to embark for Australia on 24 January 1943. The Division paraded for the Commander-in-Chief who, having inspected the parade from an open car, accompanied by the Divisional Commander, General Morshead, then addressed the troops:

> Officers, Warrant Officers, Non-Commissioned Officers and men of the Australian Imperial Force; these great days we are living in are a time for deeds rather than words, but when great deeds have been done there is no harm in speaking of them. And great deeds have been done. [The Australian Official History relates that when these latter words were spoken, it was noticeable that amongst the listless troops 'there was an imperceptible stiffening of shoulders; heads were held perhaps a little higher as the General went on to extol their prowess as fighting men' and many memories of the heat and dust of their long campaigning flooded back.]

General Alexander continued:

> The Battle of Alamein has made history and you are in the proud position of having taken a major part in that great victory. Your reputation as fighters has always been famous, but I do not think you have ever fought with greater bravery or distinction than you did during that battle, when you broke the German and Italian armies in the Western Desert. Now you have added fresh lustre to your already illustrious name.
>
> Your losses have been heavy indeed and for that we are greatly distressed. But war is a hard and bloody affair, and great victories cannot be won without sacrifice. It is always a fine and moving spectacle to see, as I do today, worthy men who have done their duty on the battlefield assembled in ranks on parade, and those ranks filled again with young recruits and fresh reinforcements. To these future warriors, I extend a warm welcome and greet them as brothers in arms who have come to join the forces in the Middle East

which it is my honour to command.

And what of the future? There is no doubt that the fortunes of war have turned in our favour. We now have the initiative and can strike when and where we will. It is we who will choose the future battlegrounds and we will choose them where we can hit the enemy hardest and hurt him most.

There is a hard and bitter struggle ahead before we come to final victory and much hard fighting to be done. In the flux and changes of war, individuals will change. Formations will move from one theatre to another, and where you will be when the next battles are fought I do not know. But wherever you go, my thoughts will always go with you and I shall follow your fortunes with interest and your successes with admiration. There is one thought I shall cherish above all others – under my command fought the 9th Australian Division.

After the address General Morshead took command of the parade. The troops Presented Arms and after the sounding of Last Post and Reveille, the Division marched past, forty abreast. Distinguished witnesses of that march past have spoken of the high emotion and splendour – an unforgettable sight. After it was over General Alexander said, 'I knew you could fight. I didn't know you could march like that.'

[After a long spell in Australia, the Division made an amphibious landing in the Huon Gulf of New Guinea in September 1943. Strongly contested by the Japanese, they fought their way to Lae. In May 1945 the 9th Division landed in Borneo in the last campaign fought by Australian troops in the Second World War.]

INDEX